The Narrative
Study of Lives

The Narrative Study of Lives

An Annual Series

The purpose of this Annual is to publish studies of actual lives in progress, studies which use qualitative methods of investigation within a theoretical context drawn from psychology or other disciplines. The aim is to promote the study of lives and life history as a means of examining, illuminating, and spurring theoretical understanding. *The Narrative Study of Lives* will encourage longitudinal and retrospective in-depth studies of individual life narratives as well as theoretical consideration of innovative methodological approaches to this work.

Guidelines for authors:

The editors invite submissions of original manuscripts of up to 40 typed pages in the areas described above. As a publication of an interdisciplinary nature, we welcome authors from all disciplines concerned with narratives, psychobiography, and life-history. In matters of style, we encourage any creative format that best presents the work. Long quotations in the protagonists' voice are desirable as well as discussion of the author's place in the study.

References and footnotes should follow the guidelines of the Publication Manual (3rd. ed.) of the American Psychological Association. A separate title page should include the chapter title and the author's name, affiliation, and address. Please type the entire manuscript, including footnotes and references, double-spaced, and submit three copies to:

Ruthellen Josselson, Ph.D., Co-Editor
The Narrative Study of Lives
Department of Psychology
Towson State University
Towson, MD 21204

The Narrative Study of Lives

Ruthellen Josselson
Amia Lieblich
editors

The Narrative Study of Lives ▪ Volume 1

SAGE Publications
International Educational and Professional Publisher
Newbury Park   London   New Delhi

For information address:

SAGE Publications, Inc.
2455 Teller Road
Newbury Park, California 91320

SAGE Publications Ltd.
6 Bonhill Street
London EC2A 4PU
United Kingdom

SAGE Publications India Pvt. Ltd.
M-32 Market
Greater Kailash I
New Delhi 110 048 India

Printed in the United States of America

Library of Congress Cataloging-in-Publication Data

Main entry under title:

The narrative study of lives / edited by Ruthellen Josselson, Amia
  Lieblich.
    p.   cm.–(The narrative study of lives, v. 1)
  Includes bibliographical references and index.
  ISBN 0-8039-4812-3 (hard).–ISBN 0-8039-4813-1 (pbk.)
  1. Psychology–Biographical methods. I. Josselson, Ruthellen.
II. Lieblich, Amia, 1939- . III. Series.
BF39.4.N38 1993
155–dc20   93-6581

93 94 95 96 10 9 8 7 6 5 4 3 2 1

Sage Production Editor: Astrid Virding

Contents

A Narrative Introduction

*O*f the many life-changing experiences that grew out of my 1990 Fulbright sabbatical in Jerusalem, one of the most meaningful and fruitful was meeting Amia Lieblich, a kindred spirit who was, like me, struggling relatively alone to find a place for the study of life narrative in psychology. For many years we had each independently been using intensive interviews with nonclinical populations to study the phenomena of development and transition in people's lives. We took this approach because we were attracted by its holism, by the richness of the data and by the sense that we were grappling with all that was missing in more distant, variable-based research (which both of us had also done extensively). Listening to people talk in their own terms about what had been significant in their lives seemed to us far more valuable than studying preconceived psychometric scales or contrived experiments.

But our orientation to research was not much valued in the psychological mainstream. Commiserating together about the difficulty in finding journals in which such work could be published, we decided to share our frustration with colleagues we knew around the world. We discovered that this was very much a shared dilemma. Many people found the study of life history meaningful, many people had creative ideas about how to approach this work, but everyone had the experience of existing journals snubbing such work as either too qualitative or too long.

We decided then to found a new journal, one that would focus on phenomenological studies using narrative methods. This would be a place where social science researchers who were interested in trying to get to the core of people's lived experience could exchange ideas and present their work. As we were exploring this idea, Jerry Bruner came to Israel to deliver the Harvard University Press lectures. We shared our ideas with him. And, in listening to the wide scholarship he quoted on the emerging interest in narrative, we became certain that our idea was one whose time had come.

We then tried to assemble an editorial board and we approached people in different fields and different countries whose work had shown a bent toward narrative or life history. We chose people who had largely been pioneers, who had led their fields in new directions. And, to our joy, the response of these people was unanimous: Everyone was willing to help; everyone agreed that there was this need. Thus we were able to assemble top scholars from psychology, psychiatry, psychoanalysis, anthropology, sociology, literature, and philosophy, all to work together to advance the study of narrative and life history. We approached Sage as a potential publisher and they were immediately interested and highly supportive: *The Narrative Study of Lives* was born. (We decided to start off with an annual because of time constraints on all of us.)

As we became more focused on our task and the mission of the Annual, we became aware of the prevalence of the word *narrative* in the academic community. Suddenly, the word had come into vogue, had invaded every field. In clinical psychology, the idea of restoring narrative had become a new approach to psychotherapy, following Spence's (1982) brilliant analysis of the differences between narrative and historical truth. Even in genetics, people were talking about "new Narratives about Nature." Stars and black holes have recently acquired "narratives," and Dennet (1991) uses narrative as a model of communication between nerve cells and neurons. But narrative, although it has intuitive appeal to people who become weary of variables and the quantification of the positivistic approach, is relatively undefined.

We know what is not a narrative much better than we can define narrative and evaluate its quality.

And the question of what is and is not adequate narrative and narrative analysis quickly became a crucial and practical one as we began to evaluate the articles that were submitted for review. We then began to confront the really hard questions about what work in this field would have to be in order to really advance knowledge. What is a good story? Is just a good story enough? What must be added to *story* to make it *scholarship?* How do we derive concepts from stories and then use these concepts to understand people? What—precisely—would have to be added to transform story material from the journalistic or literary to the academic and theoretically enriching? And even as we asked these questions, we had to ask ourselves what even these words meant—especially now that the new scholarship is stressing the importance of the personal, the uncertainty of objective material, the vanishing distinction between subject and object, the many layers of truth, the hazy line between data and interpretation. All of these new ideas have both confused and enriched us and challenged us to clarify this new field.

We could not define exactly the realm of *The Narrative Study of Lives,* but we decided to rest with a definition in process and to allow our collective thinking to evolve. We found, in general, that the Europeans, who had not taken the intellectual turn toward American behaviorism and who had, instead, a rich heritage of phenomenological philosophy, were somewhat ahead of Americans in their pursuit of narrative study. We wanted to bring some of these ideas into the American mainstream as well, to show a range of how intelligent people grapple with narrative data.

In reading others' analyses of what makes for good narrative, we adopted some criteria to evaluate what we received. We noted the *breadth* of the material and recognized that the study of narrative must struggle with the question of how much one needs to know about someone else to feel that one can understand something about them. We responded to issues of *coherence* of the material, the way in which different parts of the story add up to a complete and meaningful picture, but we were also sensitive to the problems of dealing with human complexity and contradiction. Finally, we reacted to the always debatable criterion of the *aesthetic appeal* of the presentation, which seems necessary for meaning-making, for a narrative and its explication to make sense. And this last has been, perhaps, what has most stymied making narrative "scientific" in the logical-positivistic framework. Good narrative analysis "makes sense" in intuitive, holistic ways. The "knowing" in such work includes but transcends the rational.

Knowing, however, must also include the conceptual. Story cannot stand alone but must be linked to some theoretical context or previous knowledge. Movement to the conceptual level necessitates insight and parsimony, where a different level of interpretation allows us to see things or organize data or to generalize from this story or stories to other people or other aspects of experience. Concepts, usefully applied, would create a bridge to other life situations.

Lastly, we were interested in the question of the relationship between the author and the subject. Why did this author choose this topic? What was the meaning of this story or issue in the writer's life? But this is a new style of social science: Most of us have been educated away from this mode of expression and find it hard to speak in this voice.

Not all stories and submissions we received had all these characteristics. Our review board was an invaluable source of consultation about the papers that were submitted but we were perhaps unprepared for the amount of disagreement about what constituted a "good enough" narrative presentation and analysis. On reflection, this perhaps should not have been surprising in that this is a new field where all of us are very much experimenting with how it ought to be done, with making new rules and guideposts. We differ in what "makes sense" to us. Disagreement here is a sign of vitality and we hope that this Annual will be a stage for the much needed debate about how to take hold of narrative data. In the end, we chose to publish those papers that we feel taught us something and seemed to suggest directions for where this scholarship might develop.

In the past, there have been many approaches to the narrative study of lives, coming from different fields and research traditions. Within clinical psychology, the case study method has illuminated issues of etiology, diagnosis, and treatment, but has focused the pathological. The tradition of Allport, Murray, and White, which had tried to use similar methods in the study of "normal" people, is now on the verge of a renaissance in the United States. From this vantage point, one may look at people who represent either a process or a group. By learning about these individuals, we can see the phenomena more clearly in their context—we return to studying people rather than variables.

A second approach is to study exemplary people who have public prominence. This has been the realm of biography, but new interest in psychobiography has led to the mutual enrichment of both fields and advanced our understanding of life as lived.

Life story is the interface between life as lived and the social times; like Erikson's concept of identity, life narrative interweaves individual experience with historical reality and thus interfaces with approaches in sociology, anthropology, and the burgeoning field of oral history.

Finally, within philosophy, approaches to narrative have been concerned with truth value. Is there a "true" story or are all stories reconstructions? In a postmodern sense, we may view narrative as dynamic and changing, as itself the product of psychological, sociological, and historical influence.

Our contributors to this first volume elaborate and explore these issues. They come from six different countries and four different disciplines. Such diversity, we hope, will maximize the interchange as well as emphasize the universality of interest in the narrative study of lives.

We begin with the philosophical framework that underlies the study of narrative, returning to the roots of psychology where philosophers continued to ask questions about the intersections among life, story, narrative, and reality. Guy A. M. Widdershoven discusses, in a highly lucid presentation, the ways in which philosophical hermeneutics has tried to demarcate life and stories about life. He is concerned with the explication of meaning and how life stories may be seen as interpretations that create meaning in life.

Amos Funkenstein's chapter describes the antithesis, the loss of story, the inability to narrate. When people are deprived of the capacity to narrate, identity is annihilated and human comprehension is threatened.

What leads people to want to preserve the stories of their past? Wendy J. Weiner and George C. Rosenwald next examine, from a psychodynamic point of view, the impulse to keep private diaries. They explore why people aspire to tell stories about their lives, even when the audience is only themselves.

Gabriele Rosenthal, in the next chapter, addresses methodological issues in narrative study. She proposes a way of deconstructing narrative text that takes account of how people's narratives of the past may be used in their current psychological functioning as well as being a way of recovering how the past may have been experienced at the time. After discussing the details of her very careful method, she demonstrates its application to the story of a German man whose life history intersected World War II.

The remaining contributions are from authors who analyze narratives from a variety of points of view, using single case and multiple case studies and analyses of published autobiographies. These chapters show approaches to "making sense" of narrative material that might be models for future work.

Amia Lieblich presents a single case analysis of a Russian immigrant to Israel. In this story and analysis, she explores the dynamics of change and continuity when the developmental phase of adolescence coincides with immigration to a new culture. The theme here is the complexity of transition and Lieblich tries to show the interplay between her subject's inner experience and the context of her shifting social reality.

The issue of the individual and the social world is also central to Jane Kroger's exploration of identity contexts of New Zealanders. Kroger explores the phenomenology behind some quantitative research and wonders about whether social reality creates identity or whether people with different approaches to identity create or find the social contexts that support their identity configuration.

Terri Apter thoughtfully and carefully analyzes a set of in-depth interviews to try to understand the neglected and often paradoxical relationships between teenage daughters and their fathers. She demonstrates how careful use of narrative can capture the layering of experience so necessary to psychological understanding that cannot be apprehended by linear measurement and thought.

Although social science is discovering the narrative mode, this is actually an old form and has always been present in biography and autobiography. Mary M. Gergen and Kenneth J. Gergen turn to published autobiographical records as psychological data and explore how men and women differ in their discussion of bodily experience. Their analysis suggests some intriguing interpretations of gender differences and also demonstrates how social science can use such material.

We decided to have longer chapters in this Annual in order to allow people space to develop their ideas and to present the narrative material in detail. (Too often, when authors are limited as to space, it is the *narrative* material that gets cut.) As a result, we are publishing fewer chapters and we do not attempt to cover the spectrum of narrative approaches to life history in this first volume. In future volumes, we hope to enlarge our scope and to engage authors from a wider range of disciplines.

—RUTHELLEN JOSSELSON

References

Dennet, D. C. (1991). *Consciousness explained.* Boston: Little, Brown.
Spence, D. P. (1982). *Narrative truth and historical truth.* New York: Norton.

❧ 1 ❧

The Story of Life

Hermeneutic Perspectives on the Relationship Between Narrative and Life History

Guy A. M. Widdershoven

*T*he relation between life and story usually is envisaged in one of the following two ways: On the one hand human life is seen as something that can be depicted in stories. The stories that are told about life are measured as to the adequacy with which they describe what happens in life as it is lived. On the other hand stories are regarded as ideals that we try to live up to. Consequently human life is measured against the meaningful patterns presented to us in literary stories. In the first case life is the example that literature is supposed to follow; in the second case literature gives us the example according to which we should live.

Common to both is the presupposition that life and story can be distinguished from one another in such a way that they can be described independently. In this chapter I want to investigate some alternative approaches to the relation between life and story that do not share this presupposition. These alternative approaches, which are part of the movement of philosophical hermeneutics, start from the idea that life and story are internally related. They underline that the meaning of life cannot be determined outside of the stories told about it. Consequently life cannot be regarded as an independent touchstone for the adequacy of a story. Neither, however, can the meaning of a story be determined without any reference to human life as it is lived. Thus a story is never a pure ideal, detached from real life. Life and story are not two separate phenomena. They are part of the same fabric, in that life informs and is formed by stories.

In order to elucidate the common ground of various hermeneutic approaches of the relation between life and story, I will first discuss the relation between story and reality within the philosophy of history. I will argue that this relation is neither one of continuity—nor one of discontinuity. It is hermeneutic, in that the implicit meaning of life is made explicit in stories. I will show that this hermeneutic conception is to be found in MacIntyre (1981) and Ricoeur (1983, 1990), but that Merleau-Ponty (1945) enables us to express it more precisely. Then I will turn to the field of psychology and focus on the concept of narrative identity. I will again discuss the positions of MacIntyre and Ricoeur, and make some emendations from the perspective of Merleau-Ponty.

The upshot of the discussion will be that from a hermeneutic point of view human life is interpreted in stories. Within hermeneutics, however, there are at least three different views on interpretation. The first sees interpretation as re-enactment (Collingwood). According to the second view interpretation is a dialogue with the text, resulting in a fusion of horizons (Gadamer). The third view holds that interpretation is a process of placing a text in a different context (Derrida). I will sketch these three hermeneutic approaches and discuss their implications for the role of stories in individual life.

From a hermeneutic point of view, human life is a process of narrative interpretation. Psychology and psychotherapy aim at studying this process and furthering it. Psychology and psychotherapy are hermeneutic, in that they try to understand the story of life, and, in doing so, change it. The specific nature of the hermeneutic activity of the psychologist and the psychotherapist can be characterized in different ways, depending on the view of interpretation one endorses. In the last part of the chapter I will distinguish a reconstructive, a dialogical, and an intertextual approach within psychology and psychotherapy, and elaborate their consequences for psychological and psychotherapeutical practice.

The Continuity Thesis and the Discontinuity Thesis in the Philosophy of History

The relation between life and story is much debated within the philosophy of history. The debate is about the relation between historical past and historical narrative. According to the defenders of the so-called continuity thesis, the historical past and the story told about it by the historian are essentially of the same—narrative—character. Those who take the opposite position—the proponents of the discontinuity thesis—hold that the historical past and the historian's narrative are of a different nature—the one being without structure and the other being structured in a specific way.

A returning quote within the debate is a phrase from Barbara Hardy, who says: "we dream in narrative, daydream in narrative, remember, anticipate, hope, despair, believe, doubt, plan, revise, criticise, construct, gossip, learn, hate and love by narrative" (Hardy, 1968, p. 5). This sentence can be regarded as a neat expression of the basic tenets of the continuity thesis. It is fiercely attacked by its opponents. One of them is Mink, who simply says: "Stories are not lived, but told" (Mink, 1987, p. 60), thus stressing the ontological difference between life and literature. White (1981) takes a similar position. He argues that narratives are not fit to represent reality, because reality has no beginning and no end. Annals and chronicals stand much closer to the past than the stories of historians, says White.

Hardy's statement is quoted approvingly by the defenders of the continuity thesis. The most outspoken defender, Carr, claims that life is not just a succession of events (Carr, 1986). Our actions are structured by our anticipation of the future. Like elements of a story, human actions derive their meaning from their connection to prior and later events. Life already has a meaning, before it is a subject of stories. Life is narratively structured, and as such it anticipates historical and literary stories. In opposition to Mink, Carr claims that stories are both lived and told.

According to the proponents of the discontinuity thesis, life and story are fundamentally different. The defenders of the continuity thesis see life and story as essentially of the same nature. From a hermeneutic perspective, both these position are problematic. A hermeneutic position holds that stories are interpretations of life. Story and life are similar, in that both are supposed to have a meaning. The story tells us in a meaningful way what life itself is about. Thus the hermeneutic perspective does not support the discontinuity thesis. Hermeneutics also claims that there is no meaning prior to interpretation. This implies that the meaning of life does not exist independent of the stories that are told about it. Thus life does not merely anticipate stories, its meaning is essentially dependent on stories. In this respect, the hermeneutic position is at odds with the continuity thesis. Against both the discontinuity and the continuity thesis, the hermeneutic position emphasizes that life and story are only meaningful in and through mutual interaction.

A hermeneutic approach to the relation between life and story can be found in the work of MacIntyre (1981). He defines life as an enacted narrative, a story put into practice. Life is lived according to a script that makes it intelligible. In order to understand life, we have to have access to the stock of stories that constitute its dramatic resources. Thus the meaning of life is dependent upon the stories that surround it.

The hermeneutic relation between life and story is a central theme in the work of Ricoeur (1983). According to him, life becomes human by being articulated in a narrative way. Life has a pre-narrative structure, which is changed into a narrative structure by the plot of a story told about it. Life has an implicit meaning, which is made explicit in stories. In the process of emplotment the relatively unclear pre-understanding of daily life is changed into a more lucid literary configuration. Thus the stories told about life change it and give it a more specific form. The relation between life and story is a hermeneutic circle: The story is based on the pre-understanding of life, and changes it into a more fully developed understanding.

Although both MacIntyre and Ricoeur see a hermeneutic relation between life and story, in which both sides influence one another, they share an emphasis on the story as the instance where meaning is created. For MacIntyre, life has meaning because it is lived according to a narrative script. For Ricoeur, it is only in the story that the meaning of life really takes form. Both underestimate the role of life in the creation of meaning, which is *fundamental* in the sense that life is the base for every possible story that can be told about it. This is a central idea in the phenomenology of Merleau-Ponty (1945), which places the pre-reflexive in the center. According to Merleau-Ponty, pre-reflexive experiences are the foundation of reflexive notions. He explains this by referring to Husserl's concept of *Fundierung*. Merleau-Ponty elucidates this concept as follows:

> The relation between reason and fact, eternity and time, like the one between reflexion and the pre-reflexive, thought and language or thought and perception, is a mutual relation which is called *Fundierung* in phenomenology. The phenomenon which is the foundation—time, the pre-reflexive, facts, language, perception—is prior in so far as the phenomenon which is based upon it, presents itself as a determination or an explicitation . . . , and yet the foundation is not prior in the empiristic sense, and the phenomenon which is based upon it is not merely derived, because the former manifests itself in the latter. (1945, p. 451; trans. by Widdershoven; italics in original)

Following Merleau-Ponty we can characterize the hermeneutic relation between life and story as a relation of *Fundierung*. Life has an implicit meaning, which is made explicit in stories. Such a process of explicitation presupposes that there is already something present. What is present is, however, not just there to be uncovered. It is shaped and structured in a process of articulation. A story about life presents us life as it is lived, and as such life is the foundation of the story. In presenting life, however, the story gives life a specific sense, and makes clear what it is about. Thus a story is based on life, but it is not determined by it because it is an articulation of life that gives it a new and richer meaning.

Narrative Identity

The discussion within the philosophy of history about the relation between life and story has consequences for the field of psychology in its reference to the place of stories in individual life. Like historians who tell stories about the past, people tell stories about their life. Stories are somehow important for our identity: They tell us who we are. Again it can be asked what relation these stories have to the persons we are. Do they merely describe the experiences we had in the past, or are they in some way constitutive for our (past and actual) experiences?

An example may be helpful to elucidate the place of stories in individual life. Marcel Proust, whose work can be regarded as an illustration of the thesis that narratives create individual life (Rorty, 1989), touches upon the relation between experience and story when he describes a visit to the theater, where Berma performs *Phèdre* (Proust, 1919). The narrator tells us how he tries to retain each utterance and each expression of Berma, in order to be able to remember the experience fully. In this, however, he does not succeed. In fact, his ongoing efforts to capture the present cause him to see hardly anything. His first feeling of admiration is aroused by the applause of the public. It is only later, when he reads the report in the newspaper, that he becomes truly convinced of the qualities of the performance. The narrator describes how the story in the newspaper fuses with his own experience, and adds something to it, so that his admiration grows, resulting in the exclamation: "What a fabulous artist!" He then notices that this may seem not very honest, because the experience in the theater was not nearly as positive as his judgment after reading the critics. He warns the reader, however, not to draw the conclusion of dishonesty too easily. Our stories about what we have experienced are always influenced by those of others, the narrator says, and we derive much of the strength of our most personal ideas from familiar ideas in other persons.

This example shows that experiences have little value as long as they are not connected to, or, as Proust says, fused with stories. This is not only true of relatively unimportant experiences, such as going to the theater. It also holds for experiences that are supposed to change our whole life, for example experiences of deep love or grief. We only become aware of the significance of these experiences by telling stories about them and fusing them with other stories. In this process the pre-narrative structure of experience is articulated and changed into a narrative pattern.

What then is narrative identity? It is the unity of a person's life as it is experienced and articulated in stories that express this experience. This view of personal identity is close to that of MacIntyre (1981), but it is not completely the same. According to MacIntyre, the unity of a person's life is dependent on being a character in an enacted narrative. We live our lives according to a script, which secures that our actions are part of a meaningful totality. Our actions are organized in such a way that we can give an account of them, justify them by telling an intelligible story about them. I agree with MacIntyre when he says that our actions show a unity that can be expressed in a story. I disagree, however, with his assumption that the unity that is put forward in the story is already present in the action. MacIntyre seems to overlook that the articulation of the implicit unity of life in an explicit story is itself part of the process in which identity is created. We not only live our lives in such a way that we can tell stories about our experiences and actions. We also, in telling these stories, change the meaning of our experiences and actions. Here I can refer to the narrative of Proust, which I recapitulated above. By telling a story about a visit to the theater, and mingling this story with that of others, the experience of Berma's performance is changed from a vague and fuzzy feeling into a deep admiration. Exactly this change of experience by later stories is missing in MacIntyre's account of narrative identity.

Ricoeur (1990) criticizes MacIntyre for overaccentuating action as enacted narrative and underestimating the role of narratives outside of action. According to Ricoeur, the meaning of action is articulated in stories, which bring the action in relation to a specific plot, and thus make its meaning more explicit. Whereas actions in themselves are already part of a global plan of life, or a script (as MacIntyre says), this global plan of life can in turn be related to literary stories, which can enrich a person's life. Ricoeur states that a "detour through fiction" has its advantages (p. 188). Literature can be regarded as a laboratory in which experiences can be tested, and in which the relation between action and actor can be made visible.

Whereas MacIntyre seems to overemphasize the role of the story in life itself, Ricoeur seems to overaccentuate the role of the story outside of life. It is significant that he lays much weight on literary stories as the place where the meaning of life is really created. Ricoeur seems to forget that stories have to have a foundation in life, if they are to be effective. Moreover, he completely overlooks the stories we tell in everyday life in order to explain our experiences.

Ricoeur stresses the role of literature, and thus has a rather highbrow view of personal identity. In my opinion, the stories that people use to express the unity of their lives do not have to be literary. The narratives in which people articulate their actions are mostly quite common. They are related to everyday life and everyday experiences. Thus personal identity is not primarily created through classical works of art. It is the result of an interaction between personal experiences and personal stories, entwined with stories of others in ordinary life. Again I can take Proust for my witness. It is not through literature that the narrator learns to specify his experience of Berma's performance. His admiration develops as he hears the applause of the public, and as he reads the story of the critic. We can only learn from stories if they have a direct bearing on our experiences. Of course, literary stories may have this quality, but they are not always useful in this respect, and they certainly are not indispensable.

From a hermeneutic point of view, personal identity is dependent on a mutual relation between lived experience on the one hand, and stories in which this experience is articulated on the other hand. Personal identity presupposes a felt unity of experiences. This unity serves as a foundation for stories, which express experience and thus make its unity manifest. Here again we see an example of *Fundierung* in the phenomenological sense. Personal identity is the result of a hermeneutic relation between experience and story, in which experience elicits the story, and the story articulates and thereby modifies experience.

Stories as Interpretations of Life

Thus far we have seen that, from a hermeneutic point of view, stories are based on life, and life is expressed, articulated, manifested and modified in stories. Stories make explicit the meaning that is implicit in life as it is lived. In stories we aim to make clear and intelligible what life is about. Thus stories are interpretations of life in which the meaning of life is spelled out, in very much the same way as the meaning of a text is spelled out in a literary interpretation. In telling stories we try to make sense of life, like we try to make sense of a text when we interpret it.

The concept of interpretation is central to philosophical hermeneutics. It is, however, also heavily contested. There are various theories on the nature of interpretation. I will discuss three of them, and compare these as to their view on the relation between life and story. The first theory (Collingwood's theory of re-enactment) focuses on the relation between the past and the story of the historian. The second (Gadamer's theory of dialogue) covers both historical and literary interpretations. The third (Derrida's theory of deconstruction) primarily deals with the interpretation of texts, but is more widely applicable, because according to Derrida life itself is (inter)textual.

Collingwood's Theory of Re-Enactment

Although Collingwood is not part of the hermeneutic tradition in the strict sense, his view on the activity of the historian can be called hermeneutic, in that he states that the historian is interested in the meaning of past events. The historian tries to elucidate what these events were about, like the reader of a text tries to make clear what the text is about. Collingwood underlines that the historian has no direct access to the past, no more than the reader has a direct access to the world of the text. Both the historian and the reader are unable to leave their own world behind. The historian cannot return to the past; the reader cannot move over to the world of the text. They can only make sense of their object of study by trying to understand it from their own situation.

How then is the historian to understand the past, if he cannot transport himself in time? In answer to this question Collingwood introduces his famous theory of re-enactment. According to this theory, the historian can understand the past by re-thinking the thoughts of historical actors. Collingwood mentions the example of a historical explanation of the actions of Caesar. The historian tries to understand these actions, Collingwood says, by examining the thoughts in Caesar's mind that made him perform the actions under consideration (Collingwood, 1946, p. 215). Several commentators have criticized Collingwood, by suggesting that this procedure, instead of overcoming the need to return to the past, presupposes such a return. According to Collingwood himself, however, one does not have to go back to Caesar's time in order to examine his thoughts. The historian can re-think Caesar's thoughts without leaving his own situation behind. He can understand how Caesar drew his conclusions, without being actually present.

Collingwood compares the re-enactment of a thought from the past with the performance of a piece of ancient music. Such a performance does not take us back in time; it brings the piece of music to life in the present. The re-enactment of a thought, like the performance of a piece of ancient music, takes place in a situation that is different from the original situation. Music that is ancient in our eyes, was once modern. In the same vein, thoughts that were new for people in the past, can be familiar to us. This can be seen from the fact that ideas that took eminent scholars much work to develop are often easily learned by children of later generations.

According to Collingwood, re-enactment adds a quality to the thoughts under consideration. He says:

> To re-enact the past in the present is to re-enact it in a context which gives it a new quality. This context is the negation of the past itself. Thus, the historian of poetry, reading Dante, re-enacts the medieval experience which that poem expresses; but while doing this he remains himself: he remains a modern man, not a medieval one: and this means that the medievalism of Dante, while genuinely revived and re-experienced within his mind, is accompanied by a whole world of fundamentally non-medieval habits and ideas, which balance it and hold it in check and prevent it from ever occupying the whole field of vision. (Collingwood, in press)

In this statement, Collingwood clearly expresses that the historian cannot leave the present. He even says that the historian can understand the past because he lives in the present, which enables him to see things from a distance. By virtue of this distance, ideas can be rethought more easily than they were originally thought. Thus the distance in time serves as a prism that separates the important from the unimportant, or as a magnifying glass that gives us access to the essence of an idea.

Collingwood's theory of re-enactment can also be applied to individual life. The stories that are told about someone's life can be said to re-enact past experiences. This process of re-enactment is not a return to the past. It is a revival of the past in the context of the present. When a story is told about something that happened in the past, the event is revived, together with the thoughts and feelings that surrounded it. A story makes my past actions understandable by a re-enactment of the deliberations by which they were motivated. A story is a *reconstruction* of life, by which past experiences survive in a more pure way because the inessential is removed, so that only the essential remains. From Collingwood's point of view the narrator in *Autour de Mme Swann* reconstructs his past experience in telling a story about his visit to the theater afterwards. This reconstruction takes place in a different situation, informed by new knowledge (the newspaper report, for instance). The visit is re-enacted, and in this process the meaning of the event comes to the fore more purely.

Interpretation as Dialogue (Gadamer)

Gadamer shares with Collingwood the idea that the interpretation of the past can be compared to the interpretation of a work of art. Contrary to Collingwood, however, Gadamer holds that a work of art does not have an original meaning. Whereas Collingwood still holds on to the notion of the original meaning of the thoughts of an author or actor, a meaning that can be understood by re-enactment, Gadamer proclaims that there is no original meaning. Each interpretation not only sharpens, but also changes the meaning of the phenomenon that is interpreted.

For Gadamer the distance in time plays a more fundamental role than it does in Collingwood's theory. Collingwood says that temporal distance makes it easier to distinguish the essential from the inessential. He presupposes that the essential itself does not change. The meaning of the theorem of Pythagoras, to use one of his examples, is the same for us as for Pythagoras. Gadamer takes a different position. According to him, the meaning of a text is never fixed, but always changing in and through its interpretations. When interpreters distinguish between the essential and the inessential, they change the meaning of the work. Pythagoras saw mathematical, cosmological, and philosophical elements in his work as internally related. Later mathematicians, in saying that the cosmological and philosophical elements are inessential, change the meaning of Pythagoras' theory. According to Gadamer, temporal distance is *productive* (1960, p. 275ff). The meaning of a work is created in the history of its interpretations (the so-called *Wirkungsgeschichte,* p. 284ff).

Gadamer also radicalizes the idea that the situation of the interpreter plays a role in the interpretation. According to Gadamer, interpretation always starts with a question. A text is interpreted within a horizon. In reading a text, we apply it to our present situation. Such an application results in a *fusion of horizons,* in which the perspective of text and reader are combined into a new and more encompassing horizon (1960, p. 289ff). Interpretation is a form of dialogue, in which both participants try to come to grips with the truth in a process of mutual understanding.

Gadamer's philosophical theory of interpretation can be applied to the relation between experience and story in individual life. In telling stories about past experiences, we try to make clear what these experiences mean. According to Gadamer, this requires that we try to see what the experience has to say to us, that we try to apply it to our present situation. In this process of application, the meaning of the experience is changed, as the worldview that is constitutive for the experience is fused with the perspective that is presented in the story. Our story is part of a history of interpretations, which changes the meaning of our life. By telling a story about our life, we change our life. In doing so, the story itself becomes richer, as it is filled with life experience. Thus experience and story may be said to *communicate* with one another. This is in line with Proust, as he says that the experience of the visit to the theater is fused with the story that is told about the performance. In this process of fusion, both the experience and the story get a new meaning: The narrator comes to see his experience as a unique and rich event, and he comes to understand the story as an edifying articulation of what was going on.

Interpretation as Citation (Derrida)

Collingwood and Gadamer both underline that a text that is interpreted is transferred into the present situation. According to Collingwood the text is re-enacted in the present; this process of re-enactment enables the interpreter to understand the point of the ideas behind the text more easily than the author or his contemporaries could. Gadamer says that the text is applied to the present situation; such an application is part of the effective history of the text, in which its meaning is enriched.

The thesis that interpretation is a transfer of the text to a different situation (or context) is presented in a radical way by Derrida. Reading a text, Derrida says, implies taking the text out of its context and placing it in a different context (Derrida, 1988). Whereas Collingwood states that a text is understood through re-enactment of the thoughts it expresses, and Gadamer says that a text engages the reader into a play of question and answer, which may result in a fusion of horizons, Derrida stresses that through interpretations a text is related to other texts in an uncontrollable way. When the text is transferred to a new context, this does not imply that we come nearer to the essence of the thoughts expressed in the text—as Collingwood says—nor that we come closer to the truth—as Gadamer would have it. The transfer of the text just means that new relations are created and new meaning is produced.

For Derrida there is neither origin nor continuity in the history of interpretation. With Gadamer, Derrida refutes the idea of an origin of meaning, which Collingwood cherishes. Against Gadamer, he underlines that there is no unity in the history of interpretation. Interpretation implies a process of *différance,* diffusion of meaning (Derrida, 1972). A text is fundamentally open to new interpretations and can be infinitely transferred to new contexts. Derrida underlines the so-called principle of *intertextuality.* He says:

> Every sign, linguistic or nonlinguistic, . . . can be *cited,* quoted; put between quotation marks; in so doing it can break with every given context, engendering an infinity of new contexts in a manner which is absolutely illimitable. This does not imply that the mark is valid outside of a context, but on the contrary that there are

only contexts without any center or absolute anchoring (*ancrage*]. (Derrida, 1988, p. 12, italics in original)

When we apply Derrida's theory of interpretation to individual life, the notions of unity and continuity of life become problematic. The interpretation of life in stories that are told about it does not result in unity and continuity. Every attempt to unite experiences into a pattern creates, as a necessary consequence, also divergence. Elements that do not fit into the pattern may be momentarily repressed, but are bound to come up again. The creation of unity is part of a process of citation that is both infinite and without *telos*. The interpretation of an experience in a story implies that the experience is placed into a different context. This process goes on and on, without direction or goal. Thus the interpretation of the experience of Berma's performance can be seen as a citation within a new context. The experience is related to various texts (the newspaper reports, for instance), and thus acquires a new meaning. In the story, the experience is not reconstructed nor is its meaning enlarged through a fusion of horizons. The experience is merely transferred and brought into a new web of relations. In our life we are constantly citing ourselves and others, thus creating new patterns of meaning. Life itself is an infinite process of *différance*, creating ever new texts and new contexts.

The three perspectives discussed above elaborate the hermeneutic relation between life and story in different ways. Collingwood describes this relation as reconstruction, Gadamer sees it as dialogical, whereas Derrida uses the notion of intertextuality. Moreover, they are critical of each other's presuppositions. Gadamer and Derrida reject the notion of origin, which is characteristic of Collingwood's theory of re-enactment. Derrida questions the idea of continuity that is present in Gadamer's approach. Collingwood, Gadamer, and Derrida thus present us different images of human life and its narrative character. The consequences of these differences come to the fore more prominently as we turn to the role of narrative in psychology and psychotherapy.

The Story of Life in Psychology and Psychotherapy

From a hermeneutic point of view, life is a process of inter-pretation in and through stories. Psychologists who study life from a narrative frame of reference try to understand the mean-ing of life as it is expressed in stories. Psychotherapists who operate from a narrative point of view try to further the process of meaning-making by listening to stories and helping people to develop new stories. Psychologists and psychotherapists who share this outlook are not interested in facts, but in stories. They use, in Bruner's (1986) terms, a narrative instead of a paradig-matic mode of thought. According to Bruner, these modes of thought are fundamentally different and irreducible to one an-other. Whereas the paradigmatic way of thinking aims at con-text-free explanation, the narrative approach leads to a form of understanding that is contextual and temporal. The paradig-matic mode of thinking tries to mirror reality, whereas the narrative mode of thinking weaves in with the life it relates. In applying the narrative mode of thought, psychologists and psy-chotherapists are engaged in the same practices as the people they study and treat. They try to understand and change life by interpreting it.

From a narrative perspective psychology and psychotherapy can be compared to history. Psychologists try to understand people's thoughts and actions by telling stories, just like historians do. They try to construct meaningful patterns, which give us a context in which thoughts and actions can be understood. Psycho-therapists try to make sense of their clients' lives, working out the stories the clients tell them, like historians use the narratives of the past and turn them into a more complex narrative unity. Thus psychologists and psychotherapists try to make explicit the mean-ing inherent in lived experience by articulating it in stories. Again, the relation between story and life can be characterized in terms of the phenomenological concept of *Fundierung*. Life is the base of psychology and psychotherapy, but the meaning of life is artic-ulated and modified in the stories that are created in psycholog-ical and psychotherapeutic practice.

Following our discussion of hermeneutic perspectives—the hermeneutics of Collingwood that tries to reconstruct the point of a meaningful expression, the hermeneutics of Gadamer that is interested in the truth created through fusion of horizons, and the hermeneutics of Derrida that emphasizes intertextuality—we may distinguish three views on the relation between life on the one hand and psychology and psychotherapy on the other. In all three, psychology and psychotherapy are seen as interpretive activities, but the nature of interpretation is characterized differently. I will briefly elaborate these three hermeneutic perspectives, and elucidate their view on psychology and psychotherapy.

In the first place, the narrative approach within psychology and psychotherapy can be identified as a method that is based on re-enactment. From this perspective, psychology and psychotherapy try to understand human thoughts and actions by performing them in another situation. A metaphor used to describe the activity of the psychologist and the psychotherapist is that of *reconstruction*. A reconstruction aims at a distillation of the essential aspects of thought and action. This idea plays a role within developmental psychology, as it is said to give a rational reconstruction of the development of individuals from one stage of reasoning to the next (see Habermas, 1973, p. 411ff). The notion of reconstruction can also be found in some forms of psychoanalytic therapy that aim at a reconstruction of past experiences in a therapeutic setting in order to gain insight into the essence of a person's life history.

In the second place, narrativity in psychology and psychotherapy can be related to communication. This implies that psychology and psychotherapy are seen as interpersonal encounters that aim at mutual understanding. A metaphor that plays a central role in this perspective is that of an *edifying dialogue*. This version of hermeneutic interpretation is characteristic of those approaches within psychology that focus on concrete processes of meaning-making in individual life (see Widdershoven, 1988). The method used aims to give researchers access to the world of the individuals in which they are interested. An example in the field of developmental psychology is the work of Gilligan (1982). In psychotherapy the notion of dialogue is not unfamiliar. It is the basic principle of Rogers' client-centered approach, in which client and therapist are engaged in a process of mutual understanding that aims at an explicitation of the clients' actual experiences.

In the third place, the narrative approach within psychology and psychotherapy can be seen as a process of citation. From this perspective psychologists and psychotherapists transfer texts to new contexts. Psychological research and psychotherapeutic work are embedded within an intertextual process that involves a diffusion of meaning. A metaphor associated with this perspective is that of *redefinition*. Critics of modern academic psychology show that much of the work that psychologists do is in fact governed by the principles of intertextuality, and that their argumentation is thoroughly rhetorical (Parker & Shotter, 1990). An example in the field of developmental psychology is the work of Slugoski and Ginsburg (1989), who present an alternative reading of Erikson, which stresses the role of power and rhetorics in human life. The importance of redefinition was acknowledged earlier in psychotherapy. A good example is to be found in family therapy. The family therapist deliberately tries to create new meaning by rhetorically redefining existing family relations. Expressions are placed in a new context, and thus their meaning changes completely (e.g., the behavior of a husband, who continuously criticizes his wife, is redefined as supporting and helping).

Conclusion

From a hermeneutic point of view, the relation between life and story can be characterized as interpretive. A story interprets experiences; it makes their meaning explicit. There are, however, various theories of interpretation that may all be called hermeneutic. Collingwood sees interpretation as a way of getting access to the *point* of (historical) thoughts and actions; according to Gadamer interpretation involves a dialogue that is interested in the *truth* of the text; Derrida says that interpretation is a process of *citation*, in which text and reader are part of a process that is governed by the principle of intertextuality. Thus there are several hermeneutic perspectives on the role of narrative in life. According to Collingwood, experience is reconstructed in stories: Stories help us to recapitulate our past experiences and actions. Gadamer says that stories may enrich experience: Stories help us to express the unity of our lives and thus to create our identity. Derrida asserts that in stories experience is transferred to new contexts: Stories thus articulate the intertextuality of life.

The three hermeneutic perspectives share the idea that life and story are internally related. This implies that life is both more and less than a story. It is more in that it is the basis of a variety of stories, and it is less in that it is unfinished and unclear as long as there are no stories told about it. The intertwining of experience and story lies at the core of individual life and psychological understanding.

References

Bruner, J. (1986). *Actual minds, possible worlds.* Cambridge, MA: Harvard University Press.

Carr, D. (1986). *Time, narrative and history.* Bloomington: Indiana University Press.

Collingwood, R. G. (1946). *The idea of history* (T. M. Knox, Ed.). Oxford: Oxford University Press.

Collingwood, R. G. (in press). Outlines of a philosophy of history (1928). In *The idea of history* (rev. ed.). Oxford: Oxford University Press.

Derrida, J. (1972). La différance. In J. Derrida, *Marges de la philosophie.* Paris: Minuit.

Derrida, J. (1988). *Limited Inc.* Evanston, IL: Northwestern University Press.

Gadamer, H.-G. (1960). *Wahrheit und Methode.* Tübingen: Mohr.

Gilligan, C. (1982). *In a different voice: Psychological theory and women's development.* Cambridge, MA: Harvard University Press.

Habermas, J. (1973). *Erkenntnis und Interesse.* Frankfurt: Suhrkamp.

Hardy, B. (1986). Towards a poetics of fiction: An approach through narrative. *Novel, 2,* 5-14.

MacIntyre, A. (1981). *After virtue.* London: Duckworth.

Merleau-Ponty, M. (1945). *Phénoménology de la perception.* Paris: Gallimard.

Mink, L. O. (1987). *Historical understanding*. Ithaca, NY: Cornell University Press.

Parker, I., & Shotter, J. (Eds.). (1990). *Deconstructing social psychology*. London: Routledge & Kegan Paul.

Proust, M. (1919). *A la recherche du temps perdu. A l'ombre des jeunes filles en fleur. Première Partie: Autour de Mme Swann*. Paris: Gallimard.

Ricoeur, P. (1983). *Temps et récit, I*. Paris: Seuil.

Ricoeur, P. (1990). *Soi-même comme un autre*. Paris: Seuil.

Rorty, R. (1989). *Contingency irony and solidarity*. Cambridge: Cambridge University Press.

Slugoski, B. R., & Ginsberg, G. P. (1989). Ego identity and explanatory speech. In J. Shotter & K. J. Gergen (Eds.), *Texts of identity* (pp. 36-55). London: Sage.

White, H. (1981). The value of narrative in the representation of reality. In W. J. T. Mitchell (Ed.), *On narrative*. Chicago: University of Chicago Press.

Widdershoven, G.A.M. (1988). Models of development. *Schweizerische Zeitschrift für Psychologie, 47*, 129-134.

❧ 2 ❧

The Incomprehensible Catastrophe

Memory and Narrative

Amos Funkenstein

The Possibility to Narrate

𝒯he visitor to this exhibit of art in Theresienstadt may wonder why these artists—professionals and amateurs, known or anonymous—risked their lives in order to create illegal art. In part, no doubt, they did so as a means of mental survival. With their art, they maintained their artistic identity and creativity. Some of them, you may remember, were forced to produce utterly fictitious scenes of life in this concentration camp that the Germans called, sarcastically, "a town the Führer gave the Jews as a present." To those artists, the need to become once again faithful to their vocation was irresistible. And finally: A most urgent driving force was the need to remember and to be remembered. They wanted the unbelievable to be believed in other places and other times. Indeed, Germans forbade art but permitted musical

AUTHOR'S NOTE: This chapter was delivered as a lecture in conjunction with the exhibition "Seeing Through 'Paradise': Artists and the Terezin Concentration Camp," at the University Art Museum, Berkeley, CA, March 1992.

21

performances or lectures in Theresienstadt precisely because the latter are ephemeral whereas the former may have served to document and to remember. And so, again at grave risk, many of the pictures were hidden in most ingenious places.

Remembering the collective misery, the unbearable conditions of life, the gloom and the despair was, however, not the only purpose of these pictures. Perhaps it is not even their main theme. They abound, as you can see for yourself, in individual portraits; and even in many of the public scenes depicted, you may discern individual postures and faces. The pictures wish to also preserve the memory of individuals—the individuals pictured and the individual styles and interpretations of the artists. They wish to perpetuate the memory of concrete persons whose history is, so to say, written in their postures and in their faces. The pictures breath the urge for individuation.

Let me formulate these various considerations somewhat differently. Through their creative activity, through their commemorative efforts of the common and the individual, these artists gave meaning to their lives and the lives of their fellow human beings in that they restored a narrative. Recuperating or continuing a narrative, in a sense I shall soon explain, was the effect of all creative activities in Theresienstadt as well as in other ghettos, and this is true in particular of attempts to express, to reflect, to hold in memory the persons and the individual experiences in these horrible places. It was still possible to do so; it became impossible in concentration and death camps.

I use the term *narrative* in a precise though peculiar sense. My acting-in-the-world—be it the social world or be it the world of nature that always is, to use a phrase of Marx, "humanized nature"—is the continuous plotting of a narrative, interpreting the past and projecting the future according to my image of myself. Acting in the world involves and construes my identity continuously, and my identity is a narrative, my narrative. It is not a narrative that *needs* to be told in words (though invariably we are driven to tell it). In the very same sense in which telling my narrative is a speech-act, my actions, my involvement with the world are an act of speech, the building up of a continuous story. "*Ich wünschte ich wäre eine Beethovensche Symphonie oder sonst etwas, was geschrieben ist,*" said the young Rosenzweig in one of his letters; "*das geschrieben werden tut weh*" (Rosenzweig, 1935, p. 19). The identity of an individual and the identity of a group consists of the construction of a narrative, internal and external: the narrative construed *by* and the narrative construed *about* the subject. Such is the making of a "self"— in a process that Hegel aptly described as a process of mutual "recognition" (*Anerkennung*). A subject's identity, continuously construed, *is* his or her history.

I cannot resist quoting from the "Oration for the Dignity of Man," by one of the greatest of Renaissance humanists, Pico della Mirandola (1956). Of all living species, he said, humankind alone lacks a fixed nature. Being a true microcosm, endowed with the seed of every kind there is, he can become everything he wishes to become:

> At last the best of artisans ordained that the creature to whom He had been able to give nothing proper to himself should have joint possession of whatever had been peculiar to each of the different kinds of being. He therefore took man as a creature of indeterminate nature and . . . addressed him thus: ". . . The nature of all other beings is limited. . . . Thou, constrained by no limit, in accordance with thine own free will, shalt ordain for thyself the limits of thy nature. . . . Thou shalt have the power to degenerate into the lower forms of life, which are brutish. Thou shalt have the power . . . to be reborn (*regenerari*) into higher forms, which are divine." (pp. 224-227)

The human self, Pico della Mirandola tells us, is made, not born: The making of the self is what I called its narrative.

Every so often we are told by historians or other students of the Holocaust how difficult if not impossible it is to construe a narrative from the indisputable facts about it, how impossible it is to represent the experiences of concentration camps as a coherent story. My friend and colleague Saul Friedlaender recently organized a conference dedicated to the limits of representation of the Holocaust—the outcome is now available in a handsome volume. Those of you who have seen Landzman's unforgettable *Shoa* will remember how fragmented the memory of survivors was; a fragmentation now documented manyfold in the recent book by Lawrence Langer (1991), *Holocaust Testimonies: The Ruins of Memory.* This fragmentation of memory is only partly and insufficiently accounted for by the trauma, the pain of remembering—all the more so because many of them now *want* to remember. Let me suggest a simpler circumstance that compounds the difficulty of remembering. In the sense just elaborated, most inmates of concentration—and death—camps *had* no narrative to remember later. The Nazis robbed them of their identity, of their capacity to construct a narrative, of investing the events their lives with meaning and purpose. They lost their individuality; and survived or died, as Primo Levi describes, as if they were human atoms. This may be the deeper reason why even survivors find it so difficult to reconstruct individually a meaningful sequence or pattern of events afterwards—except for those who, like Primo Levi, had the fortune within their misfortune of a little bit of a shelter: He was used as a chemist in the I. G. Farben plant.

Things were different in the ghettos, as they were in Theresienstadt. Indeed there, too, people lived in the daily shadows of death. But there was still some latitude, some space for creativity, for decisions, for expression, in short: for the construction of narrative. It is these expressions that you saw today, in this exhibit. Through their works of art, the artists both described the individual lives of others and, by so doing, expressed also their identity, constructed their own narrative.

The Incomprehensibility of the Holocaust

These considerations lead us inevitably to other closely related ones. Historical narratives are the way we comprehend the past. Every so often, even serious students of the Holocaust speak of the "incomprehensibility" of the events. How can we hope to *understand* the mentality of the perpetrators or the experience of the victims? The concentration camps—even the ghettos—were "another world," "another planet." Those responsible for the genocide certainly did not act out of any recognizable political, economic, or other logic of *raison d'état*. Nothing in our historical or personal experience can be found by way of an illuminating analogy. And so, some of the best students of those times, whose knowledge in these matters surpasses mine by leaps, insist that there will always be an irreducible, elusive enigma.

I wish to oppose this stand vehemently. I wish to claim, to the contrary, that it is the duty of historians, psychologists, sociologists, and philosophers—in short, of all who reflect upon the human condition—to make every possible effort to comprehend the catastrophe in all of its aspects; and they ought to be guided by the reasonable expectation of success. Perhaps historians ought to learn something from physicists or mathematicians—namely that one can still hope to understand where imagination fails; for who can imagine a fourth or *n*-th dimension? or a singularity? The crimes committed by the Nazis were of immense proportions. They defy any patent rationale, their horror transgresses our capacity of imagination, yet it is possible to understand them, because understanding does not presuppose empathy for the perpetrators or the reliving in the mind the experiences of the victims. Even if the perpetrators were madmen who lost all touch with reality, a reconstruction of their mentality and patterns of action would be possible—inasmuch as psychiatry makes it possible. But they were not madmen, at least not in the clinical sense of the word. If madness entails loss of sense of reality, then no entire society can be called mad, because reality is—as Luckmann and Berger taught us—a social construct through and through (Berger & Luckmann, 1967). The prehistory of the genocide, its necessary condition, and the logic of its unfolding can be illuminated more and more by the collective, cumulative efforts of interpretation.

Let me sketch a possible narrative—an account of the mental mechanism by which Nazi ideology led to mass murder, step by step. All anti-Semitic ideologies since the end of the 19th century had in common that they were directed less against traditional, Orthodox Jews who could be recognized *as* Jews, and much more against those Jews who became well acculturated and assimilated. Assuming, as anti-Semitic ideologues more and more came to assume, that being Jewish is an indelible, innate character, which no conversion or acculturation could obliterate, it seemed to follow that the assimilated Jews deceived others and perhaps even themselves. In the best case, they may believe that they are capable of becoming full Germans or Frenchmen; in the worst case, their assimilation is a conspiratorial pretense to undermine the healthy texture of society from within and gain world power. The way to undo the damage was to isolate the Jews again, to revoke their legal emancipation, to turn them back from citizens to subjects. This program—and no more—was thoroughly implemented, step by step, during the first 7 years following the Nazi *Machtergreifung* in Germany—mostly with the tacit or explicit approval of the population. Jews were isolated and forced to emigrate so as to leave Germany *Judenrein.*

But the National Socialist ideology contained the germ of a much more ruthless so-called solution of the Jewish Question. In its dramatic-apocalyptic reading of world history, Jews were not only an inferior race on the order of Slavs or blacks, but rather a much more dangerous, unique counterrace, a hypostatized negation of sanity, creativity, health, sanitation, and order, a secular antichrist. If other so-called races—say the Slavs or the Semites—were subhuman (*Untermenschen*), Jews throughout history were nonhuman (*Unmenschen*), a counterrace to the *Herrenrasse,* a vermin, a bacillus that can live only a parasitic life by seemingly adjusting to its host organism so as to destroy it. Isolating them was not enough; and with the onset of the war it became impossible to force their emigration. As the war broadened, Germany—and certainly the Nazi leadership—slipped into an acute sense of an apocalyptic "total war." Jews had to be exterminated, and their extermination was again spoken of in terms of hygienic medicine—as the extermination of rats (*Jud Süß*) or bacteria.

Realizing a Metaphor

The isolation of Jews in ghettos under subhuman conditions, their systematic degradation and murder in the camps, were not only the *result* of Nazi fantasies about the Jews but also the way in which these fantasies were translated into reality. They were instruments to deprive Jews of their identity, of their humanity, to make them into that which Nazis thought they were to begin with: nonhuman. *Entlausung* was the terrible realization of an ideological metaphor. The Jews, themselves lice in the Nazi terminology, had to be deloused (*entlaust*) entering the camp or the death chambers. They were to be made into lice, forced to live in the most unhygienic conditions, worked to death, dehumanized even in their own eyes, deprived of name, of even a minimum of personal possessions, of anything reminding of one's identity, and finally exterminated as lice. Symbolism and reality became almost one.

Franz Kakfa's famous story, "The Metamorphosis" (*"Die Verwandlung"*), that also deals, as many of his stories, with the dissolution of identity, may serve to explain further what "the realization of a metaphor" may mean. Gregor Samsa, you will remember, wakes up one day to find himself *"ein riesen Ungeziefer"* (Kafka, 1967). At first, his physical and mental behavior is still rather human. Slowly, gradually, through a subtle interaction between his family and himself, he acquires more and more the mentality of a roach; and he dies like one. At the end of the story, after his death, we discover that, in a sense, he was always something of a bug, even before the story commenced: The family, seemingly once depending totally on him, gets along splendidly without him. He was always superfluous: "becoming" a bug was not a coincidence after all, but rather the continuous translation of a symbol or of a metaphor into reality. Kafka, by the way, may well have been deported to Theresienstadt had he been alive.

The ghettos and even more so the concentration camps thus were mechanisms that functioned to concretize, to visualize, the rationale for extermination. Theresienstadt was different. Though the shock of coming there was devastating, and the daily misery and anxiety unspeakable, its inmates were not deprived of their identity; they held to it desperately, and the pictures you saw are a proof of it. Why the Germans permitted even that much is not obvious: perhaps to have prominent Jews as hostages, perhaps for propaganda reasons. But they did.

The point I wanted to make is that, without a shred of empathy, one can give an account, a narrative as it were, of Nazi acts and motives. They are not incomprehensible. It is not even true that the extermination of the Jews was carried out at the cost of the war effort. On the contrary: One of the lessons of the Holocaust, as of other later genocides such as in Cambodia, is indeed the realization of how easy it is to commit genocide, with what few resources and manpower it can be done. We cannot excuse ourselves from the obligation of understanding the acts of the Nazis, to construct their collective and individual narrative, if we want to condemn them, let alone if we want to prevent similar crimes from being committed again.

But is not the experience of the victims incomprehensible? Did I not say myself that they were robbed of their identity, of their narrative? More than other students of the Catastrophe, theologians seem to emphasize the "incomprehensibility" of the Holocaust and the "madness" of those who caused it because they, the theologians, cannot find any theological meaning to it—certainly not in the language of traditional theodicies (Funkenstein, 1989). Perhaps also because they hardly dare to say that if one were to believe in transcendent agencies, the Holocaust could prove the autonomy of evil, an evil manifested not only by the number of its victims but also by its sheer inexhaustible inventiveness, by the almost infinite varieties of systematic degradation and killing. If, however, one turns from God to humanity, the Holocaust is neither incomprehensible nor meaningless. It was neither bestial nor pagan. It was, indeed, an eminently human event that demonstrated those extremes that *only* human beings and their society are capable of doing or suffering. It pointed at a possibility of human existence never known before, a possibility as human as the noblest instances of creativity and compassion, a possibility that Pico della Mirandola could never anticipate—that human beings can destroy not only their own form but also that of others. We can be deprived of our identity against our will. It is our duty to understand that and how it can happen, and to rescue as many life stories—identities or, if you wish, narratives—as we can out of the ashes. History is always the history of individuals.

References

Berger, P., & Luckmann, K. (1967). *The social construction of reality.* Garden City, NY: Doubleday.

Funkenstein, A. (1989). Theological responses to the Holocaust. In François Furet (Ed.), *Unanswered questions: Nazi Germany and the genocide of the Jews* (pp. 304-320). New York: Schocken.

Kafka, F. (1967). *Die Verwandlung* [The metamorphosis]. In *Kafka's Erzählungen* (B. Flach, Ed.). Bonn: Fischer.

Langer, L. L. (1991). *Holocaust testimonies: The ruins of memory.* New Haven, CT: Yale University Press.

Pico della Mirandola, G. (1956). Oratio de hominis dignitate. In E. Cassirer, P. O. Kristeller, & J. H. Randall (Eds.), *The Renaissance philosophy of man: Petrarca, Valla, Ficino, Pico, Pomponazzi, Vives* (pp. 224-227). Chicago: University of Chicago Press.

Rosenzweig, F. (1935). *Briefe* (E. Rosenzweig, Ed.). Berlin: Schocken.

❧ 3 ❧

A Moment's Monument

The Psychology of Keeping a Diary

Wendy J. Wiener
George C. Rosenwald

*"The horror of that moment," the King went on, "I shall
never, never forget."
"You will, though," said the Queen, "if you don't make
a memorandum of it."*

Lewis Carroll

*W*hen Freud likened the life histories of hysterical patients to
"an unnavigable river whose stream is at one moment choked
by masses of rock and at another divided and lost among shal-
lows and sandbanks," he was referring to the ravages of insin-
cerity and repression rather than suggesting that comprehensive, smoothly flowing narratives are the rule (Freud, 1905, p.
23). On the contrary, most life stories are strings of episodes and
generalizations punctuated by gaps and uncertainties. However,
blank spaces are usually tolerated by the narrators and investigators unless they happen to frustrate a particular inquiry.

Rather than ask what life experiences have survived repression, we might accordingly do better to study what the subject has selected for preservation. For the act of remembrance is a choosing, a highlighting, a shaping, an enshrinement (even when it hurts). A life story is not simply that which has escaped forgetting.

Some subjects preserve experience in diaries, and when they do, biographers and students of life narrative plumb them eagerly. But how is one to read a diary? Unless one regards diaries as straightforward records of the past—windows on worlds of fact and experience no longer retrievable by other means—one must wonder what prompted the diarist to make the entries and why in a particular way. What is the utility of the diary to the diarist? This—the psychology of keeping a diary—is the topic of this chapter.

Our interest is not well represented in the research tradition. More often investigators have regarded diaries as records of a (secret) truth. But if we replace this voyeuristic notion with a pragmatistic one, we can no longer interpret diaries the same way: We are then watching the diarist at work rather than mining hidden facts.

Is the diary a narcissistic indulgence? Or perhaps a prosthesis for the writer's memory? Is it a communication with a nameless, even unconsciously intended audience? Allport (1951) suspected that it is addressed only to the author him- or herself. Hoffer (1946), Stein (1977), and Stewart, Franz, and Layton (1988) have used the content of diaries to draw psychological conclusions about the owners of the diaries. By contrast, the psychology of keeping a diary has been largely ignored.

Literary biographers and historians have to some extent addressed the diary as a genre or a cultural phenomenon,[1] and the self-reflective remarks of a few of the better known published diarists give us some glimpses of how the diarist experiences him-or herself as a diarist.[2] However, there has been remarkably little systematic attention paid to the meaning of diary writing as an activity or commitment, or to the personal meaning of being a diarist. For the most part, discussions in the psychological literature are limited to the educational or therapeutic uses of assigned journals in writing classes as well as in certain cognitive and behaviorally oriented treatments.

In one of the few studies of diary-keeping as such, Sosin demonstrated the "relational and developmental functions of a diary" (1983, p. 93). Writing about the diaries of adolescent girls in particular, she argued that the diary functions as a transitional object for such girls. In reviewing the literature about adolescent diaries, she rejected the traditional focus upon the content of a diary, and instead examined the "diary-diarist relationship," that is, the role and function of the diary in the person's life. Drawing on the concept of transitional object introduced by Winnicott, she argued that the diary can serve as one of these "soothing psychic structures" that bridge the gap between the "me" and the "not me" (p. 95). The purpose of a transitional object in infancy is to allow secure differentiation from the mother and may be experienced by the child ambiguously as neither part of the self nor completely different from it. Sosin argued that in the second individuation of adolescence, transitional phenomena, of which diary-keeping is an example, take a more symbolic form. Although adolescents know that the diary is not literally a part of their body, they may experience it quite intensely as just that—part of themselves and yet also as another person, confidante or lover, for example. Sosin's interviews with young women revealed that the diary provided its owner with a means for discovering her own self as separate from her parents. Sosin concluded that "diary writing is a phase-appropriate developmental phenomenon . . . [that] functions as a transitional object by generating calm, integrating affect and thought, and facilitating differentiation" (p. 96). Dalsimer (1982) also attributed an object-relational function to adolescent diaries.

Because these findings pertain to only one stage of the life cycle with its specific developmental tasks, it seems worthwhile to explore to what other dynamic and integrative uses diaries can be put. The objectivation of the self, inherent in the process of writing about oneself, is bound to be meaningful in different ways for all diarists. Further, the meaning of diary-keeping itself, of the contents written about, and finally of being a diarist are apt to be diverse and complex.

Overview

Material for this chapter is drawn from a study of 12 people between the ages of 18 and 50, who volunteered to be interviewed for one to three hours about their experience of keeping a diary. Four of them were college students, five were graduate students, and three were professionals, including one who was also a part-time graduate student. Five were men, and seven were women. Their backgrounds, goals, and life experiences varied but we made no effort to create a representative sample. Instead we looked for respondents of some diversity who could provide us with instructive examples. These diarists were asked to describe their personal backgrounds and the history of their diary writing and to speak in general about themselves, their thoughts and feelings about the diary, and how it fit into their lives. They were assured from the outset that no attempt would be made to penetrate the privacy of the diaries themselves. The intention was rather to explore the meanings with which diaries are invested by diarists and the uses to which they are put.

Together with the contents of diaries, the psychology of keeping a diary is still largely a secret. Because diaries are not only among the biographer's and the life history researcher's favorite resources, but ostensibly play an important role in the understanding and development of the diarist's self, students of life history are apt to benefit from a lifting of the veil. A multiple case study approach was chosen with the intention of exploring the range of possible uses and meanings of diaries (Rosenwald, 1988). Rather than pursuing empirical regularities or seeking to construct the typical diarist's personality profile, our aim is to learn what psychological possibilities a diary offers the diarist. This requires an understanding of diarists' diverse experiences. Thus our goal is to sensitize rather than generalize. We shall therefore present the findings from our open-ended interviews under several headings, each of which represents a perspective relevant to what it might mean to keep a diary. Because we had no access to the respondents' diaries, but only to their own reflections on keeping them, we do not document our findings with actual entries. Our eye is on the *subjective* utility of diaries. Diaries themselves might shed additional light on this. Therefore, it might be worthwhile to follow this investigation with others in which diarists are asked to comment on specific entries. Above all, we wish to stress that many different complicated meanings were attached by the respondents to their diaries. In a concluding section we offer a hypothesis about the diarist's overall commitment to the diary—beyond the practice of day-by-day writing. We relate this commitment to issues of memory and personal development.

We undertook the project with the following orienting questions: To what extent might the diary, even in adult life, function in some sense as an "other"; that is, might diarists think of the diary as another person? And if so, in what ways might they think of it other than as the "Dear Understanding Ear" of Sosin's adolescent diarists? To change perspectives, might writing in the diary be a performance as well as creating the audience for it? If so, does the idea of the diary figure as a representation of the performing diarist's self? What are the possible meanings of writing about—or to, or for—oneself?

Because diaries are usually kept private, they easily become featured not only as repositories of secrets, but as a representation of secrecy itself. It is only natural to wonder about the role of shame and concealment in the act of diary keeping. This question proves difficult to address, eliciting contradictory reactions; it seems that the subject of secrecy is intrinsically elusive. Finally, the keeping of a diary is an activity extended in time and one that marks and describes the passage of time. What meaning might the consciousness of this have for individuals, and what role might it have in shaping their development?

But these were only the initial questions. Others arose as the complex meaning of diary-keeping unfolded in the interviews. The diary, we were reminded, is at once an object, a place, and an activity. As these ambiguities shifted depending on which aspect of the diary became the focus of a particular interview, we became alert to the role diaries play in defining and manipulating boundaries of many kinds—including those among aspects of the self, among points in time, and between self and others.

The processing of emotional experience is another topic to which our attention was unexpectedly drawn. But no perspective or topic is separate from the others. For example, the theme of boundaries includes, as subsets, boundaries involved in the experience of emotions and boundaries involved in the experience of the self. However, emotional experience processed in the diary need not be limited to the creation or dissolution of boundaries; it can also involve the evocation of an "other" to witness or respond to the emotion. Thus the categories under which our comments are organized should be regarded as overlapping, and it should be kept in mind that some of our respondents activate psychological functions of diary-keeping that play only a slight role in the accounts of others.

Setting Boundaries

We will begin by addressing the different ways in which a diary can be used to establish and maintain boundaries. These can be boundaries between different "selves" when the diarist experiences himself or herself as many people. They can also be boundaries between different experiences and emotions that the diarist wishes to separate from one another. The scope of what can be bounded by the diary seems as broad as the ways the diary can be defined: as an objectivation of the self, for example, or as a container for experiences and emotions.

The use of multiple diaries to compartmentalize and separate experiences even further is not uncommon. One subject illustrates this establishing of boundaries among aspects of the self and among emotional states. Hester, a recently married college student, who was a victim of sexual abuse in childhood, patiently describes her use of five separate, simultaneous diaries, each with its own prescribed domain. Her use of the diary resembles what Sperling (1948) called "the spacing of emotions." This concept refers to a specific example of the defense mechanism of isolation evident in those cases in which "out of fear of an excess of emotion, the affect is subdivided and the parts experienced at different times" (p. 232).

One of Hester's diaries is for what she calls "documentary" purposes. This one is the least private and unlike the others will not require destruction before her death. In fact, this diary, paradoxically the only one with a lock, is to serve future biographers if she should become famous. An aspiring and talented artist, she does in fact have realistic expectations of fame. Hester deliberately writes only brief, factual accounts of important events in it, as she considers this a journal of her "whole life," and hopes not to use it up until her whole life is over. In contrast, her other diaries treat more specific topics. She has what she terms her "married life journal," which she began at the time she planned her wedding and in which she writes on anniversaries and about things pertaining to her marriage. She hopes to pass this diary on to her future children. She also has an "angry journal," in which she cannot write loving thoughts. In this book she cannot include "daydreams about my husband" because "it's just too full of nasty ugly things." She also has a "spiritual journal, where I only write about my spiritual growth and thoughts about God." Recently she acquired yet another journal that she considers to be specifically for a transition she is now making in her life as she graduates from college, takes a career-related trip, and resettles, temporarily without her husband, in another city to begin advanced training. It is important to keep specific moods and subjects separated in particular diaries. Additionally, as will be further discussed below, she experiences herself as somewhat fragmented, in the context of her childhood abuse, into different selves who do not know each other well and are represented in the different diaries.

Sam, a graduate student, describes keeping two diaries, one for keeping track of miles he has run and another for recording daily events. Within this second diary he establishes several more boundaries. He prefers to use diaries of the type designed to be appointment books in which a page is provided for each week, with boxes for the days and a facing blank page. Sam "forces" himself to record the day's factual events in the box and then sometimes uses the facing blank page for "rumination." However, he emphasizes that this rumination is restricted to a written search for a solution to various problems, mainly involving how to do better at tasks he sets for himself. In this way he isolates external facts from internal thoughts and further separates even these thoughts from feelings, which are excluded altogether. "Phobias, fears, fantasies, flights of fancy are not included," he remarks. Thomas Mallon (1984), in the introduction to his survey of published diaries, mused on his own diary-keeping, which bears some similarity to Sam's experience: "I try to write each night, but I often don't get around to writing up a day until several more have gone by. But I manage to keep them all separate. . . . I suppose it's a compulsion" (p. xiii).

As can be seen (and will be further discussed under a later heading) diaries separate not only domains of experience from each other but also episodes and segments of time. John, who keeps a carefully composed "journal" as well as a portable, casual "thought book," compared his diary-keeping to dental hygiene: "I do it every day because it feels good, and it's good for me."

What are these diarists attempting to do by establishing these rigid boundaries with and within their diaries? What is being isolated? One can see in this act an isolation of affects, but one can also view it as a separating of different self-images from one another. Whereas Sam is a person who seems to prefer to remain unemotional, Hester is quite involved in her own emotions, using them professionally in her art as well as personally. Indeed she describes at length how she hopes to gain access to her true emotions through writing because she seems often to cut herself off from them self-protectively—a habit of distancing she attributes to her experience of abuse in childhood. Her separation of aspects of the self into different books appears to be akin to the dissociation observed in people with multiple personality disorder, in many of whom the pathology is traceable to childhood abuse. At the same time it may be thought of as the written manifestation of an already existing dissociation of selves. Such separation allows her greater control over the part-selves as well as contact among them that is unavailable to a person with multiple personality disorder. Even in well-functioning persons such complex self-structures are serviceable (Dixon & Baumeister, 1991).

The defense mechanism of isolation is usually discussed in relation to affects that are separated from the ideas originally accompanying them. Diaries may point our way to a subtler understanding of this process because they can create various other segregations and compartmentalizations, including components of self, episodes, activities, ideas. It should be noted, however, that these separations are only relative. Their allocation to different places in diaries is reversible; the pieces can, at the will of the diarist, be reassembled, if only temporarily. The isolation can be undone, and it appears moreover that its reversibility is one of the attractions of writing in diaries—the retrievability and reappropriation of what has been objectivated.

Managing Emotions

Diaries can control and contain emotional experience in various ways, for instance, by evoking and shaping it in the act of writing. Some subjects report that they write only when in a good mood, others only when depressed. Bruce, a graduate student, remarks that his diary gives a distorted picture of his life because he only writes in it while depressed; when he is happy he has no motivation to analyze his mood. Victoria, a college student, observes the opposite; her diary creates a false impression because she cannot bring herself to write about sad events and only writes when something good has happened to her. Yet another subject, Virginia, a graduate student and aspiring novelist, elaborates this idea further. As a child she had a fear she had never been able to write about because she worried that writing about something could make it come true. An interesting question raised by these comments that will be addressed later is the meaning of creating an impression of any sort. Who is the audience to this self-portrait?

A diary can be used to control or contain negative emotions without the creation of rigid physical boundaries. James, a scientist, presents himself as mild-mannered and claims never to raise his voice in anger. His journal contains all of his

> negative emotions . . . feelings of remorse and loss. . . . Jealousy, anger and swearing come out in unabashed tones. . . . The diary is like raw ego screaming. . . . When I write, I can get much rawer. . . . I don't have to worry: Am I hurting somebody? Am I inflicting pain?

Here the diary as sole repository for negative emotions helps to isolate emotions from the rest of life. By contrast, Sam keeps fantasies, fears, and emotions out of his diary. Whereas Sosin's adolescents treat the diary as a " 'vent for the emotions' " (p. 99), James has little sense of the diary as a particularly tolerant, receiving object that might offer an alternative to intolerant parents. The diary is simply a safe place or container for the emotions.

We can also understand James's experience by thinking of diary writing as an activity during which the diarist is in a special state of mind in which thoughts and feelings are free from their usual controls. In the diary one can safely try out unusual or unacceptable ways of being without fear of disrupting one's everyday life. Creativity can thrive on such an interlude. As Hester put it:

> It's the moving up and out of thoughts and feelings. . . . If I sit and think, I can get real tense, but if I put it into an activity like writing . . . it takes shape. The feeling that I have as it takes shape is the same. (What is that feeling?) Creation! I'm not planning it, it just comes out through language, and shapes. . . . It just bypasses something—straight from my mind, or heart to form, without, what would you call it, cerebral *analyzation*!

Elizabeth, a graduate student who describes herself as an unusually emotional person, grew up feeling that her emotions were overwhelming to others and that they did not wish to receive them. To get what she needed, she had to present herself to others in a rational, orderly manner. Her use of the diary helps her to comprehend and organize her emotions. Sosin discussed the role of the diary for her adolescent subjects as an accepting "object the diarists sought when they felt besieged by confusing or intense emotions," because it "tolerates the discharge of all affects" (p. 99). She also noted its related use as a "self-soothing mechanism." One of her subjects described the experience of writing when upset as akin to

> taking a sedative. . . . A lot of times I would feel angry, sad, or anxious and . . . sitting down and just outlining what was going on, it really almost always made me feel a lot better. (p. 98)

To Elizabeth, the diary is not simply a repository for these overwhelming feelings. It is a place where she tames and molds them into presentable shape. The attempt to rationalize and gain control of her feelings is primary. Writing in the diary is often a prelude to a conversation with a real other person, usually her parents, but also friends and lovers.

> (What happens when you need to write?) Mostly emotional extremes, one way or the other. . . . It's what I use to figure out what's going on in my head . . . to sort of puzzle things out. (How does that work?) I usually just start stating the problem: "Just hung up with my parents and I'm feeling confused about thus and such, or angry about thus and such." Then I usually proceed to describe what I think I'm feeling . . . just trying to figure out what it is I'm feeling and then try and isolate what I'm feeling and figure out what the causes are and what I feel about it. So I'll say, you know, I'll describe what's going on and kind of pick it apart. It's a fairly analytical process. . . . It can be a

preliminary step to going back and working it through with whoever was causing the problem.

This use seems to go beyond self-soothing or discharging affects. Rather, organization and analysis let the diarist feel more in control of her feelings and able to make use of them interpersonally. In addition, it is possible that the active nature of writing facilitates this process. Brand and Powell (1985) suggest that writing always effects a change in emotions, tending to increase positive feelings and weakening what they term "negative passive emotions." Litowitz and Gundlach (1987) argue that "as there is a lessening of affect through mediation from experience to speech, there is a further weakening of affect in writing. Writing can therefore serve to tame and control emotions that threaten to overwhelm the subject" (p. 86). Diaries, in which the management of emotions is often so central, may be useful windows on the processing of emotion more generally.

Dissolving Boundaries

Rather than tame affects, a diary can mobilize and focus them. Hester uses her diary to give her emotions free play but also to help herself learn about them. Without the diary, she sometimes experiences them as belonging to separate selves between which there is little communication. She sees herself as someone who "stuffs down" emotions and suffers various symptoms of irrational anxiety and depression as a result. In the diary, she says,

> I speak to myself. I let it out on paper, like a secret with myself. [Even in the diary] there are parts of myself that don't get to know the secret. I just quiet them and say "You're not there" and let the voices speak. . . . It's a way for me to hear voices within myself that I've been unwilling to hear because the other voices were louder and drowned them out. So if I can get the louder ones to be quiet and sneak it out onto paper, then I can see it and eventually when I've seen it I can confront it.

In recounting her recent discovery of previously repressed memories of sexual abuse, she relates how the diary helped her to remember:

> Often it's the voice of the little girl that speaks through my pen, that didn't have enough courage to speak to the voices that've been drowning her out all these years. . . . It feels so good, discovering this child within me, I'm meeting someone, getting to know someone and it feels good to hear what she has to say and know she's there because I never thought, as far as I was concerned, I was never a little girl. . . . If something's painful she'll want me to write . . . I'll have to write to get to her.

Whereas many diarists search for control, Hester regards the diaries as a place to relinquish control and to allow repressed material to surface. This occurs through a "dialogue" with distinct "selves." It is noteworthy that she experiences her own writing as though it had been written by someone else, someone to whom she refers in the third person. In this way she makes the self into an "other." This is a common feature of many diarists' projects. At the same time, this trend is also reversed here, as Hester attempts to pull perceived "others" together into an integrated self. Hester not only accords a franchise to a voice that was previously muffled; she also privileges it and assigns it agency, even predominance over other voices. The little girl is not only experienced as an other in a manner confirming the theory of transitional objects; "she" also "wants" Hester to write certain things, and Hester in turn writes to her. The little girl therefore exercises preponderance not only over the other competing voices but over Hester herself. The diary, by separating voices from each other as well as bringing them into confrontation, functions as a stage for magical self-transformations—like pulling oneself out of the mud by one's bootstraps.

Several subjects refer to the dissolving of boundaries. Some feel that quite separate parts of them exist, that these are in some cases out of contact with each other, and that the diary functions in a way to restore such contact. Says James, who is interested in meditation,

> [In my journal] I might be having a conversation with different parts of myself. . . . After meditating, a part of myself that's more enlightened addresses parts of myself that are more habit-driven. . . . For me, the diary is a way to get in contact with my more personal self, my more inner self, the part of myself that's less external.

This use of the diary illustrates that aspects of the self existing at more primitive levels of ego organization can be brought together. It seems plausible that the discipline of writing itself subjects fleeting, fragmentary identity components to the relative rigors of the secondary process—somewhat like dissecting a dream, explaining a joke, putting a revery into words. The objectivation of the self temporarily shifts the center of agency away from the writer to the written page and then restores it to a transformed invigorated subject.

The Self in a Mirror

In regard to all diaries questions arise about the objectivation of the self inherent in diary writing. For some diarists this "mirror" function of the diary, that is, the observation of the objectivated self, seems especially salient.

The use of the diary to keep a tight rein on oneself can be coupled with its use to chart the progress one is making along the path toward self-improvement. One subject uses the diary to keep track of his accomplishments and examines his shortcomings in a somewhat self-chastising way. Sam "forces" himself to record daily events in a limited space in his diary even though he considers the writing out to be a "burden" that would only be increased if he fell behind. In the diary he "ruminates" about "how to get things done, how to control myself better, how I can help my wife, how I'm doing on my dissertation." In another diary he keeps count of the number of miles he has run. Victoria practices a similar self-monitoring. She spent her early years in a European country and moved to the United States at the age of ten, whereupon she began to keep a journal. Among the things she wrote in it were her frustration over learning English. However, she would also reassure herself about her progress with the language as she practiced it there. Victoria, too, feels an obligation to write and becomes angry with herself when she has nothing to write about or feels unable to verbalize her experience adequately.

This self-observational quality of the diary is not necessarily self-punitive or self-controlling in nature. Bach's (1977) elaboration of Lacan's notion of the "mirror stage" of development sheds light on alternative aspects. At this stage the infant becomes capable for the first time of a self-reflective stance, realizing that the self is not merely a fragmented, sensate body but something that can be viewed as an integral object. In narcissistic individuals, Bach argued, the use of something similar to a mirror or what he calls "narcissistic 'phantoms' such as transitional objects, imaginary companions . . . the creative product itself [and, we might add, diaries] may be regarded as readaptation phenomena to correct distortions in the sense of mental and physical well-being" (Bach, 1977, p. 215). He described the experience of the child discovering itself in the mirror as "triumphant exhilaration" (p. 216).

Some people seem to use the diary in the same way and with the same effect. By writing about oneself in the diary one creates a picture of the self as a whole. One may also become aware of the self as divided into subject and object, the experiencer and the observer of experience. Beyond the transitional object function of the diary, which serves to help the self differentiate from others, this mirror function of the diary helps to distinguish not only the "me" from the "not-me"; it also embodies the division between "I, the subject" and "me, the object" of reflection. This division may accompany the growth of reflective self-awareness and the awareness of others as also "owning" subjectivities. This is a more complicated function than that highlighted by the "transitional object theory." Boundaries are simultaneously constructed *around* the self and *within* it through this experience. Bach conceptualizes the self as "a mental content rather than a psychic structure . . . having to do with people's theories about themselves including their fantasies, both conscious and unconscious, about self-integration and self-disruption" (1977, p. 213). Many diarists refer to the discovery or creation of the self in this sense and to the development of its complexity through objectivation.

Several subjects demonstrate that the diary can be used as a way of gazing admiringly into a mirror—defining the self by objectivating and then observing it. Virginia, who is struggling constantly with separating herself from her very tightly knit family and with guilt feelings about her desire to do things only for herself, demonstrates this. On the one hand, she expresses joy in being completely self-absorbed, in becoming the kind of person she wants to be, and in allowing herself pleasure. On the other hand, she is plagued by guilt and fear that her complete self-absorption might cost her all connection with other people. Her struggle against being owned by others and restricted rather than free has a long history. She recalls seven years in her childhood when she suffered a terrible and completely secret fear of becoming possessed by the devil. Although she first attributed this to a repressive Catholic education, she acknowledges that a more pervasive fear of being "possessed" has stayed with her throughout her life and that her withdrawal from relationships with others is a subject that causes her some concern. She recently had what she called "my summer of abandon," in which she experimented sexually and indulged herself generally, recording the experiences in her diary. At the time of the interviews she is absorbed in her schoolwork and writes in her diary about that, including her plans to write a novel. She speaks about these experiences and plans with great excitement and a kind of boastfulness. It is likely that she feels a similar excitement in writing about them and in looking over what she has written.

> It has to do with how I perceive myself and how I want others to perceive me, it goes back to what I'm going to

write in my journal. . . . You can be whoever you want
when you're writing; that does become your history. . . .
What I'm writing is how I want to be perceived. . . . I
write it for myself. I notice in my journal writing, I
don't dedicate that much to other people, because it's
more for me, and that could be selfish. . . . It's the one
thing that's mine.

Bruce, who expresses much concern about what others think
about him or how he is viewed and who has a particular interest
in being thought of as a worthy, clever, creative, and special
person, also illustrates the mirroring potential of the diary,
though in a strikingly different manner from Virginia. Although
she seems to be enraptured with the image of herself and
fleetingly concerned lest she be distracted from it by someone
or something else, Bruce gives the impression of a person engaged with others most of the time but constantly glancing into
the mirror to see what effect he might be having on them. In this
way he reassures himself that he is there:

I'm a you-think-of-me-therefore-I-am kind of person. A
lot of my sense of self is contingent upon being alive in
the minds of others. [My journal] is a device that I use
to stifle that impact. It provides a legitimate confirmation
that I did exist, and did have feelings. Everyone could
go away and I'd still have that.

A diary provides objectivation without alienation. Most other
products of human creativity—even the simple word spoken to
another—are susceptible to expropriation and distortion. This is
so because expression is never identical with the originating
experience. The arising ambiguities may bring it about that the
socially mediated objectivation turns against its subjective sources
and betrays them. The diary, as we can see from this illustration,
provides protection against such uncontrollable breaches. Bruce
need not wait for others to prove his self's reality or to instigate
its development. Proof and goad are at his beck and call. Further,
being a journal keeper is itself an important part of Bruce's

reflection in the mirror of his diary. The diary "makes me feel like I have a history," Bruce explains.

> I always thought that if people knew I kept a journal, it would show that I had a depth—"Oh, he keeps a journal!"—which a lot of people don't have. . . . I'm always impressed when other people keep journals; I think it shows that a person has depth.

Virginia's experience is remarkably similar: "[The journal] shows that I have depth, I'm not just superficial." About her firm distinction between her earlier "diary" and her present "journal" she comments,

> I guess . . . I am dictated by appearance. . . . Diary sounds so juvenile, journal is more intense. . . . If I'm keeping a journal it's much better than keeping a diary.

As students of the psychology of diary-keeping, we cannot help wondering whether diarists become dependent on their mirrors for the sense of self, that is, whether the self's center of gravity shifts to its objectivation.

Managing Time

Gail Godwin referred to diarists as "incomparable purveyors of sequential self-conscious life" (1988, p. 50). Although the self-consciousness has been addressed in several of our earlier comments, the notion of a sequential life or, more generally, the peculiar relation of the diarist to time, has yet to be discussed. The diarist's relation to time is almost inevitably ambivalent because his or her access to past events and feelings easily overleaps all the usual boundaries whereas the setting down of these experiences in a chronologically ordered book that can be closed and even locked invites a rigid imposition of limits. For the diarist, the past is both more and less changeable than it is for other people. Although it is clear that many diarists use their writing to gain distance from aspects of their selves or their feelings, putting them in perspective or transforming them altogether, it is noteworthy and paradoxical that time appears to be condensed in the diary. The past is preserved and made present. Indeed, there is often an implied sense of prescience or anticipation of the future in the entries of a diary. We shall have more to say about this.

Some of our subjects are mainly concerned with the here-and-now in their diaries. They seldom if ever look back on earlier journal entries. Nevertheless, many of these subjects see the journal as not merely a record of what has gone before, but almost as a part of themselves, a living preservation of the past. Bruce, who keeps his journal on a computer disk and makes periodic printouts, once accidentally deleted a file: "I lost a part of my life. Throwing away my journal would be like throwing away the past. . . . It would be liberating to throw it all away, but I'm not ready to be liberated. . . . The past is an anchor." James echoes this thought in uncannily similar language: "My identity is anchored to the journals." Once when he had moved to a new home, he feared having lost a box of old journals: "I felt some remorse, some sense of relief too that they weren't around anymore and maybe this was a clean slate in my life." John's remark that his diary preserves past events almost as brushing and flossing preserve his teeth reflects the degree to which the past, as it appears in the diary, can be experienced as something essential to the diarist. One diarist likens his diary to "saving receipts" and muses whether he might not be "hoarding" the past.

Bruce remarks on the alarming and intriguing ease with which history could be altered or completely fabricated, relating this to his use of a computer. Godwin noted:

> sometimes, to set the record straight, I jot down a word or two in old diaries to my former self—to encourage, to scold, to correct, or to set things in perspective. (1988, p. 54)

In this complex statement there is an acknowledgment that history might be altered as one's perspective changes. Even more striking is the notion of communicating with the former self that is apparently experienced as a separate person. In this condensation of time, past and present selves can speak to one another. Clearly the past, as represented by the journal, is subject to control and exerts control on the diarist at present—a control that is felt to be oppressive but ultimately reassuring. Above all, we see here the possibility of rereading the diary as one writes in it further—a token that one has changed in one's own eyes. The recorded past signifies the present.

Not surprisingly, the attitude of the diarist to the future is an interesting one as well. Many diarists explain that they write for their future selves; some seem to write *to* their future selves. The diarist's acute consciousness that what is now being recorded will one day be past creates for some a sense of prescience. Without knowing precisely what the future will hold, they express a sense of being able to look into the future. This envisioned future may of course be masked by the diarist's sense of control over time; all points in time can be collapsed into a written document. Virginia tries to express this in the broader context of her thoughts about time. "I'm consumed by time," she remarks, adding that she must write in her diary in order for the day to be over, that a day feels to her like a creation she has accomplished. "It's exciting to see blank pages. . . . I'd like to look ahead, to know what's in store for me." This phrasing suggests that the blank pages contain invisible writing. Control over the passage of time is experienced through the recording of events by some diarists: James frequently describes his life as a "locomotive that runs me along a track" and the journal as a tool for mastering that "sense of helplessness." This, too, expresses the intimation that the present signification can tame the future by assimilating it to the present intention, in short, it illustrates the binding of time.[3] Mallon noted that he has

> often anticipated small disasters—in love, at work—in
> the diary, and written that if the bad thing I have in

> mind happens, it really won't hurt so much. . . . When good things have glimmered around the corner, I've sometimes hesitated to hope for them in the diary because the gods can hear and mustn't be tempted. (1984, p. xiv)

These suggestions of magical thinking, omnipotence fantasies, and timelessness indicate a shift toward primary process functioning. This is consistent with the hypothesis that the diary functions in part as a transitional object. Such temporary circumscribed regressive shifts can serve to advance adaptation (Hartmann, 1939).

Bach (1977) observed "narcissistic states of consciousness" in several psychoanalytic patients. His essay provides some insights into an experience of time that resembles the experience of many diarists. Issues of time control are prominent; such patients, like many diarists, do things like "trying to make time stand still or regress." Many cling "obsessively to temporal benchmarks as a way of linking things up in the absence of experiential self-continuity" (p. 231). Whether or not diarists put their "sequential" lives into writing so as to compensate for a lack of experiential self-continuity—an idea worth considering—many of them do manifest concerns with time and its demarcation that approximate this description.

Conclusion

We began this study with the observation that life stories are always incomplete and episodic and that the diary is a favored depository for the segmental narratives. Taken together, the topics surveyed in this chapter suggest that the chief psychological interest of diaries emanates from the reflexive uses to which diarists put them rather than from their secrecy or from their supposed address to an unconsciously intended audience.

We have been able to show some of the developmental and integrative benefits associated with keeping a diary: The manipulation of boundaries between self and others and among the various domains of experience facilitates the management of emotions and self-regard. Also, the diary permits the evocation of fantasies about the self, and the sedimentation of these fantasies on the written page becomes the diarist's mirror, sometimes flattering, sometimes reproving. In short, writing in the diary transforms the diarist, however briefly or superficially.

Two considerations may help to explain the diary's mutative potential in a preliminary way. One, the diary is multifaceted as a "space" and an "object" (in the psychoanalytic sense of an other); as a process and a product; as a container, its contents, and the experience of containment. The diarist's ability to shift subjectively from one to another of these facets may account for the diary's psychological utility.

Two, the diary involves a characteristic use of language. The act of private writing occurs in a transitional space within the circumscribed area that Vygotsky (1986) described as the place where thought and language meet. Distinguishing this area from the poles of pure nonverbal thought and pure nonintellective speech, he defined it as including logical, discursive speech as well as "inner speech." He traced the development of inner speech from the child's differentiation of the egocentric and social functions of speech. The diary seems to represent a compromise insofar as it makes "inner" speech also "outer." The egocentric speech of children, noted by Piaget, is considered to be inner speech—a function developmentally prior to the ability to talk to oneself mentally without verbalizing externally. The diarist's writing may be understood as inner speech of a similar sort. If it is true that many adults externalize such inner speech in their diaries, we may wish to reconsider whether egocentric speech is properly regarded as simply a developmental phase appearing in small children. Rather, egocentric "speech," in such media as diaries, may persist throughout the life span.

Although these may be useful perspectives on the process by which the diary plays its transforming function, they can account only for the effect of each entry experienced by itself. They shed no direct light on the diarist's commitment to the diary as a whole, beyond the daily problems and solutions. If the diarist proposes to construct the story of his or her life within the frame of the diary, of what use is this practice in general? This abstract question could not be put directly to our respondents. It is actually a question about the diary's temporality. This temporality attaches not merely to the act of writing itself—as though one simply wrote entries on a tear-off calendar and each day discarded yesterday's notation, replacing it with today's. Rather, temporality defines the keeping of a diary as an activity that binds time. Our speculation concerns this binding of time.

It goes without saying that all writing is meant to be read. In the case of diaries, however, two specific intentions mingle. As the very first entry—and every subsequent one—is made, the writer expects not only to reread it later but to add further entries. We emphasize the intention rather than its fulfillment. Whether the diary is in fact kept up is not decisive. But this double intention informs the moment of writing; one makes an entry as though one were going to return as reader and writer. Each entry is the notation of a precedent not fully realized; only subsequent reflection will round out its meaning.[4] Each writing is a commitment to continuity.

In this orientation, the question for us is no longer how well diaries excerpt life or how to draw inferences from what is written to what is not. Rather, we ask what we can learn from the diarist's practice about how lives are extended or built up out of their own recollection. How does the diarist work on himself or herself, writing anew within a field furrowed by prior writings that were deemed worthy of remembrance? For each writing, no matter how seemingly fresh and redirected, remains beholden to former writings, staying within or transgressing the existing horizon. Thus each writing is significantly a commentary on what already stands; it is a re-writing. Similarly, what one reads again, one reads differently. It is a re-reading from a new perspective fulfilling the intention that accompanied the past moment of writing. This is how the diary becomes the possibility and the record of constancy and transcendence.

Living one's life and recounting it are not distinct as reality and representation, but as two kinds of action—re-reading as recollection; new construction as re-writing—both acts of the imagination (Rosenwald, 1992). Seen in this light, the keeping of a diary involves the mobilization of memory in the service of new living. What was constructed and ventured at one point becomes revalued as a memory and a premise at the next.

Among the fundamental tasks of any historical or biographical research is the deciphering of the traces of the past within the present—even if the present dazzles us with its apparent new beginnings (Rosenwald & Wiersma, 1983). Our question concerns the active, shaping force of un-self-conscious memory, memory that is lived out rather than recited. How Freud, who broke through to the recognition of the full force of reminiscence, incorporated the conditions of his hermeneutic procedure into his notion of the mind is the subject of an essay by Derrida (1978). To conceive the presentness of the past—to conceive memory—involves "the necessity of accounting simultaneously for the permanence of the trace and the virginity of the receiving substance" (1978, p. 200). Freud attempted this once with the distinction between ϕ and ψ neurons (1895/1989d), then with a quasi-histological model (1920/1989a), and finally—"graphematically"—in the "Note On the Mystic Writing Pad" (1925/1989c). In this "small contrivance" (p. 228) he thought to have discovered a splendid analog (inconceivable at the time of his first attempt 30 years earlier) to the systems and dynamics of the psyche. Each model, in its own way, showed that the psychic system that receives new impressions cannot also be the one that is modified by the reception. But the terms he brought together in these atemporal models—path-breaking, registration, representation, transcription, psychic quality—center on the inscription of traces and their subsequent revival.

In search of an analog to the inextinguishable self-assertion of the past within and against the present, we find the diary superior to the Mystic Writing Pad. "Freshness of surface and depth of retention" (Derrida, 1978, p. 217) are combined in the materiality of pages filled up and waiting to be filled, their relative weight steadily shifting to the former. Writing in a diary lays down a trace that is not merely a lasting potential, retrievable "in suitable light" (p. 230) but rather an energy that reaches forward and prefigures new impressions—in short, a trace that lays claims against the openness of the future.

We have hypothesized that writing in one's diary is an act of anticipative memory. It carries out a resolution to preserve an experience for recall. In trying to understand this resolution, which, in its generalized form, involves the commitment to keep a diary, we can draw instruction from two related phenomena— the "command to remember" and the sense of *déjà raconté*, both familiar from the context of free association.

It is not uncommon for a patient in psychotherapy, about to relate a memory, to have the sudden strong conviction that he or she has already communicated this on an earlier occasion. On closer examination it is found that the memory in question could not have been related before but that it is associatively connected with, and thus serves as a cover or screen for, another idea that has been repressed (Freud, 1914/1989b). The partial representation of the repressed contents (idea, feeling, or event) in the remembered screen acts as a kind of safety valve, diminishing the tendency of the repressed to seek a return to consciousness. The illusion of *déjà raconté* regarding this screen obviates the risks of articulation. To put the point briefly, the repression has subdued a psychic danger, and the paramnestic impression secures this success by declaring the rescue operation over and done with, in no need of review.

The command to remember involves a similar transformation of a psychic danger. "When children are struggling to effect repressions they have a kind of 'hunger for screen experiences'; that is, when they experience anything which they can use as a screen memory they sometimes feel a kind of inner injunction: 'You must make a [mental] note of that!' They obey this injunction, and this enables them to forget something else" (Fenichel, 1953, p. 153).

Just as the injunction to make a mental note seeks to extend the psychic victory into the indefinite future, the impression of *déjà raconté* seeks to establish such a victory as a completed, irreversible achievement. What the first does for the subjective future, the second attempts for the subjective past. Each seeks temporal anchors for what feels precarious in the present. It is this sense of precariousness that demands transformation.

These two phenomena, common in the registers of the psychopathology of everyday life, have their parallels in the keeping of a diary. By informing the moment of present writing with the double intention of rereading and rewriting, the diarist activates a hypermnestic function combining the *déjà raconté* with the command to remember, the backward with the forward gaze.[5] However, we hypothesize that the diary, as an aid to memory, has a wider scope. It secures not only repression but a variety of other advances in adaptation, and it frames these within a mirror for the self. We have sampled various such advances in our survey: differentiations and consolidations of self, versatility and coordination of ego functions relevant to emotional experience and expression, and to a host of other more specific tasks like those connected with the balancing of impulse and defense, the challenges of work, and the management of one's progress toward idealized states. The diary can preserve these advances because as a present object it transcends the temporality of its making. It projects the past onto a plane of simultaneity. This likens the diarist's self-portrait to the way ordinary people think about the self in time: "The self has a time dimension. . . . We include into our experience of our self the life that is still ahead of us . . . [and] those aspects of our personalities which were at some phase possible—potentialities that existed but were not actualized" (Lichtenstein, 1965, p. 119). It seems likely that this dimension of the diarist's experience of self is affected by the concrete presence of the past "potentialities." Perhaps the diarist's activity exemplifies a more general tendency to store an accumulation of past experiences and future possibilities within the idea of the self.

The specific potentialities that our respondents preserve in their diaries appear to be the ones they yearn to realize and preserve in their lives—flaws mended, limitations and isolations overcome, capacities refined. Of course, our hypothesis would have to be rejected outright if it were taken to imply that diaries are bloated with complacency. Quite the contrary, they record struggles with various threats—anxiety, dilemmas, inhibitions. Our speculation holds that writing about each of these threats reduces it somewhat, that these reductions are desired transformations, and that the diarist obeys an inner injunction and "makes a note."

We do not propose that diarists enjoy an overall advantage in living compared with nondiarists. After all, there are other ways to reconcile recollection and new living action. Nor do we overlook that psychological processes are not decisive. The path to a more rewarding life is blocked for many by more formidable obstacles than mere obliviousness. But it appears plausible that a personal sense of identity depends on continuing efforts to integrate the theory and practice of one's own life in a manner that facilitates constructive continuance. In this project diaries seem helpful.

Freud regarded the explanation of memory as fundamental in a science of the mind (1895/1989d). Similarly, it may be that the psychology of the diary, merging the intentions of rereading and rewriting, is our most serviceable model of how we learn from experience when building up our lives. Biographical memory saves our most promising projects of self-transformation, and new living action seeks to complete and extend these. The diary preserves both poles of the transformation. Like a screen memory, it contains a partial representation of that which was in need of mastery as well as the record of its overcoming. The reminders of old frailty have been covered over with a chronicle of acquired fitness. From this archive of triumphs small and large— from this palimpsest—the diarist draws confidence for the struggles ahead. The diary is a *memento vivere*.

Notes

1. Examples of this treatment of the diary include Blodgett (1988), Lifshin (1982), Mallon (1984), and Rosenblatt (1983).
2. Diarists who are also psychologists have taken this approach; among them are Horney (1980) and Milner (1987). Among literary figures, self-reflection on being a diarist has been pursued by Boswell, Barrett Browning, Woolf, and numerous others.

3. An acquaintance of the authors reports:

> I recall vividly an occasion in my own adolescence when I was involved in some exciting event, whose outcome was unknown, and was so eager to find out what would happen that I experienced the irrational urge to turn to the end of the diary I kept so as to take a peek. In fact, I skipped to the last page and wrote a note there: "When you get here, tell me what happened with ––," as though my present self would be discontinuous with this future self, which would be permitted to know the resolution, and as though the future self, on becoming the present self, would be able to communicate through writing with the now present, but soon to be past, self.

This contribution illustrates the time-binding function of the diary.

4. Elizabeth: "I go back to things I wrote years ago, concrete memories that don't change with time. I can reinterpret them but they're sort of frozen in time. . . . I couldn't afford to see then what I see now. It functions on so many levels—my processing at the moment and the reinterpretation when I go back to it later. . . . What I wrote back then has a whole different significance now."

5. John: "It's really a letter to the future me. . . . I go back and I realize that a lot of little everyday things will seem important in the future. . . . The little things that escape me will seem really shocking. . . . It's really kind of nostalgic and it's kind of to clue me in as to what I was like."

References

Allport, G. (1951). *The use of personal documents in psychological science.* New York: Edwards Brothers.

Bach, S. (1977). On the narcissistic state of consciousness. *International Journal of Psychoanalysis, 58,* 209-233.

Blodgett, H. (1988). *Centuries of female days: Englishwomen's private diaries.* New Brunswick, NJ: Rutgers University Press.

Brand, A., & Powell, J. (1985). Emotions and the writing process: A description of apprentice writers. *Journal of Educational Research, 79*(5), 280-285.

Dalsimer, K. (1982). Female adolescent development: A study of the diary of Anne Frank. *Psychoanalytic Study of the Child, 37,* 487-522.

Derrida, J. (1978). *Writing and difference.* Chicago: University of Chicago Press.

Dixon, T. M., & Baumeister, R. F. (1991). Escaping the self. *Personality and Social Psychology Bulletin, 17*(4), 363-368.

Fenichel, O. (1953). On the inner injunction to "make a mental note." In *Collected papers* (Vol. 1, pp. 153-154). New York: Norton.

Freud, S. (1905). Fragment of an analysis of a case of hysteria. *Collected papers* (Vol. 3, pp. 13-146). London: Hogarth Press.

Freud, S. (1989a). Beyond the pleasure principle. In J. Strachey (Ed. and Trans.), *The standard edition of the complete psychological works of Sigmund*

Freud (Vol. 18, pp. 1-64). London: Hogarth Press. (Original work published 1920)

Freud, S. (1989b). Fausse reconnaisssance (déjà raconté) in psychoanalytic treatment. In J. Strachey (Ed. and Trans.), *The standard edition of the complete psychological works of Sigmund Freud* (Vol. 13, pp. 201-207). London: Hogarth Press. (Original work published 1914)

Freud, S. (1989c). A note upon the "mystic writing pad." In J. Strachey (Ed. and Trans.), *The standard edition of the complete psychological works of Sigmund Freud* (Vol. 19, pp. 227-232). London: Hogarth Press. (Original work published 1925)

Freud, S. (1989d). Project for a scientific psychology. In J. Strachey (Ed. and Trans.), *The standard edition of the complete psychological works of Sigmund Freud* (Vol. 1, pp. 295-397). London: Hogarth Press. (Original work published 1895)

Godwin, G. (1988). A diarist on diarists. *Anteus, 21*, 50-56.

Hartmann, H. (1939). *Ego-psychology and the problem of adaptation.* New York: International Universities Press.

Hoffer, W. (1946). Diaries of adolescent schizophrenics (hebephrenics). *Psychoanalytic Study of the Child, 2*, 293-312.

Horney, K. (1980). *The adolescent diaries of Karen Horney.* New York: Basic Books.

Lichtenstein, H. (1965). Toward a metapsychological definition of the concept of self. *International Journal of Psychoanalysis, 46*, 117-128.

Lifshin, L. (1982). *Ariadne's thread: A collection of contemporary women's journals.* New York: Harper & Row.

Litowitz, B. & Gundlach, R. (1987). When adolescents write: Semiotic and social dimensions of adolescents' personal writing. *Adolescent Psychiatry, 14*, 82-111.

Mallon, T. (1984). *A book of one's own: People and their diaries.* New York: Ticknor & Fields.

Milner, M. (1987). *Eternity's sunrise: A way of keeping a diary.* London: Virago Press.

Rosenblatt, P. C. (1983). *Bitter bitter tears: Nineteenth century diarists and twentieth century grief theories.* Minneapolis: University of Minnesota Press.

Rosenwald, G. C. (1988). A theory of multiple-case research. *Journal of Personality, 56*(1), 239-264.

Rosenwald, G. C. (1992). Reflections on self-understanding. In G. C. Rosenwald & R. L. Ochberg (Eds.), *Storied lives: The social politics of self-understanding.* New Haven, CT: Yale University Press.

Rosenwald, G. C., & Wiersma, J. (1983). Women, career changes, and the new self. *Psychiatry, 46*, 213-229.

Sosin, D. (1983). The diary as transitional object in female adolescent development. *Adolescent Psychiatry, 11*, 92-103.

Sperling, O. (1948). On the mechanisms of spacing and crowding emotions. *International Journal of Psychoanalysis, 29*(4), 232-235.

Stein, M. (1977). A psychoanalytic view of mental health: Samuel Pepys and his diary. *Psychoanalytic Quarterly, 46*, 82-115.

Stewart, A., Franz, C., & Layton, L. (1988). The changing self: Using personal documents to study lives. *Journal of Personality, 56*(1), 41-74.

❦ 4 ❦

Reconstruction of Life Stories

Principles of Selection in Generating Stories for Narrative Biographical Interviews

Gabriele Rosenthal

*W*hat can be done with life stories?" This question was posed by Daniel Bertaux (1981) in the introduction to his *Biography and Society*. At that time, research interest in life stories was largely concerned with using them as sources of information about a reality existing outside the text. Meanwhile, however, especially in West Germany, this question has taken on another meaning: The life story itself, seen as a social construct in its own right, has increasingly become the focus of social-scientific research. Empirically founded concepts and programmatic outlines of biographical theory have been put up for discussion by such sociologists as Martin Kohli, Fritz Schütze, and Wolfram Fischer-Rosenthal.[1] Methodology and methods of reconstructing life histories out of oral biographical presentations are being continuously developed: "Researching the biographical as social entity implies both the question of the social function of biographies as well as the question of the social processes that constitute biographies (Fischer-Rosenthal, 1991, p. 253).

Conceiving of biography as a social construct comprising both social reality and the subject's experiential world raises the next question, which is, how can one set about reconstructing a social structure that is constantly being reaffirmed and transformed in the interaction between biographical experience and socially defined schemata? Or, more simply, how does one proceed from a given autobiographical text to life itself? To what extent is one receiving an account of an "actual" life history[2] and to what extent is one being presented with the autobiographer's present construction of his or her past, present, and future life? This chapter attempts to answer some of these questions by emphasizing methodological and procedural aspects of reconstructing narrated life stories. Before we can make assumptions about the social reality to which a text is referring, we must first gain some understanding of the structure of the text, or data base, itself. In the following, the data base consists of the transcribed texts of a series of biographical-narrative interviews (Schütze, 1977, 1992). In all of these interviews, the autobiographical narrators—so-called biographers,[3] were asked, by means of an initial opening question, to give a full extempore narration (as opposed to an argument or a theoretical exposition) of events and experiences from their own lives. The ensuing story, or "main narrative," is not interrupted by further questions but is encouraged by means of nonverbal and paralinguistic expressions of interest and attention, such as "mhm." In the second part of the interview—the "period of questioning"—the interviewer initiated, with narrative questions,[4] more elaborate narrations on topics and biographical events already mentioned. In addition the interviewer asked about issues that had not been addressed.

Analyzing such narrated life stories, we distinguish two levels: (1) the analysis of the lived-through, the experienced life history (the genetical analysis) and (2) the analysis of the narrated life story. The purpose of the genetical analysis is the reconstruction of the biographical meaning of experiences at the time they happened and the reconstruction of the chronological sequence of experiences in which they occurred. The purpose of the analysis of the narrated life story is the reconstruction of the present meanings of experiences and the reconstruction of the temporal order of the life story in the present time of narrating or writing. This analysis is particularly concerned with discovering the mechanisms of selection guiding the biographer's choice of textual elements (or stories) in relation to the general thematic orientation of the interview. The objective of this analytical step that we call thematic field analysis is to reconstruct the form and structure of the narrated life story, that is, the way in which it is temporally and thematically ordered in the interview.

The goal of a hermeneutical case reconstruction is on one hand the reconstruction of the life history, that is, the experienced, lived-through life history, and on the other hand the reconstruction of the life story, or the narrated life story. Life story and life history always come together. They are continuously dialectically linked and produce each other; this is the reason why we must reconstruct both levels no matter whether our main target is the life history or the life story.

Thematic Field Analysis

Thematic field analysis involves reconstructing the subjects' system of knowledge, their interpretations of their lives, and their classification of experiences into thematic fields.[5] Our aim is to reconstruct the interactional significance of the subject's actions, the underlying structure of the subject's interpretations of her or his life, which may go beyond the subject's own intentions.

Because it is easier to understand this kind of method by following it as a dynamic process, I shall demonstrate this step of analysis using a simplified interpretation of an actual interview (see section below on interview with Hans Lohs). This is the life story of a German witness to National Socialism, who became a member of the Hitler Youth in 1933 and participated in World War II as a soldier.

But before embarking on the actual thematic field analysis of this case, some theoretical remarks about the structure of life stories in general, about the complete procedure of a hermeneutic case reconstruction, and about the thematic field analysis in particular, will be presented.

The Structure of Narrated Life Stories

One of the major objectives of biographical research is to encompass the total life of an individual (Kohli, 1986a). A naive understanding of this could, theoretically, lead to the expectation that a person's whole biographical experience should be reconstructed and analyzed in its entirety.[6] This, of course, would have overwhelming consequences both for subject and researcher even in the phase of data collection, ideally requiring ongoing interviewing throughout the subject's lifetime. So the term *total life* clearly cannot be taken to mean simply a review of every single event that ever took place in a person's life. It must rather be interpreted in the gestalt sense of biography as a comprehensive, general pattern of orientation that is selective in separating the relevant from the irrelevant. In practice, this means that the oral account has to be even more selective (Kohli, 1986a, p. 93). The narrated life story represents the biographer's overall construction of his or her past and anticipated life, in which biographically relevant experiences are linked up in a temporally and thematically consistent pattern (Fischer, 1982). It is this biographical overall construct that ultimately determines the way in which the biographer reconstructs the past and makes decisions as to which individual experiences are relevant and included.

The stories that are selected by the biographer to present his life history cannot be regarded as a series of isolated experiences, laid down in chronological order like so many strata of sedimentary rock; individual experiences are always embedded in a coherent, meaningful context, a biographical construct. They are a part of the overall pattern of thematic and temporal relationships that make up the experience of a lifetime. Reconstructing his or her own life history, the subject connects and relates single events, actions, and experiences with other events, actions, and experiences according to substantive and temporal patterns that do not necessarily follow the linear sequence of the "objective time" but rather conform to a perspectivist time model of "subjective" or "phenomenal" time (Fischer, 1982, pp. 138-215). The present perspective determines what the subject considers biographically relevant, how he or she develops thematic and temporal links between various experiences, and how past, present, or anticipated future realities influence the personal interpretation of the meaning of life.

We can thus assume that the process of selection being carried out by the biographer while presenting his or her life story is not haphazard or arbitrary, merely reflecting possible interactive influences of the interview situation or a passing mood. A life story does not consist of an atomistic chain of experiences, whose meaning is created at the moment of their articulation, but is rather a process taking place simultaneously against the backdrop of a biographical structure of meaning, which determines the selection of the individual episodes presented, and within the context of the interaction with a listener or imaginary audience. This texture of meaning is constantly reaffirmed and transformed in the "flux of life." It is constituted by the interweaving of socially prefabricated and given patterns of planning and interpreting together with biographically relevant events and experiences and their ongoing reinterpretations. These reinterpretations are usually hidden from the conscious access of the biographer; they are constituted by the biographical overall construction—sometimes manifest in the narration as global evaluation, molding the past, present, and anticipated future (Fischer, 1982).[7] The order we can discover in a life story is brought about by the "world-experiencing life" (*welterfahrendes Leben*), to use Edmund Husserl's term. It is the order of the primordial interrelation of "world" and "I".

The narrated life story thus represents a sequence of mutually interrelated themes[8] that, between them, form a dense network of interconnected cross-references (Fischer, 1982, p. 168). The *thematic field* is defined as the sum of events or situations presented in connection with the theme that form the background or horizon against which the theme stands out as the central focus. It is these fields that are reconstructed in the thematic field analysis (see Fischer, 1982; Gurwitsch, 1964).

Returning to the central objective of biographical research mentioned above, that it should ideally comprehend the total life of an individual, we can now express this in different terms: What we are in fact attempting is a reconstruction of both the narrator's biographical overall construction and the biographically relevant experiences. The relationship between the overall construct and the relevant experiences must be conceived of as reciprocal: The construct determines the relevancy of an experience and the cumulative relevant experiences form the construct. When reconstructing a life history, the first step is to analyze this interaction between construct and narrated experiences; only then can one embark on the analysis of the accumulated experiences themselves. Only when some insight has been acquired into the structure and form of the data base, the life story, can general propositions be made about the importance of the separate episodes and their meaning for the narrator and the further course of his or her life.

When reconstructing the narrated life story we have to take into account another phenomenon: Each interview is a product of the mutual interaction between speaker and listener. Narrators do not simply reproduce prefabricated stories regardless of the interactional situation, but rather create their stories within the social process of mutual orientation according to their definition of the interview situation. The neopositivist research tradition would regard this aspect as an irritant that must be eliminated, reduced, or at least controlled. In our view, trying to eliminate a "problem" such as this amounts to a quixotic fight against imagined giants, giants that in the final analysis are revealed to be not even windmills but rather the "winds" of the everyday world. The "wind" driving the mill that is creating biographical constructs cannot be eliminated without eliminating the constructs themselves, because this wind is in fact the ongoing interaction between the biographer and his or her social world. Life stories, taken as constructs, are inseparable from these interactional processes; they themselves evolve out of the genetic process of interaction, just as their presentation in the biographical research interview is a product of the interaction between narrator and listener.

Within the interactional framework of the interview, the biographer relates his or her life story in a thematically focused context based on negotiations about what the interactants consider relevant. Life stories are not finished products ready to be "served up" on demand. The story evolves around a thematic topic, usually established by the interviewer, in a manner judged by the narrator to be of interest to the listener.[9] The topics can center on a certain period of the biographer's life, on experiences arising in connection with certain historical or social events, or on a single biographical strand such as the person's occupational career. By putting forward such topics, the interviewer is providing the biographers with a framework for selecting the stories to be included. How the interviewees actually interpret the topic suggested, whether they keep to it or whether they orient their narration primarily toward what they suppose to be of interest to the interviewer or to themselves—these are all empirical questions that can only be answered in the individual case analysis.

To sum up, one could say that the narrated life story, as it evolves around a specified thematic focus, represents a general construct of biographical experiences that is a coagulate derived from past interactional episodes and future expectations, and is simultaneously a product of the biographer's present situation. This biographical overall construct, a coagulate of the past and future and a creation of the lived present, determines the selective principles guiding the narrator's choice of stories to be related in the interview. This construct, which is not at the biographer's conscious disposal, constitutes not only the selection of experiences out of memory. It also constitutes how the biographer perceives these experiences today.

The methodological consequence of this is that, before embarking on an analysis of the stratified biographical experiences themselves (the genetic analysis), one must reconstruct these selective principles, the underlying structure of the text.

Hermeneutic Case Reconstruction

Before starting on the thematic field analysis itself, a few general comments on the method of hermeneutic case reconstruction are necessary (cf. Rosenthal, 1987, 1990).[10]

Two principles are of fundamental importance in the hermeneutic reconstruction of texts: the principle of *reconstructive analysis* and the principle of *sequentiality.* In contrast to a logically subsuming classificatory approach, reconstructive analysis avoids confronting the text with predefined systems of variables and classifications. Instead, the researcher progresses "reconstructively from the explication of concrete social sequence to the general structural type" (Oevermann, 1983, p. 246). Following Charles Sanders Peirce's theory of abduction, theoretical knowledge is applied as a heuristic: "Abduction makes its start from the facts, without, at the outset, having any particular theory in view, though it is motivated by the feeling that a theory is needed to explain the surprising facts" (Peirce, 1933/1979, p. 7.219).

The principle of *sequentiality* makes allowance for the process aspect of social activity. It starts from the assumption that every action represents a choice between the alternatives potentially available in a certain situation. Action sequences that are manifested in texts as reported activities are thus processes of selection that, independently of the narrator's perspective, result in certain subsequent actions while at the same time eliminating certain other possibilities. Translated into practical terms, a methodological approach therefore requires a procedure of analysis that takes into account such aspects as the range of possibilities open to the subject in a certain situation, the selection made, the possibilities ignored, and the consequences of the decision. It was on the basis of these theoretical considerations that the method of sequential analysis was developed: Interpretation is thus the reconstruction of the meaning of the text following the sequence of events. In terms of the method of abductive reasoning, sequential analysis involves generating hypotheses about the possibilities contained in a given unit of empirical data, hypotheses as to possible further developments (follow-up hypotheses) and, in a third step, contrasting these with the actual outcome (empirical testing).

The aim of this process is to reconstruct the structure of the case. This leads to questions such as whether the biographer, in opting for a particular course of action, systematically eliminates other possible interpretations or actions, that is, whether there are certain underlying rules to be discovered that influence decisions. For this reason, we begin our case analysis with trying to imagine which options are potentially open to the person in a particular situation. We then look at the actual choice and so try to determine to what extent, in different situations, certain potential options tend to be systematically excluded.

In the biographical analysis of life stories, sequential analysis is carried out at two levels: *genetic analysis*—that is, the analysis of the reproduction and transformation processes in the narrator's life history—and *thematic field analysis,* which is the analysis of the biographer's biographical overall construction in the narrational present.

In genetic analysis the attempt is made to reconstruct as far as possible the actual sequence of events in the course of the biographer's life. Thematic field analysis is concerned with the sequences as they are presented in the text. In order to avoid false interpretations the social researcher is forced to reconstruct both levels, regardless of whether the primary research interest is to reconstruct a life history or to determine the narrator's present perspective and biographical construction.

The genetic analysis of a text that has evolved in the spoken or written present and refers to an experienced past that requires a previous analysis of the form and structure of this data base. The first question to be put when analyzing a text is not what really happened at that time or how accurately is the contemporary witness reporting events, but what is the biographer's present perspective and which selective principles are guiding the choice of stories. And vice versa, before one can draw conclusions about the biographical overall construct, about the biographer's present perspective, one must be in possession of certain information about his or her life. For example, one cannot make assumptions about displacement in time (such as that the biographer is displacing an unpleasant memory out of a period generally considered to have been pleasant into an earlier, less pleasant phase) if the actual chronological sequence has not been reconstructed beforehand in a separate analytical step.

Procedure. The analysis of such biographical self-presentations, which are selected for single case analysis after a global analysis of all interviews according to the model of theoretical sampling (Glaser & Strauss, 1967, pp. 45-78) is based on a full transcription of the audiotape. The steps of analysis are:

(1) analysis of the biographical data
(2) thematic field analysis (reconstruction of the life *story*)
(3) reconstruction of the life *history*
(4) microanalysis of individual text segments
(5) contrastive comparison of life history and life story

Analysis of the Biographical Data. Before embarking upon thematic field analysis, the "objective" biographical data are interpreted in the manner suggested by Ulrich Oevermann et al. (1980). All data that can stand more or less independently of the narrator's own interpretation are extracted from the interview. In contrast to thematic field analysis, which analyzes the material in the order in which it was presented during the interview, this first step attempts to reconstruct the actual chronology of the life history itself. This becomes backdrop for the *thematic field analysis,* which allows us to see which biographical data are blown up narratively and in which sequence they are presented.

Reconstruction of the Life History. After the thematic field analysis, which will be discussed in more detail in the next section, the task is to reconstruct the perspective of the past, to reconstruct the biographical meaning that the experiences had at the time they happened.

Microanalysis of Individual Text Segments. In this part of the analysis all hypotheses—those developed in earlier steps—are checked by detailed analyses of single text segments.

Thematic Field Analysis

The object of this analytical step is to reconstruct the form and structure of the narrated life story, that is, the way in which it is temporally and thematically ordered in the interview. In preparation for the analysis the interview text is first sequentialized, that is, briefly summarized in the form of a list of separate units that are divided up according to the following criteria: turn-taking (changes of speaker), textual sorts (changes in style of presentation, such as argumentation, describing, or narration,[11] cf. Kallmeyer & Schütze, 1977), and thematic shifts.[12] *Narrations* transmit former experiences, whereas *argumentations* represent the perspective of the present (cf. Schütze, 1976b). The sequences, themes, or stages of the life story at which the biographer argues, describes, or narrates are noted. The narrative segments are also categorized according to the various styles of narration, such as whether they are reported (sequences of events are chained together without expanding upon individual situations) or whether the biographer picks out individual situations to elaborate in detail and tells a story. The analysis of the sequentalization thus necessarily follows the structure of the text, each individual sequence being interpreted as it arises. The possible significance of each sequence to be interpreted is then considered without reference to or knowledge of subsequent units.

The following questions guide the hypotheses that are developed:

(1) Is the biographer generating a narrative or being carried along by a narrative flow in the story-telling?

(2) How much is the biographer oriented to the relevance system of the interviewer and how much to his or her own?

(3) In which thematic field is the single sequence embedded: What is the hidden agenda?

(4) Why is the biographer using this specific sort of text to present the experience or theme?

(5) Which topics are addressed? Which biographical experiences, events, and periods are covered, and what is left out? What comes up in the second part of the interview (after further questioning by the interviewer) that had been omitted in the first part, the "main narration" (after the initial opening question)?

(6) In which details are the single experiences or themes presented and why?

All possible hypotheses about each sequence are formulated: for each hypothesis a follow-up hypothesis is considered according to "what comes next in the text, if this reading proves to be plausible." These hypotheses are then contrasted with the text sequences that follow: Some of them gain plausibility whereas others are falsified.

What we are aiming to interpret at this stage is the nature and function of the presentation in the interview and not the biographical experiences themselves. For this reason, certain questions will inevitably arise at the beginning of analysis, such as, why does one biographer begin with the death of her father in her infancy, although she had actually been asked to relate her wartime experiences? To explain her choice of an introduction to her story, various possible modes of selection are suggested. In the course of further analysis certain of these gain plausibility whereas others have to be eliminated.

Thematic Field Analysis of the Interview With "Hans Lohs"

The interview with "Hans Lohs"[13] is taken from a research project on "Coming to Terms With the National Socialist Past," carried out at the *Freie Universität* in West Berlin under the supervision of the author (cf. Rosenthal, 1986, 1987, 1989). In this project, completed in 1984, 24 biographical-narrative interviews were conducted with former members of the Hitler Youth organization, *Hitler Jugend* ("HJ"), all of whom were born between 1923 and 1929. Two interviewers were present at each interview.

In conducting the actual interview the interviewer followed the narrative interview method developed by Fritz Schütze (1977, 1992).[14] The biographers were asked to tell the interviewers about their experiences in the Hitler Youth, as well as about their life in general during the war, their experiences during the collapse of the Third Reich, and about how their everyday life settled down to normal afterwards. We indicated at the beginning of the interview that we would not interrupt while they were talking, but would take notes in order to be able to ask some questions later.

The main narration following the initial question generally lasted between 90 minutes and 3 hours. The biographers talked in great detail—usually without any additional questions by the interviewers—about their lives within the suggested temporal framework and sometimes beyond. Most narratives were not confined to the Hitler Youth or wartime experiences but were extended to many different aspects of daily life during the entire period. When the main narration was finished, we asked for more details about themes and events that had thus far only been touched upon. Toward the end of the interview we regularly asked about particular historical events, such as the death of Adolf Hitler, assuming that such events could potentially be of special biographical relevance.

The recorded interviews were transcribed in their entirety, word for word as spoken, that is, with no respect for the rules of written language.

The interview presented here was conducted by myself and a student. "Hans Lohs" is a pseudonym. Before the discussion of the thematic field analysis of this interview, I give a short survey of the biographical data that could be extracted from the whole interview.

Hans Lohs was born in Berlin in 1923, the second son of a working-class family. His brother was 9 years older. His father was originally a member of the German Communist Party but joined the SA, the military-like fighting organization of the Nazis, in 1933, when the Nazis came to power. In the same year Hans, aged 10, became a member of the *Jungvolk,* the section of the Hitler Youth for 10- to 14-year-olds. However, he stopped attending the meetings and activities of the *Jungvolk* after one year.

Toward the end of 1937 he started an apprenticeship as toolmaker, which was finished in 1940, the second year of the war. In 1941 he was called up and opted to join the paratroopers. After a period of basic training he was sent to join the armed forces (*Wehrmacht*) in Italy in 1942, first to Salerno, Sicily, and then to Monte Cassino, where he stayed until autumn 1944. He was then posted to the Front, serving in Poland, Lithuania, and finally in East Prussia. Trapped behind the Soviet lines, he was one of a small group that fought its way through to Silesia, where he remained in active service until his dismissal from the army on May 5, 1945. He managed to avoid being captured by the Allies and to make his way back to Berlin, where he was taken on in the auxiliary police force. A year later he took up a career as racketeer on the black market, which was brought to an end on May 12, 1949, with the end of the Berlin blockade. In 1956 he emigrated with his future wife to Canada, but returned to Germany in 1962. At the time of the interview, in spring 1982, he was living in early retirement in West Berlin, aged 59.

Looking only at these data we can assume that, asked by the interviewer to talk about his time in the Hitler Youth and during and after the war, Hans Lohs would have much to present. Merely his war experiences at different frontiers should do to generate a flow of narrations. In contrast to all other informants in the sample, however, Hans Lohs seemed unable to let himself go and be carried along by an easy flow of story-telling. He was finished with the main narration within 30 minutes, less than a third of the time taken by most of the others. During this phase he also repeatedly asked the interviewer for questions to help him on his way. Only during the second part of the interview, when we asked for details about specific topics and events, was he motivated to produce more elaborate stories, which continued for another 3 hours.

Working on the assumption that there must be some explanation for Hans Lohs's difficulties in producing the expected form or gestalt of his life story, we did in fact come upon just such an explanation while reconstructing the selective principles underlying his text production. In other words, by applying the methodological principle explained above, that the style or structure of self-presentation in such an interview must be related to the narrator's biographical global construction, we were able to achieve a fruitful analysis of this otherwise sparse interview. The following analysis will show that Hans Lohs's difficulties in narration are manifestations of his biographical construction of the entanglement of his life history in National Socialism.

The Thematic Field Analysis. We shall confine ourselves here to analyzing the first part of the interview, the "main narration," which lasted 30 minutes (see Appendix A).

In response to the standard opening question, Hans Lohs begins, not with a narrative, but with an argument. He points out that in metropolitan Berlin the initial reception of the National Socialist movement was at first not as exaggerated as in, say, many small provincial towns.

What does Herr Lohs want to convey to the interviewers with this claim that in Berlin the response to National Socialism was not so intense as elsewhere?

Two hypotheses were put forward:

(1) Lohs wants to explain that he has little to say about National Socialism, that is, the argument is related to the issue of his competence as an informant; or,

(2) He wants to convey that as a "Berliner" he was not a fanatical Nazi, that is, he wants to legitimize his own and his environment's behavior and is trying to establish a certain image of himself.

Let's see how Herr Lohs continues and which of the two hypotheses can be verified.

There follows a short narration (11 lines) about a situation soon after Hitler came to power, in which his father was pressured by neighbors to join the Nazi party. It was after this that his father did in fact join the SA Reserves. In the transition from the initial argument to this narration Herr Lohs uses the word *but,* thereby indicating a connection between the two statements, his meaning being: National Socialism was not so extreme in metropolitan Berlin *but* there was still a certain amount of pressure.

Whereas he is arguing in the first sequence, he now is narrating his father's joining the Nazi party.

One can put forward the hypothesis:

(3) Herr Lohs tries argumentatively to play down the influence of the Nazis, but his narrations discover another reality. For the following presentation we assume: He will try to convey by means of biographical global evaluations that the Nazis had little influence, but his narrated stories will contrast with this. In other words: Today he tries to present his life as having been independent from National Socialism, but the experienced entanglements will nevertheless determine the thematic field of his narrated life story.

After this narration Lohs switches to a brief report (13 lines) on his time in the *Jungvolk,* which he introduces with the utterance, *"well then, so naturally I joined the Jungvolk."* His joining is directly linked with his father's membership in the SA, the expression "naturally" conveying how self-evident this step was and that it requires no further legitimation. However, far from being self-evident, this was in fact quite an exceptional move at that time; it was not at all common for a 10-year-old boy to join the *Jungvolk* as early as 1933, the year when it came into being.

How is this presentation of a self-evident joining of the *Jungvolk* to be interpreted?

The following hypotheses were set up:

(4) That he is expressing his perspective at that time (past perspective), which was that it was "natural" for him to follow his father's examples and do what was expected of him, or

(5) seen from his present perspective, the narrator feels the need to present a problematical move as nonproblematical and so to legitimize it; today and in the context of the interview Herr Lohs wants to play down his membership in the Nazi youth organization vis-à-vis the interviewer or, indeed, to himself. In the same way as he belittled in the first sequence the influence of the Nazis in Berlin, he now tries to minimize his own entanglement in National Socialism.

The hypotheses should have made it quite clear by now what this step of thematic field analysis is aiming at. It is not an interpretation of the event of his joining the *Jungvolk*—this is the task of the genetic analysis—but it is concerned with how this piece of information is presented in the context of the interview.

The next step is to interpret why his presentation of his career in the Hitler Youth, which apparently lasted one year, is so very brief.

(6) Herr Lohs reports so little because there is little to tell; this period was unproblematical and had no further relevance for the rest of his biography, making greater elaboration unnecessary;

(7) he does not wish to talk about this period because of unpleasant associations he would rather forget;

(8) he chooses to reveal so little because his actions and experiences at that time do not match his present perspective and the self-image he is trying to put over to the interviewer (cf. Hypothesis 5).

Lohs follows up his report on his experiences in the *Jungvolk* with another report on the time of Hitler's assumption of power. He describes how his father was unemployed before 1933, offering this as a different explanation for his father's political change than the one he had used before.

Here we can formulate the hypothesis:

(9) Hans Lohs is put under legitimizing pressure with respect to the entanglement of his family in National Socialism (see above).

He is also quite conscious that his father was to a certain extent convinced by the Nazis and did not just join the SA Reserves because of the neighbors' pressure.

He closes this report with an argumentation: *"if you kept your mouth shut, nothing happened to you"* and finishes with the statement that his dropping out of the Hitler Youth—after one year—had no negative consequences for him.

This argument probably pinpoints the decisive global evaluation that determines the way in which the biographer wishes his stories to be understood.

Hypotheses on the meaning of this line of argument:

(10) Herr Lohs wants to show that Germany under National Socialism was not as restrictive as is usually claimed. In a way this argumentation serves to demonstrate the innocence of the National Socialist State and has to be seen in relation to his initial argument on the limited impact of Nazi politics on everyday life in "metropolitan Berlin." The latent biographical overall construction underlying this presentation is the attempt to construct a life history detached from National Socialism (cf. Hypotheses 2 and 5).

(11) He is explaining that one was not forced to join the Hitler Youth, thus repudiating the argument frequently put forward nowadays that "one was forced to participate" in the movement. Thus he also expresses that he is not able to set himself free from his life-historical entanglements.

Having made this point, Herr Lohs introduces the topic "Jews." The content of this sequence reveals that what follows is a theme located in the same latent thematic field as well as in the same manifest global evaluation as what went before. Hans Lohs begins with, *"well, we had—oh yes, as I was saying, about Jews, we didn't know about that either."* The expression *"as I was saying"* indicates that his previous argument had also intended somehow to include the claim that "they"—probably his family—were unaware of what was going on.

From this follows Hypothesis 12, that the general legitimation "we didn't know about it" was also intended to apply to his father's and his own membership in Nazi organizations—thus placing both arguments in the same thematic field containing the themes of National Socialist entanglements. If this hypothesis is correct, we can expect some evidence of his biographical entanglement in the persecution of the Jews from one of the next sequences.

His introduction is followed by an exemplifying narrative[15] about *"the chess game with the Jews,"* to demonstrate that, at that time at least (i.e., probably before the Nuremberg laws were passed in 1935), the narrator himself had nothing against Jews. This whole theme is dealt with in three lines.

Hypotheses on the short presentation of this topic:

(13) For the narrator, anti-Semitism and the persecution of the Jews are not problematical subjects that demand more extensive discussion. Hans Lohs does not see himself as having been involved in any way with this aspect of the Nazi past and feels no sense of collective and personal guilt.

(14) The biographer tries to avoid this topic, because some further elaboration would disclose his biographical entanglement in this part of the Nazi past. The theme "chess game with Jews" is appresenting—to use a phenomenological term—the theme "what happened with these peaceful and civilized Jews later." This is a theme that Herr Lohs—as well as most other German witnesses of the Nazi period—tries to avoid.

After this very brief exemplifying narrative Lohs offers a general evaluation of what he has said so far: *"Well, so that was the average, is that what you wanted to know, was that about the average?"* He is obviously referring to the introduction to the interview, when one of the interviewers somehow mentioned this word "average." Lohs now wants to check whether he "was doing it right" in his role as interviewee; he is not quite sure whether he is fulfilling the interviewers' expectations. Further we may assume that this question at that point in the interview dealing with the topic "Jews" is not accidental, but supporting the hypothesis that he tries to avoid the topic.

Having put this question he goes straight on, without a pause, to give a 15-line narrative (the longest narration so far) account of how he was summoned to attend an obligatory Hitler Youth event in 1940, which he did. We can assume that the interviewer gave some sort of nonverbal response, such as a nod, to his question, making it unnecessary for him to wait for an answer. Further, the quick connection indicates the rhetorical meaning of the question and its function to evade the topic "Jews."

Lohs continues with an argument that even after this summons his further avoidance of Hitler Youth activities still had no negative consequences for him. He closes with *"you didn't have to go anywhere, no uniform, nothing."*

By this time the dialectics of his general global evaluation regarding National Socialism and of the thematic field of his life story becomes quite evident. His evaluation could be paraphrased as follows: One was not forced to join the Nazi movement and, whatever crimes were committed at that time, he and his environment did not know about them. Again one may ask whether Lohs is trying to refute the common argument that claims "participation through coercion," or whether his intention is to play down the restrictive aspects of the Nazi State (cf. Hypotheses 10 and 11).

His account of the summons is followed by a 3-second pause, then he asks, *"so, now you're looking at me like that (laughing), what else do you have, what else shall I tell you? About before, before the war?"*

Hypotheses on his questions and lack of narrational flow:

(15) Hans Lohs still has not quite understood what is required of him, that he is meant to give an account of his biographically relevant experiences up to the postwar period. The interviewers may not have given him the right instructions or support at the outset.

(16) Lohs is not able to enter into a full narrative account as required because he does not know what is relevant and what is not; he is trying to orient himself to the interviewers' relevances.

(17) Hans Lohs does not wish to get involved in a full-scale narration, because he does not want to present his experiences of the time; this would disclose his involvement in the National Socialist regime, and there are experiences connected with this phase of his life that he does not want to thematize.

(18) Lohs is not able to enter into a full narrative account as required, because the set topic as he understands it is irrelevant to him personally. Whereas he supposes the interviewers' interest in National Socialism, he himself believes his life to be independent of it.

(19) Hans Lohs wants to evade the topic of National Socialism, but feeling himself under a legitimizing pressure he is not capable of developing another thematic field unrelated to National Socialism.

The interviewer now asks Lohs to relate his own experiences, to talk about what was important to him personally. After a pause of 4 seconds Herr Lohs says, *"well, yes, for me it was actually (3 sec. pause). I got an apprenticeship, did a training...."*

His education and training for a job are now presented as biographically relevant, although neither area have been mentioned so far. Hypothesis 18—suggesting that Hans Lohs was not able to narrate fluently because he had been orienting himself to the relevances of the interviewers and the topic held no direct biographical relevance for himself or he wants to avoid it (cf. Hypothesis 17)—receives some support from this reaction. Now that he has been asked explicitly to talk about his own personal experiences, he would—if the hypothesis fits—finally enter into an easier flow of narration.

Hypothesis 20 is advanced at this point: Herr Lohs sees no connection between his own occupational training and National Socialism.

After another short argumentation claiming that, in spite of his continued lack of interest in the Hitler Youth, he had no difficulties as an apprentice either, he briefly refers to his leisure activities apart from the Hitler Youth (2 lines). He then goes on to report about a friend of his who was in the Hitler Youth and later joined the SS. This leads on to a somewhat more detailed narration (23 lines!) of the events of the so-called *Reichs-kristallnacht*—the pogrom against the Jews in November 1938—in which this friend was directly involved. He begins with the same evaluation that he used before to introduce the topic of the persecution of the Jews: "we didn't know that." However, he then narrates what he experienced himself during this pogrom. He remembers, for example, that in front of a shop where he had bought a wristwatch shortly before, there were watches scattered in the street.

With this sequence Hans Lohs stays in the thematic field *"my experiences with National Socialism."* Hypothesis 19, that he cannot evade the topic because he feels a legitimizing pressure, is thus supported. Hypothesis 13, that the topic "persecution of the Jews" is irrelevant to him, is falsified by this.

Again in this sequence he seems to be producing a contradiction to his biographical global evaluation. On one hand it becomes obvious that his life (at least via the friendship with somebody who actively took part in the persecution of the Jews) is connected with the National Socialist politics and practice of persecution. Talking about what he experienced of the persecution is also in contradiction to the statement that he knew nothing. One wonders if he himself realizes this contradiction. Let's see how he continues.

Rounding out this part of his narration, Herr Lohs concludes that *"you had to keep your mouth shut"* because *"if you spoke out against it then it could happen that—uh—(2 sec. pause) you somehow got locked up."* But then he goes on to describe a series of situations that in fact demonstrate just the opposite: that in his firm, for example, nobody used the greeting *Heil Hitler* and that a colleague of his, who had previously been in the SPD (Social Democrats), agitated openly against the Nazis without getting into trouble. Once, he himself got into an argument with a member of the *Werkschutz,* the Nazi organization in industry, and nothing happened to him.

This is obviously a contradiction: first he takes up the typical standpoint, "you had to keep your mouth shut," and then goes straight on to prove from his personal experience that this was not true.

Hypothesis 21 addresses this contradiction:

In situations that impinged upon him personally, Herr Lohs was ready to defend himself, but as long as the persecution of the Jews did not affect him directly, he felt no need to respond to it one way or the other. In other words, his references to anti-Semitism are a product of his present perspective and not related to what was important to him at the time. The legitimations he produces are part of a present attitude and would have been irrelevant to him at the time.

This clarifies why Hans Lohs stresses again and again the lack of coercion. His problem today is that he cannot free himself from his biographical entanglement in the National Socialist politics of persecution by the argument of coercion, because one was not forced to go along, as he experienced himself when he simply stopped going to Hitler Youth meetings. But what does he feel guilty about? Are there onerous experiences that he does not relate?

His narration of all these various situations is drawn to a close with the same argumentation with which he had opened the interview: that metropolitan Berlin was different, that things there were more anonymous and that nobody was forced to join the movement. Then he adds, *"before the war practically nothing happened."*

So Hans Lohs is still in the global evaluation "there was no coercion to join and I didn't have much to do with National Socialism." Again Hypothesis 10, postulating that he wishes to play down the repressive element of the Nazi state, gains support. Further, Hypothesis 11, suggesting that he wants to invalidate the common claim about "coercion to join," can also be maintained. Furthermore, Hypothesis 1, set up right at the beginning of the analysis, proposing quite simply that he thinks he had little to tell, is also confirmed: at least until the beginning of the war nothing important happened to him personally in connection with his chosen theme of "National Socialism and coercion to join." This leads on to Hypothesis 22, that he may

have experienced something during the war that bears a closer
relation to the topic and that he feels is worth recounting in
more detail.

After the last argument Herr Lohs pauses for 8 seconds and
then asks, *"anything else? do you have anything else (clearing
his throat), don't hesitate to ask."*

He is indicating that he wants to cooperate but still expects
definite individual questions. This utterance also implies that he
has a feeling that the interviewer might not dare to ask.

Now the interviewer asks him to continue his narration from
the point where he was summoned to the Hitler Youth event.
She is trying to encourage him to produce a biographical story
in chronological order.

There follows a lengthy biographical narrative, uninterrupted
by further questions, depicting his life throughout the period
established at the outset as the framework for the interview.
After a very brief summary of these sequences we will select
certain details for closer analysis.

Lohs begins, *"and then, yes, I completed my apprenticeship."* He remembers his final exam and expands upon this in
more detail than has been the case so far (23 lines). He did badly
because his hair was too long. He describes joining the army and
then comes out rather suddenly with: *"yes, then I was—, in Italy
they locked me up."* There follows a long dramatic narrative[16]
about how he was court-martialled for *wehrkraftzersetzende
Aussagen* (seditious statements). After 3 months of imprisonment on remand he was acquitted. The whole story is concluded
with the evaluation, *"so those were my war experiences, that
was all there was that was to do with Hitler."* He continues with
a short report on his National Socialist commanding officers.
Then, opening with the temporal marker, *"well, in '45 the war
was over"* and beginning with his discharge from the army on
May 5, 1945, he plunges into a full-length epic narrative,[17]
containing a whole series of dramatic stories covering no less
than six pages of transcript, in which he narrates how he found
his way back to Berlin and tells about his experiences and career
during the postwar period. He gives a detailed account of his

year in the auxiliary police and subsequent career as a racketeer, closing rather abruptly with the short argument, *"at the beginning of the fifties things got better economically."* Without mentioning how he made a living after that, he goes on to report briefly on his emigration to Canada and his return to Berlin and, after a pause lasting 6 seconds, asks the interviewer, *"so, now (7 sec. pause) you are reasonably satisfied with that, I suppose."*

The interviewer's last question clearly had the effect of enabling Hans Lohs to enter into a narrative flow and keep to it, without further encouragement, right up to the end of the period set by the interviewer at the outset of the interview, when he had been asked to relate his experiences up to the time *"when his everyday life settled back to normal."* With this, the first part of the interview, the main narration, came to an end.

It is important to note that the narrative flow released after the interviewer's last question cannot be explained purely as an interactive product of the interview situation, but was clearly related to the development of the theme itself. As had been predicted beforehand in Hypothesis 22, Hans Lohs did in fact experience something during the war that was—in his interpretation—directly related to the issue of National Socialism; an experience where he personally was brought up against the repressive pressure exercised by the system upon the individual. The story of his court martial was the first of such length (2 pages); the charge brought against him stands out as his global evaluation of "National Socialism and coercion." Beyond this, he says nothing about his experiences as a soldier but talks instead about Nazi commanding officers, that is, he again turns to a subject directly related to National Socialism. This is extraordinary in view of the fact that he experienced 3 years of active service at the front, taking part in campaigns both in Italy and the East. The hypothesis gains plausibility that the stock of the thematic field of this life story is "my experiences with National Socialism."

Hypotheses on his failure to describe his own war experiences:

(23) For Lohs there is no connection between his time in the army and the topic of National Socialism. The army and Germany's

role in the war have—in his opinion—nothing to do with the Nazi State. Hence his own wartime experiences are not relevant to the topic at hand as he has understood it. Hans Lohs puts important phases of his life—as he did with his apprenticeship—aside from National Socialism and thus tries to understand his life as independent from National Socialism.

A different hypothesis would be:

(24) He does not want to talk about his life as a soldier because his experiences were so upsetting that he would rather not mention them. There are also other onerous experiences, which he attempts to evade.

Only when he reaches the period following his discharge, that is, after the collapse of the National Socialist regime, does he again enter into an elaborate epic narrative. As long as he was talking about wartime, Hans Lohs kept strictly to the thematic field: *"my experiences with National Socialism";* only when he got beyond this period in his biography was he able to give rein to his reminiscences and draw from personal experience without setting limits. Only from this point could he orient his story toward himself and rid himself of the pressure to move in a thematic field he would rather evade. The fact that he was not able to leave the set thematic field until the narration of the end of the war demonstrates and expresses a need for legitimation. Hans Lohs tries hard to present a life story independent from National Socialism, but this attempt fails, because he feels guilty for something about which he probably "kept his mouth shut."

Here we come to the end of our analysis of the main narration. Some of the hypotheses have become more plausible whereas others can be excluded altogether. A good many, however, have still not been clarified one way or the other. For example, the question of why Hans Lohs tells so little about his experiences in the *Jungvolk* or to what extent he feels personally involved in the issues of anti-Semitism and the Holocaust, remain unanswered. The analysis of the second part of the interview provided material for a great many further interpretations. For example, it came out later that his time in the Hitler Youth was associated with an unpleasant experience (cf. Hypothesis 7): his Group Leader committed suicide upon discovering that he was of Jewish origin. Furthermore, in the microanalysis of individual passage from the text, hypotheses could be tested yet again. Thus, on the subject of the Holocaust, the microanalysis of a reference to prisoners in a concentration camp revealed how very concerned the narrator is to deny any personal involvement in this chapter of German history. As a soldier, Hans Lohs had to guard KZ (concentration camp)-prisoners and he witnessed how they were brutally mistreated by SS guards and he refused to keep the guard. His superior accepted. Again he experienced that one was not forced to do such things. But obviously this refusal did not take the burden from him; up until today he has to ask himself what he could have done against the maltreatment of the prisoners.

In summary, it seems to have become clear during this analysis that Hans Lohs does not wish to see his own life during the Nazi period as being in any way connected with the National Socialist system as a political phenomenon. He perceives himself as somebody who went his own way, more or less independently of social conditions. Being under legitimizing pressure, however, he cannot evade the thematic field "my experiences with National Socialism" and narrate instead those experiences unrelated to this. In his opinion, such stories do not belong to the subject.

This interpretation finds further confirmation in the analysis of the second, inquiring part of the interview, which lasted for another 3 hours. It could be demonstrated that Hans Lohs not only rejects all personal responsibility for the German Nazi past but also denies having consciously "suffered" under the conditions of the time. He does not feel the need to justify himself with such common collective explanations as "that was the way we were brought up" or "we were too young"; neither does he come out with typical collective interpretations of his own suffering along the line of, "they tricked us out of our youth" or "the Nazis used us as cannon fodder."

Similarly, the interruption of his working career and his experiences as a soldier had nothing to do with National Socialism. When asked directly about his years at the front, he did in fact narrate in great detail dreadful experiences that give him nightmares to this day. But he still did not relate these experiences to the "subject in hand"; even in the face of such extremities, he failed to perceive a connection between what happened to him and social conditions in general.

The attitude demonstrated so very clearly in the interview with Hans Lohs explains why, in such interviews, the interviewer's opening question does not trigger an easy narrative flow. Such "failures" cannot be accounted for as "bad interviewing" or a lack of narrational competence on the part of the biographer. It is rather a manifestation of the biographical overall construct and the structure of meaning underlying the biographer's understanding of social reality and his life story. If people do not conceive of their life as being related to social conditions, they are simply not able to talk about it under such a heading.

Lohs's presentation of a life detached from the political context of the Nazi period cannot be interpreted as a random interpretation or, worse still, as cognitive incompetence on his part. It has a particular function in coping with the Nazi past. It has been demonstrated in a more recent study (Rosenthal, 1990), in which various strategies for normalizing the Nazi past were reconstructed by means of comparisons between generations, that depoliticizing the Nazi period is a common strategy employed particularly by Germans older than the Hitler Youth generation to avoid facing up to the whole issue of National Socialism. In this study we chose a different opening question ("Please tell us your life story—concentrated on your war memories") that avoided mentioning National Socialism as such. We found that especially the older generation (those who had already experienced World War I in their youth) frequently told their life stories without a single reference to the Third Reich. Whereas these very old people tend in this way to depoliticize the Nazi past implicitly, Hans Lohs does it quite explicitly with his repeated assertions that he had little to do with the Nazis.

Summary

In general, we may assume that how biographers react to the opening question, how they interpret the set topic, and which thematic field they develop as framework for their narrative is dependent on their biographical overall construct. This was obvious in the case cited here but can be generalized to apply to all biographical interviews. For example, in interviews concentrating on the subjects' working lives, the question would also arise about which parts of their everyday lives are connected with the thematic field in question. It might also be asked whether the narrator talks about the influence of his or her work on other biographical areas and which connections he or she sees or fails to see between the various spheres of his or her life. It is possible to reconstruct all of these aspects in such a study. Generally, the reconstruction of a life history first requires an analysis of the data upon which it is based. Before reconstructing the biographical meaning of single experiences and events, it is necessary to find out how the narrator or biographer has understood the given topic, how it is used as an orientation and in which thematic field individual experiences and events are located. Only if an insight is gained into whether the informant is orienting toward personal or the interviewer's relevances can the analyst make propositions on the intersubjective meaning of the narrated events and experiences. In other words, it is not possible to interpret a text naively on the assumption that everything the biographer relates is of personal biographical significance.

The intersubjective meaning of individual stories cannot be reconstructed by subsuming the stories presented by the narrator under the categories set up by the interviewer nor by interpreting single text passages independently from the narrative context. Hermeneutic analysis requires that contextual interpretation take the entire interview into account; in the case of biographical analysis this means that each narrated experience must be identified and localized within the framework of the biographer's overall construction, as defined through the biographical strands and thematic field presented in the interview.

88   THE NARRATIVE STUDY OF LIVES

At first glance, however, it is not possible to determine to which thematic field a particular story belongs; this can only be done in a painstaking step-by-step analysis.

Appendix:
Sequentialization of the Interview With Hans Lohs

page/line

1/4-1/8	Argumentation:	National Socialism in Berlin not so exaggerated
1/8-1/17	Narration:	Father joined the SA
1/17-1/30	Report:	The time in the *Jungvolk*
1/30-2/3	Report:	Father was unemployed before 1933
2/3-2/25	Argumentation:	"If you kept your mouth shut, nothing happened to you"
2/25-2/28	Argumentation:	"we didn't know about that either"
	Exemplifying Narrative:	The chess game with the Jews
2/28-2/30	General Evaluation:	"That was the average, is that what you wanted to know?"
2/39-3/8	Narration:	Summons to attend a Hitler Youth event

3/8   Question to the Interviewer: "What else shall I tell?"
Answer from the Interviewer: What is important for you
Interviewee: Apprenticeship, training

3/28-3/30	Argumentation:	No difficulties because of absenteeism from the Hitler Youth
3/30-3/32	Report:	Leisure activities
3/32-4/1	Report:	My friend who joined the SS
4/1-4/29	Narration:	The *Reichskristallnacht*
	Argumentation:	"you had to keep your mouth shut"
4/29-5/1	Report:	*Heil Hitler*
5/1-5/16	Narration:	Problems with the *Werkschutz*
5/16-5/29	Argumentation:	National Socialism in Berlin not so exaggerated
	General Evaluation:	"before the war practically nothing happened"

Notes

1. Cf. Kohli, 1986a, 1986b; Schütze, 1983, 1984; Fischer-Rosenthal, 1989, 1991.

2. By *life history* we mean the lived through life; by *life story* we mean the narrated life as related in a conversation or written in an actual present time.

3. We prefer the term *biographer* to *autobiographer;* the latter does not account for the social constitution of the subject and the social construction of his or her life history.

4. The goal of narrative questions is to elicit further narrations. They must not be put in such a way that they trigger argumentations or legitimizing accounts. The biographer is asked to elaborate in greater detail on a previously mentioned experience, event, or period of life.

5. This stage of analysis is largely founded on the methodological approach of Fritz Schütze (1976a, 1983), as well as on suggestions put forward by Wolfram Fischer (1982) on thematic field analysis; these in turn refer to the theoretical works of Aron Gurwitsch (1964).

6. This was in fact postulated by W. I. Thomas and Florian Znaniecki (1918-1920/1958, II, p. 1832), who claimed that "life records, as complete as possible, constitute the perfect type of sociological material."

7. *Biographical overall construct* is the term for that context of meaning that is not consciously at the disposal of the biographer; by *biographical global evaluation* we mean the biographer's conscious interpretations.

8. In Aron Gurwitsch's (1964) terminology, the individual themes are "elements of a thematic field."

9. If the interviewer does not set a specific topic but asks the biographers in a general way to tell their life story, the biographers themselves will select those topics that are relevant. This method has the advantage of allowing the researcher to learn how the biographers—if at all—are embedding the topic of research interest in the presentation of their life story.

10. The procedure is based on Ulrich Oevermann's objective hermeneutics (Oevermann et al., 1979, 1980), on the method of narrative and text analysis developed by Fritz Schütze (1983) and on the thematic field analysis of Wolfram Fischer (1982).

11. *Narrations* refer to single sequences of events from the past; sequences of actual or fictitious occurrences that are related to one another through a series of temporal or causal links. *Descriptions:* "the decisive feature distinguishing them from narrative is that descriptions present static structures" (Kallmeyer & Schütze, 1977, p. 201). *Argumentations:* abstracted elements occurring outside the story-telling sequence—*theorizing:* declarations of general idea. They show the narrator's general orientation at the moment.

12. Cf. sequentialization in the appendix.

13. For more details of this narrated life story see the discussion of Hans Lohs's interview in Rosenthal (1987).

14. The aim of this interview method is to elicit and maintain a full narration by the interviewee, with the help of a set of noninterfering techniques applied by the trained interviewer. The method is based on the assumption that the

narration of an experience comes closest to the experience itself. Narration of biographical events gives the chance to glimpse some of the motives and interpretations guiding the actions of the biographer.

15. Exemplifying narrative: adds plausibility to a line of argument.

16. In "dramatic narratives" a number of main chains of events are drawn together in common situations (cf. Kallmeyer & Schütze, 1977, p. 187).

17. *Epic narratives* are "narratives containing much descriptive elaboration, in which sequences of events are skimmed over in summarized form (e.g., by means of abbreviated repetitive formulae such as 'there we were, driving along . . . from one village to the next . . . always trying to ask, me jumping out the whole time") in order to keep to one main narrative strand" (Kallmeyer & Schütze, 1977, p. 187).

References

Bertaux, D. (1981). *Biography and society*. Beverly Hills, CA: Sage.

Fischer, W. (1982). *Time and chronic illness. A study on social constitution of temporality*. Habilitation thesis, University of California, Berkeley.

Fischer, W. (1989). Perspektiven der Lebenslaufforschung. In A. Herlth & K. P. Strohmeier (Eds.), *Lebenslauf und Familienentwicklung* (pp. 279-294). Opladen: Leske & Budrich.

Fischer-Rosenthal, W. (1991). Biographische Methoden in der Soziologie. In U. Flick, E. v. Kardorff, H. Keupp, L. v. Rosenstiel, & St. Wolff (Eds.), *Handbuch Qualitative Sozialforschung* (pp. 253-256). München: Psychologie Verlags Union.

Glaser, B., & Strauss, A. L. (1967). *The discovery of grounded theory: Strategies for qualitative research*. Chicago: Aldine.

Gurwitsch, A. (1964). *The field of consciousness*. Pittsburgh, PA: Duquesne University Press.

Kallmeyer, W., & Schütze, F. (1977). Zur Konstitution von Kommunikationsschemata. In D. Wegner (Ed.), *Gesprächsanalyse* (pp. 159-274). Hamburg: Buske.

Kohli, M. (1986a). Biographical research in the German language area. In Z. Dulczewski (Ed.), *A commemorative book in honor of Florian Znaniecki on the centenary of his birth* (pp. 91-110). Poznan, Poland: Naukowe.

Kohli, M. (1986b). Social organization and subjective construction of the life course. In A. B. Sorensen, F. E. Weiner, & L. R. Sherrod (Eds.), *Human development and the life course* (pp. 271-292). Hillsdale, NJ: Lawrence Erlbaum.

Oevermann, U. (1983). Zur Sache: Die Bedeutung von Adornos methodologischen Selbstverständnis für die Begründung einer materialen soziologischen Strukturanalyse. In L. v. Friedeburg & J. Habermas (Eds.), *Adorno-Konferenz 1983* (pp. 234-289). Frankfurt a.M.: Suhrkamp.

Oevermann, U., et al. (1979). Die Methodologie einer "objektiven Hermeneutik" und ihre allgemeine forschungslogische Bedeutung in den Sozialwissenschaften. In H.-G. Soeffner (Ed.), *Interpretative Verfahren in den Sozial-und Textwissenschaften* (pp. 352-434). Stuttgart: Metzler.

Oevermann, U., et al. (1980). Zur Logik der Interpretation von Interviewtexten. In Th. Heinze, H. W. Klusemann, & H.-G. Soeffner (Eds.), *Interpretationen einer Bildungsgeschichte* (pp. 15-69). Bensheim: Päd extra.

Peirce, Ch. S. (1979). *Collected papers of Charles Sanders Peirce* (C. Hartshorne & Paul Weiss, Eds.) (Vol. 7). Cambridge, MA: Belknap Press. (Original work published 1933)

Rosenthal, G. (Ed.). (1986). *Die Hitlerjugend-Generation.* Essen: Blaue Eule.

Rosenthal, G. (1987). Wenn alles in Scherben fällt . . . In *Von Leben und Sinnwelt der Kriegsgeneration.* Opladen: Leske & Budrich.

Rosenthal, G. (1989). May 8th, 1945: The biographical meaning of a historical event. *International Journal of Oral History, 10*(3), 183-192.

Rosenthal, G. (Ed.). (1990). Die Auswertung. Hermeneutische Rekonstruktion erzählter Lebensgeschichten. In dies.: "Als der Krieg kam, hatte ich mit Hitler nichts mehr zu tun." Zur Gegenwärtigkeit des "Dritten Reiches" in erzählten Lebensgeschichten (pp. 246-251). Opladen: Leske & Budrich.

Schütze, F. (1976a). Zur Hervorlockung und Analyse von Erzählungen thematisch relevanter Geschichten im Rahmen soziologischer Feldforschung. In Arbcitsgruppe Bielefelder Soziologen (Ed.), *Kommunikative Sozialforschung* (pp. 159-260). München: Fink.

Schütze, F. (1976b). Zur linguistischen und soziologischen Analyse von Erzählungen. In *Internationales Jahrbuch für Wissens- und Religionssoziologie* (Vol. 10, pp. 7-41). Opladen: Westdeutscher Verlag.

Schütze, F. (1977). *Die Technik des narrativen Interviews in Interaktionsfeldstudien.* Arbeitsberichte und Forschungsmaterialien Nr. 1 der Universität Bielefeld, Fakultät für Soziologie.

Schütze, F. (1983). Biographieforschung und narratives Interview. *Neue Praxis, 3,* 283-294.

Schütze, F. (1984). Kognitive Figuren des autobiographischen Stegreiferzählens. In M. Kohli & G. Robert (Eds.), *Biographie und soziale Wirklichkeit* (pp. 78-117). Stuttgart: Metzler.

Schütze, F. (1992). Pressure and guilt: War experiences of a young German soldier and their biographical implications. *International Sociology, 7*(2), 187-208.

Thomas, W. I., & Znaniecki, F. (1958). *The Polish peasant in Europe and America* (Vol. 2). New York: Dover. (Original work published 1918-1920)

❧ 5 ❧

Looking at Change

Natasha, 21: New Immigrant From Russia to Israel

Amia Lieblich

*I*n Berkeley, spending a sabbatical year away from the Hebrew University, speaking English all day long (rather than Hebrew, my native language), I often remember the young students, new immigrants from Russia, whom I interviewed last year in Jerusalem. Searching for a missing expression or an unknown address, forlorn in front of the new computer, their experience of being strangers in an unfamiliar culture emerges for me in its polarity of helplessness and courage. My situation, of course, is a lot easier than theirs: I have not lost my home and friends, because I will return to Israel at the end of the year; I know the language used in this country, I am secure with proper housing and a job.

AUTHOR'S NOTE: The interviews with Natasha, which provide the material for the present chapter, took place in the framework of a research project conducted at the Hebrew University by Dr. Orly Bach and myself on "The New Soviet Immigrants to Israel: Lives in Transition," financed by a grant from the Bruno Goldberg Memorial Fund, American Friends of the Hebrew University, New York. I wish to express my deepest gratitude to Orly Bach and Paul Weinberger for their part in formulating the research design and the outline of the interviews, and to Levia Fiurko for her review of the literature on immigration.

In my case, the main loss is in status, from being a well-known-re-spected-author-and-professor in Jerusalem, to just-another-visiting-scholar-with-a-strange-accent in this community. However, when I experience loss of familiar orientation, such as being unable to find my way (lost!) on the freeway or among the stacks in the university library, I shudder for the immense loss of my young Russian new-immigrant students. Natasha, 21, is one of them.

In the following narrative I will present Natasha's acute transition in the midst of the normal, developmental transition of her age group. The "acute" issue is the personal experience of immigration: the loss of one's old home and country on the one hand, and the necessary accommodation to a new society, language, and culture on the other.[1] The basic, "normal" issues for Natasha at this stage are a search for identity and values, and separation-individuation vis-à-vis her parents (Lieblich, 1989; Wiseman & Lieblich, 1992). Natasha must make a dual transition. She must deal with choices in the realms of career and relationships, in the context of the upheavals of immigration.

Natasha (not her real name, naturally) is one of 12 Hebrew University students whom I interviewed in depth during the academic year of 1990-1991. When I met them for the first time, they were less than 6 months after emigration from the USSR. Most of them were enrolled in the "preparatory year" designed specifically for newcomers to Israel, to provide intensive courses in Hebrew and English. I saw each of them individually for 2 to 4 hours at the beginning of the school year, and again 6 months later. Several of them requested additional meetings with me in between.

In our conversations, my open-ended questions covered their present situation, past history, and future plans. I conducted the interviews in Hebrew or English, after clumsy, unsatisfactory attempts to let them speak Russian and work with an interpreter. The evolving procedure was, therefore, to search for individuals who were able to express themselves in Hebrew or English, to present my questions slowly and in "Hebrew for beginners," and to use help from an interpreter present in the room (in most of the sessions) whenever the students could not understand me or express themselves. Although good rapport was established, this emerging procedure had, of course, its drawbacks: the selection of more verbally gifted individuals, the limitations imposed on the communication due to the remaining language barrier, and the effects of the presence of another person in the room. Given that I wanted to conduct the interviews myself (see previous work based on similar techniques in Lieblich, 1978, 1981, 1986, 1989; Wiseman & Lieblich, 1992) but cannot speak Russian, I believe that this was the optimal solution to our communication problems.

Part I: Life in Transition

The Present Situation

My first impression of Natasha was of a colorless and subdued young woman. She seemed to be skinny and pale, her black eyes enormous and sad, her smile polite and somewhat shaky. Apparently, she needed dental work on her front teeth. For our first meeting she was wearing a gray plaid skirt and a matching sweater—unusually elegant garments for a student. She sat erect in the armchair, her legs crossed.

Natasha reported that she was a regular full-time student, in addition to her special classes in Hebrew and English. For the first 3 months she went to the Ulpan (intensive Hebrew course) with her parents in the town where the family had settled, and then continued for 2 months at the summer Ulpan for students of the Hebrew University in Jerusalem. Because she had already been a university student for 3 years back in the USSR, in Kishinov, Moldavia, she was allowed to take the entrance examinations for the Hebrew University right away, and was accepted for third year in Slavic Literature and first year in Linguistics. At the initial stage of our interviews I commented on Natasha's acquisition of the new language.[2]

> I: So you are taking lectures in Hebrew, together with
> the Israeli students," I inquired.
>
> She: Yes, of course. I can listen for about 15-20 minutes,
> and then it gets too hard to concentrate; I'm exhausted
> [in perfect Hebrew!]. And I take my notes in Russian,
> which is funny. I have lots of classes and it's hard to be
> on campus all day long. I cannot commute to my
> dormitories during the day for rest, because it's too far,
> and the bus is too expensive. Often I go to the library
> to rest for a while, but it is no good.

One of my earliest impressions of Natasha was that she did
not dare—or allow herself—to complain. She described her difficulties with detachment, speaking neutrally, her calm voice
uncorrelated with the contents of her account. (In later meetings I noticed the tears welling up in her huge eyes, reflecting
her inner state more accurately than her voice.) When I offered
possible solutions to the problems she mentioned, such as
taping the lectures, she had two typical reactions: "I'm fine,
please don't worry about me," and: "If I take this step—the
situation might get worse." Here I detected for the first time the
reluctance to change in the midst of changing, or her holding
on to the slight stability that was available during the general
turmoil she was experiencing inside and outside. Take the following encounter as an example:

> I: Perhaps you should ask to be moved to the dormitories
> here on Mount Scopus; I could help you in that.
>
> She: Oh, no. I have a nice roommate, an Israeli girl, and
> I can speak a little Hebrew with her. If I move up here,
> who knows who will be my roommate.

Only much later did I find out that her relationship with that
roommate was quite unsatisfactory. At the same time she did not
mention that she had a number of Russian-speaking friends in
the dormitories where she roomed, and probably was afraid of
losing this support group.

As our meetings continued, I was able to see Natasha as a very attractive young woman, tall and slim, warm and highly intelligent. The "concealed quality" of her personality and beauty did not result from the cultural barrier between us alone. She was, at this stage, especially with Israeli strangers, a person-in-hiding. Generally, I understood Natasha's situation at the beginning of the academic year as that of a person exerting a tremendous struggle to cope with the crisis of immigration. Although she was doing very well from an objective point of view, this struggle drained her of energy (color), and dulled the power and charm of her personality.

In order to understand this we should look into Natasha's past, and the terms of her loss through emigration from her native world. Later we will go into Natasha's new choices and relationships and her ambivalence toward changing as required by her age and transition.

Natasha's Past in Moldavia

Natasha's grandparents on her father's side were the rich owners of a bakery. When the Russians occupied Moldavia and enforced a communist regime on the country, they exiled the Jewish capitalist and took all his property. Natasha's father grew up in Siberia, where his father died at the age of 46. Thereafter, the widow and her son were permitted to return to their native city. Natasha's father was admitted to the university in Moscow, where he obtained a degree in engineering (a tremendous achievement for a Jew, indicating his excellence). Coming back to Kishinov, he met the woman who would become his wife at a wedding, got married, and had two children. He worked as a construction engineer in a cooperative, and his wife built a career as an economist in a factory. In spite of the relatively good income of the couple, the family lived in a tiny two-room apartment together with both grandmothers, who took care of the children.[3]

Natasha was accepted at school at 6, a year ahead of other children, because she started to read and write on her own. She went to a good school, was an ardent reader, and obtained excellent grades until she was 13. She said that studying in an elite school (specializing in physics), where half of the students and most of the teachers were Jewish, protected her from being exposed to anti-Semitism, as were others in her town. She became tearful when describing the intimate friendships that developed among the children studying together in the same school for 10 years.

Two features stand out in the account of Natasha's later childhood or early adolescence: the extreme parental authority over children (apparently a common phenomenon in that culture, see Mirsky, 1991), and the experience of an early, intense, and unreciprocated love relationship.

Natasha's parents emerge from her account as two highly delicate, fragile personalities. (This may, of course, be a projection of Natasha's own sensitivity.) She used to see them, especially her father, as "friends" and as "sentimental people." They are by no means "thieves"—Natasha's term for people who can easily make it in the jungle of life. At the same time, during her childhood and adolescence in the USSR, she depicts them as having absolute authority over her conduct. One instance follows:

> She: I was in an archery team, and I used to train every afternoon, going for games and competitions out of town, too. It was great fun. When I was 15, however, my father decided that I should stop this hobby, and dedicate all my time to studying, so that I would graduate with the best possible record.

Examples of this sort appear repeatedly. Her parents applied a strict curfew rule on their daughter, demanding that she be always home by 9 p.m., even when she was a student and 20 years old. When she graduated from high school and wanted to study in Leningrad "my Mom wouldn't allow it. She said: you are not independent enough to leave home." When her parents decided to emigrate from Moldavia (Natasha was already 20, and a third-year student at the time) they simply informed their children, not asking for their opinion or presenting it as their choice.[4] In Natasha's narrative, Father is the authority figure, with Mother providing silent support to his decisions and acts, and generally having a minor role in the story.

Yet this type of parental attitude did not produce any rebellion on Natasha's part. Moreover, she could still see her father as a person. In a different context, describing her father in the USSR, Natasha says, in tears:

> In spite of the fact that he had lost his father in Siberia, he believed in the communist system, and said that only in the USSR can children be provided with a good education. He is naive. He is not a strong man. He just loves books, you know. Give him books and he doesn't want a thing in his life.

For me, growing in a more permissive culture, it was strange to realize that this man, who was "not strong" and certainly did not use any physical power, had absolute authority over his children's lives. Power could apparently be obtained from the traditional role of a father, notwithstanding the person in the role.

Natasha's parents interrupted her relationship with the boy she loved in school, too—which brings us to the second feature of her youth in Moldavia. When Natasha was 13, she fell deeply in love with a boy of 14. They were "going out together" for 2½ years, during which Natasha said she had "suffered immensely from the boy's infidelity." "I loved him terribly," she tells in a dramatic voice, "and I cried all the time. I don't think that he loved me. He did awful things to me, always dating my girlfriends at the same time he was with me." When she turned 15, Natasha's parents announced that this should stop, because the boy was not Jewish. (His parents ordered the same—because she was Jewish.) "I loved him until we graduated from school, but I stopped seeing him or speaking to him, as my parents demanded. Actually, I did not have such a deep love for anyone ever since."

Disregarding for a moment the extreme demonstration of parental authority and interference in their children's lives, one tends to speculate about the place of a relationship of that sort in Natasha's development. According to her story, such an intense emotional attachment is not so rare at that age in Russia. One outcome of the affair from Natasha's point of view was a loss of her interest in school work, especially in mathematics, which later effected her career choice. Another outcome, which Natasha mentioned in a different context, was her tendency to brood and reflect a lot about herself, a trait she disliked.

On a deeper level, however, I see this long episode as probably having additional implications. Such a deep involvement in the life of a teenager indicates an early need to separate from the psychological dominance of her parents, and develop an emotional world of her own (Blos, 1962). The maintenance of the relationship for so long, in spite of the pain it caused her, indicates maturity beyond the average on the one hand and a trend toward romanticism on the other. The experience of rejected love may have produced the depressive aspect in Natasha's personality and her basic insecurity about her worth. Insecurity is demonstrated by a saying she repeated several times in a variety of contexts: "To be successful, one needs to be lucky. Otherwise, a person has little control over fate." On the other hand, being a romantic, slightly depressed and insecure to begin with, may explain how Natasha felt drawn to such a relationship and prolonged it beyond its expected duration. Whatever the direction of the causal chain, the complexity of Natasha's future contacts with people, her tendency to doubt and introspect, and her inability to find simple happiness in the options open to her in reality, are characteristics that are accentuated by the psychological state of an immigrant, as unfolds in the remaining parts of her life story.

The Beginning of Transition: Natasha's Years as a Student in Moldavia

At the age of 16, after graduating from high school, Natasha was accepted at the local university to study Russian language and literature. Although while going through the admission procedure Natasha became personally aware of discrimination due to anti-Semitism for the first time, and in spite of the fact that she was not allowed by her parents to leave home and study elsewhere, the account of her student life in Kishinov is the most joyful chapter in her life story.

> For the first 2 years it was like a paradise. I enjoyed my studies and thought that my professors were the best. I had lots of free time to spend with my friends and develop my hobbies. I was active in the students' theater and newspaper. Every afternoon I took long walks with my friends, talking about books we read, and later sat in certain coffee shops until they were closing them, at 8:00 or 9:00 in the evening. It felt like I was leading the life of students in Paris, about whom I read.

The outstanding features of this stage were the close friendships with some other students, Natasha's sense of autonomy within the permitted framework, and academic interest in her work. The experience of "paradise" was, however, brief. After the first 2 years at the university, Natasha's narrative takes a turn, and the theme of loss that governs future stages begins to surface.

> Our problems started with the Perestroika. Due to the emergence of Moldavian nationalistic sentiments, all foreigners, whether Russians or Jews, were unwelcome anymore. Studying Russian literature was not encouraged, and some of my best professors vanished from school. The ones who took their places taught us in the Moldavian language and were often stupid. At first we believed that the reforms would bring some good to the country. But gradually it dawned on us that they were just talking and talking, while actually the situation became worse. That is when my parents realized that there was no future for us in the USSR and decided to immigrate to Israel.

The process of transition in the life of an immigrant can be divided into two stages: (a) In the country of origin, between the decision to leave and the actual departure—the stage of "severing the ties." (b) Adjustment and building a life for oneself in the new country. Because of bureaucratic difficulties, the first stage lasted for about 2 years for Natasha's family. In Natasha's account, this chapter brings back the familiar sad and moody atmosphere. Her interest in studying declined drastically; she completed the third year, and then decided to drop out with the excuse that she needed to help her family with all the arrangements. In fact, her parents did all of those by themselves, and protectively excluded their children from the burden as well as the sense of participation in the family process.[5] If the economic situation in Moldavia deteriorated, Natasha says she had only very vague picture of it: "I never stood in lines for food, and I could always find enough to eat in our refrigerator."

Natasha's reaction to her parents' decision to emigrate was ambivalent. "I didn't really want to go to Israel. At the same time, I was attracted to the idea of a new beginning, in a new place." Not being interested in her academic work anymore, and not taking part in the family chores, Natasha seemed to have been drawn into a void where separation from her close friends loomed large as an approaching disaster. "My friends have always been the most important thing in my life, that is—being able to open my heart to another."

I confronted Natasha by suggesting that she might have remained behind, while her parents and young brother would leave. "I thought about that, but I couldn't. My parents are such sentimental people, it would have broken their hearts, and my mother has high blood pressure anyway, she is not well." Again we see that Natasha's parents exert their authority in weakness as much as in strength, provoking guilt feelings in their daughter.

Departure and Arrival

Sadness is the prevailing feeling in Natasha's account of her life at the time of separation from the place where she was born and grew up. The family left by train in April 1990. In the days prior to departure Natasha saw all her friends, having intimate talks with them. Her female friends told her things they had never revealed before, because they knew this was their last opportunity. The separation itself is described in a dramatic fashion: A group of about 40 people came to the train station to say good-bye to Natasha (not counting her parents' friends and relatives). She was given gifts and plenty of flowers, hugged and kissed by people who never went beyond a handshake. A lot of her girlfriends cried, as did her mother's friends. Natasha mounted the train with all the flowers, and only after its departure did she start to weep. "It was horrible, horrible. I suddenly realized that I really left this place for ever and ever, never to return. But the full realization took perhaps 3 months more to sink in."

Natasha's moods swing swiftly. In the airport in Bucharest she meets young Israeli men who are in charge of the immigrants' security.

> They were so handsome and strong. I spoke English to them, and it was fun. This helped me stop thinking about my friends. . . . In the airplane we were given plenty of food, and people were so happy to see the lights of Tel Aviv as we approached to land. I, too, was extremely happy, I felt it in my stomach.

Euphoric feelings and idealization of the experience characterize the first few weeks in Israel.

> My first impression was that everything in this country is so pretty, and the people so nice. All the clerks at the airport were extremely polite and efficient [This is as far from reality as one may get! AL], and our relatives came to pick us up. It was late at night but I didn't want to sleep, just to see and hear and absorb what was happening. In the morning I saw the view, it was all so green and beautiful. I had always dreamt of living near the seashore, and here I saw the Mediterranean from my cousin's window. Oh, and I remember just as we

descended the airplane the delightful smell of orange groves, it was everywhere. For the first month I ate oranges all the time, until I couldn't stand their taste anymore.

The oranges memory obviously stands for the return to reality, with its promises and disappointments, and the growing aware ness of what Natasha left behind and lost.

Part II: What Was Lost?

Immigration creates a tremendous chasm in the midst of the immigrant's life. In the present section I will present the major areas in which Natasha experienced her losses, the way she described them in our interviews.

Parental Authority

The transition to Israel resulted in the decline and loss of parental status vis-à-vis their children, a process that normally occurs in adolescence or the stage of transition to adulthood.[6]

The process of immigration exposed Natasha's parents—in her eyes—as old, weak, and insecure, thus accentuating and accelerating the normal process of breaking away from one's parents at this stage. The matter of the age of her parents, who in the new country seem to Natasha as elderly all of a sudden, is repeatedly brought up. In our first interview she said about her father: "He is 52 years old, that is too old to begin a new life. Yet he has to do it." And about her mother—

> My mother is not well, she has high blood pressure and cannot learn Hebrew. She doesn't really try. She says that at 44 it is too late for her, while I tell her that she cannot live in a country without speaking its language and she has her entire life before her.[7]

When her parents wanted to join a kibbutz, where the family would be spared most of the economical struggle, they were rejected, because Natasha's father is too old to become a member. (One wonders whether the idea that Natasha herself is a young person, is something she clings to as a promise for better future adjustment.)

Natasha sometimes describes her parents as depressed, and at some other times as being fully accepting of the hardships involved in the immigration "with no regrets whatsoever," as long as they see that their children might have a better future in the new country. Whatever the emerging picture of her parents, it was clear that they could not and would not remain the same authority figures she had been used to in the past. Thus, Natasha lost her idealization figures, the images of people who could have guided her further in her new life. At the end of her first year in Israel, Natasha, who had been a carefree and protected child in Moldavia, feels that her parents need her support, and she views them with compassion.

Friends and Social Network

When Natasha mentions her classmates in school or the university, her eyes fill with tears. "I had such good friends in my school, I can never forget them. I loved them and the things we did together." Natasha is clearly suffering with longing for them. In comparison, she declares: "I still don't find satisfaction with my new friends that I made here."

Why is she using the term "can never forget," though? Does this mean she tries to forget her friends to avoid the pain of mourning, but she cannot? Will forgetting them make her feel guilty? Natasha's account leaves such questions unanswered.

A recent occasion in which this loss was highly salient for Natasha was the wedding day of her best friend in Kishinov:

> I received the invitation to the wedding by mail, and
> she even sent me the menu of the party. It was good to
> realize she had not forgotten me. I sent her my wishes

in a letter, which probably didn't arrive on time; I had
no money for a gift. The day of her wedding I cried all
day. It was so painful not to be with her and with all
our group of friends.

Not only friends, but a wider network of people who provided support and meaning to Natasha's life were lost in the
transition. At the end of our first meeting, rising to go, Natasha
said to me:

You know, you are the first adult outside my family with
whom I had the opportunity to talk at length since my
arrival. In Kishinov, I had this mother of my close
friend, with whom I often confided. All the things I
couldn't speak to my own Mom about, I discussed with
that woman. Sometimes you feel like you want a
grown-up to talk to. My parents are okay, but talking to
them is just not the same.

Loss of Status

Natasha experiences status and self-respect in relation to two
reference groups—the general group of new immigrants from the
USSR, and her own family. The status of these two groups affects
her own self-respect as a separate individual.

Belonging to the group of Russian new immigrants is an
experience of marginality. To express this, Natasha uses a popular phrase among the immigrants: "In Russia we were told:
you're different, you're Jews; Here we are told: you're different,
you're Russian." Natasha speaks about Israelis who are nice and
polite, yet she also comments on others, lacking patience for
newcomers who cannot express themselves quickly and clearly
in the new language, or who wear different kinds of clothes.

Furthermore, Natasha senses frequently that as a group, Russian new immigrants are looked down upon by Israelis. The
press and the media present them in an unfavorable way. Natasha
is personally offended and hurt by the negative stereotype,

because it seems to be referring to her as well. In our second session she told me the following:

> I read in the papers that the new immigration from Russia is evil. [This is the term she used, picking the English word when she could not express herself in Hebrew.] They say that all the Israeli physicians and engineers will be out of jobs because of competition from the Russians, and, even worse, that in the new elections all the Russians will vote for the extreme "hawkish" parties in Israel, and good-bye to the process of peace-making with the Arabs. It was a terribly bad article,

she said indignantly, "but some Russians (new immigrants) really behave in such a manner that I feel ashamed to belong to this category.

In terms of her family, there is a dramatic decline in the status of her parents. Natasha's father, who had been a well-paid construction engineer, is now a part-time menial worker in a bakery; her mother—the former economist—tends an old lady. "They will never be able to go back to their professional lives, and they seem to have accepted this for a fact. They come home from their separate jobs at 2 p.m., and eat together," described Natasha, tears in her eyes.

> Then they both go out to a cleaning job which they do as a team in a computer company nearby. They tell me that people treat them so well there, inviting them to their homes to visit, or bringing them gifts for the holidays. I believe these people realize that my parents are not the kind you would expect to find in cleaning jobs. Well, what can I say, it's hard.

In comparison to Natasha's former experience of belonging to an elite group, relatively respected and economically secure, she is now aware of having a marginal and lower status in Israel.

Loss of Clarity of Norms

There are two major families of norms that seem to be changing for Natasha in her new life. Her former norms were clear and well grounded in expectations and traditions, whereas the new norms are vaguely understood. As Natasha tells me about exploring new norms, I could sense her confusion and her embarrassment to the point of feeling lost in a maze of contradictions.

Natasha's dilemmas concern the areas of gender expectations and parent-child relationships, namely: How should a young, single woman behave, especially in the context of a possible development of heterosexual relationships? How to educate children—specifically, how should children be brought up to behave toward their parents?

Concerning the first area, Natasha disclosed:

> Back in Kishnov, I was already 20, yet my parents never allowed me to be out of the house later than 9 p.m. It was not to be argued. They used to say: "You are not married, so you are in our responsibility. Once you have your own family, you'll be able to go out as late as you want."

In comparison to these strict norms: "Here in Israel they don't say this anymore. They see that everybody else goes out as late as they want."

But Natasha is confused with the new freedom, and applies her own rules and regulations, as we will later see in discussing the relationship with her boyfriend. This is a tale of four cities: where Natasha lives, where David lives, where he studies, and where she studies. Meeting places and even telephone calls between these two busy students are saturated with conflicts, from Natasha's point of view. For example, she never calls him on the phone, and expects him, "the active, courting male," to be responsible for their communication. David, who is Russian-born but has lived in Israel since early childhood, does not accept this pattern and sees in it lack of emotional involvement on Natasha's part. Living in the dorms where telephones are shared, Natasha, on her side, finds it extremely unbecoming to be asking for him. Similarly, it is fine as long as he comes to visit her in her parents' house, where he frequently stays overnight during weekends, but she refuses to reciprocate. "A girl does not go to the man's house," she said, sounding unsure of herself, as if asking for my opinion. "If I go to sleep in his family's home, I'd feel obliged to him in a way. That's how I was raised, I can't change now."

"So the man and woman in a relationship are not in symmetrical positions," I commented.

With pain in her eyes she said: "Well I know it doesn't sound right, but that's how I'm used to behaving, and it creates problems with David all the time."

Although Natasha and David go on trips together, where he takes the role of the host showing the sights to the newcomer, she tells me about long deliberations on her part about how to behave, and many conflicting encounters that burden their relationship almost to breaking point. In our later conversations, and even on the phone, between scheduled meetings, Natasha asked for my advice in that area, expressing bewilderment and embarrassment about norms and expectations in the area of heterosexual relationships.[8] Although even within a cultural context young men and women find the period of forming a relationship quite confusing, the bewilderment would be much more severe when cultural transition is added to the "normal" sensitivities concerning intimacy and personal boundaries.

Concerning the area of parent-child relationships, Natasha expressed mixed feelings about the way children are raised and behave in Israel. She noticed that children were not polite or respectful toward adults, and specifically toward their parents. "Parents here pamper their children terribly. They drive their children wherever they need to go, they let them shop for anything they fancy, it's too much. I think that they are spoiled and allowed to date and party much too early for their own good." Reflecting on that opinion, and probably remembering herself at 13, already deeply in love, she added:

This is very strange. My parents used to discipline me
severely, and I thought it was wrong. But here it's the
opposite, and I find this is also wrong. I used to think
of myself as nonconservative. I wanted the freedom to
come and go, to dress as I wished. Here I have second
thoughts, especially concerning discipline in the
upbringing of children. I think I have become more
conservative. . . . Oh, God, How will I know how to
behave with my own children?

A long dialogue developed at this point about time and
change, which will be discussed later. Here it suffices to say that
in the second time point, Natasha expressed admiration for what
she perceived as the freedom and courage of children and young
people in Israel, although she was still quite critical of what she
saw as "lack of polite manners among Israelis of all ages. In
Russia it was very clear," she says,

when you see an old person in the bus, you give them
your seat. If you're a man, you open the door for a lady,
and hold her arm as she steps down from the bus. It's
kind of nice. But David makes fun of these manners,
and says that I look down on people if they don't
behave in this hypocritical way. So who is right here? I
don't know.

Loss of Self-Confidence

It is hard to evaluate whether Natasha was a highly self-con-
fident young woman back in her home town; After 3 years in the
university, apparently she was. The transition to a new country
and society, speaking a different language, studying within a
university that operated according to an entirely different system than the one she had known—all these undermined her
former level of self-confidence.

Natasha speaks to me about this loss in divulging how extremely sensitive she has become to others' views about her. "I

have become really anxious about what people here might think about me, what would they say about my Russian accent, about everything. I wish I could care less and be my own self again!"

A salient manifestation of Natasha's loss of self confidence is expressed in her sense of being observed. Although it is agreed that most adolescents have a strong feeling of being observed by their peers, and continuously compare their appearance with their reference groups, Natasha at 21 is again experiencing this earlier state. Right in our first meeting Natasha told me that she felt tested and observed all the time. In the presence of her boyfriends' parents, for example, she feels under judgment whether she is "good enough for their son, who is a genius," this being complicated by the fact that she is "too old for him" (to be clarified below). Six months later, she provided many more instances for her sense of being observed, and combined it with what she labeled as "fear of the Israeli society," and I label as intense need to belong on her own terms.

"For example," she explained, "I love long skirts and I think I look well in them, but David says that in a skirt I look Russian or, worse, as a Jewish orthodox lady. So I wear my blue jeans all the time, but I'm fed up with it." (I have to admit that Natasha looked prettier to me in every consecutive meeting. She often came in tight jeans, and once in a short miniskirt, sitting demurely, crossing her long legs, as if not entirely at ease in that disguise.)

> A week ago I met an older guy, who asked me why did I never wear skirts. Encouraged by him, the following evening I put on one of my long skirts and a blouse. I went out with David and his friends to a Burger place and they were all staring at me like I don't know . . . I felt so uncomfortable that I walked out to the courtyard, where they had some swings and games for kids, and I sat in my skirt on the swing, all by myself. Suddenly I realized that I was watched through the windows. I had the sense that these strangers were pointing at me: "Look at her, look at her." I had to leave.

"You see," she continues to explain, "I often feel ashamed here." In matters of clothing, as a most outward sign of one's identity, Natasha reported that she used to like original, uncommon outfits back in her native city. Here in Israel, however, lack of confidence drives Natasha toward the most common and popular forms, which seem to promise acceptance.[9]

Another topic that reflects on Natasha's loss of confidence in Israel has to do with speaking in public, even in Russian: "I feel uncomfortable in many of the classes I take, and as a result I never speak up in public. I used to be very active in classes back home, but here I speak less than anyone else. I feel as if I have a wall right here (pointing at her chest) which I cannot overcome." Even in a pair, Natasha finds it hard to defend her opinions:

> Often I do my home assignments in Linguistics with an Israeli girl. Whenever we disagree, she says that I didn't understand what the professor said, and we end up doing what she thinks right. When we get our papers back, it often turns out that I was right and she was wrong, yet I still feel unable to stand my ground.

Loss of a Sense of Cultural Belonging

The issue of cultural belonging cuts through several of the former areas presented in this chapter. Whenever Natasha is uncertain about the expected norms of behavior or the dress code, she experiences her cultural alienation or marginality due to the loss of former roots in a familiar cultural environment. Cultural loss has many manifestations:

> In Kishinov, which is the capital of Moldavia, there were lots of theaters and places to go, it was the center of our civilization. Here, I miss the pulse of the city. Also, not being able to go to the theater is hard—at first I couldn't understand the language. Now, I can understand more, but it is too expensive.

Back home she knew some young writers and poets who made it in Moscow—whereas here she was a stranger to the cultural scene. She also told me, sadly, that the family left its entire private library, which was huge, back in Kishinov. She grieved for her books, and complained that she lacked books for reading (although she had very little free time to feel this loss too often). In another context she says: "I used to enjoy the study of language, but here, when I decided to major in Linguistics, it was a mistake. For after all, this is not my language."

Clarity of Career Path

Whereas in Russia Natasha was already a fourth year student in a 5-year program leading to a master's degree, building a future career as a teacher, this path was interrupted by the family's decision to emigrate. Now we find Natasha as if re-gressed to a prior stage, making her vocational choice for her future in a relatively unknown society. Thus choosing her major in the university is hard and confusing; Natasha, who is remark-ably intelligent, claims that she still does not comprehend the credit system of our university. She argues that a counselor misinformed her about the program in Linguistics, which is her second major. "I am often bored in classes, or I don't under-stand," she says.

At the end of her freshman year in that subject, she said clearly:

> I made a mistake in starting this major, and I will have to change again. It is not so bad, actually, I have already some plan in mind. The problem is greater for my parents—being "Soviet personalities" they don't take into account the possibility of having alternatives to choose from, or the option of change. They are afraid of changes. Nobody in Russia ever makes a change like that, once they're in school. All they can do is drop out. My parents believe that if I'll change my major, I'll

prove that I'm not serious about my work. Moreover, I'll
be kicked out of the university, or lose my scholarship.

Her interrupted career training, which appears in the beginning of the academic year as quite a loss, becomes, however, at
the end of the year, an area for making new choices, namely:
Natasha is pleased about the new possibilities unfolding before
her. In this instance, change is not experienced solely as a loss,
but as an opening and a challenge.[10] She also feels a clear sense
of superiority here in comparison with her parents, and admits
it without pain, guilt, or regret. Although they are afraid of
changes, Natasha is less so. This attitude indicates the resump-
tion of the interrupted process (by immigration) of normal
separation from her parents.

Looking boldly for new career options is possible because
this is an area in which loss, too, was concrete and easy to
formulate. It is perhaps after the experience and/or expression
of loss, as in mourning (Parks, 1979) that changes become
challenges and the process of growing up may go on.

Part III: Changing and Not Changing

At one time, in our interviews, Natasha and I had a direct
conversation about change. This happened after Natasha said
that, because of the different traditions of the two cultures she
lived in, in the future she probably won't know how to raise her
children. I answered Natasha that she had plenty of time for that.
In her response she said: "Maybe I'll change. My brother, who
is 16 now, has completely changed already; He goes out every
evening, like the Israeli boys."

A long dialogue about "change" followed. Natasha's arguments can be summarized in three points:

(1) Some Russian new immigrants are very quick to adopt Israeli
norms of behavior, such as in dress, for example. Some also
change their first or second names to Israeli names, a step that

she scorns. (She has a female acquaintance who did that, and suggests that I interview her, to realize the difference.)[11]

(2) In fact, Russian mentality can be compared to a chameleon; many Russians are highly conforming to external messages and demands in their behavior—the so-called Soviet personality—and she detests this.

(3) Natasha herself did not change, according to her view. The only exception, she said on this occasion, was in her relationship with her parents.

The underlying theme I discerned in this part of the interview was Natasha's search for stability in the midst of a changing, confusing, perhaps even turbulent world. The admission that she did change "only" vis-à-vis her parents, sounded naive to me, because as a psychologist I obviously consider this area to be at the core of people's personalities and of utmost significance for their transition to adulthood.

Let us listen to the changes that have taken place in Natasha, as told, half-told, and denied throughout our interviews.

First Signs of Changing

Looking at Natasha's account of her first experiences in Israel, idealization of what had been perceived from the outside, and plasticity of her own personality from the inside, both stand out clearly. She spoke with what sounded like exaggerated enthusiasm about the physical and social reality first encountered in Israel. She discovered a good, new world. We heard that Natasha had wished for a "new beginning," and indeed her expectation seemed, at the very first, to be coming true.

The "plasticity" of Natasha's personality could be discerned first of all in the amazing manner of her mastering of the new language (Grinberg & Grinberg, 1989). This was certainly more than an intellectual feat. She went to a beginners' Ulpan with her parents, where the teacher was "wonderful and full of knowledge on all

Jewish topics; I loved and admired her." After a month she felt that she knew everything and asked to transfer to a higher grade, where she attended daily classes for 6 weeks more. There, again, she excelled. Simultaneously she started to prepare for the psychometric admission examination for the university—apparently making up her mind about her future plans. As mentioned before, she was accepted for studies in the Hebrew University without the usually required "preparatory year"—all indicating her ability to make an extremely fast psychological transition.

When I pushed Natasha to tell me what was hard about this time, she seemed to be groping for a response. Whether it was really her experience that "all went so well," or her reluctance to complain, or a process of denial of loss and difficulty, one cannot determine. After some deliberation, Natasha told me about the bureaucratic mishaps and hassles she had experienced when, after 3 months in the country, she moved all by herself to Jerusalem. Problems came up in getting admitted to the proper Summer Ulpan in the university, in obtaining dormitory space (because she was late in registration), and so forth, and more than once she had been "almost in tears." "But all had ended well, you see," she concludes. On the surface, it looks like a tremendously fast and successful adjustment.

Establishing New Friendships

As time went on, Natasha formed new relationships in Israel. She has several male and female friends who are also new immigrants from the USSR. All are students living in the same dormitories, and they seem to lead a fairly active social life as an informal group of about 10 members. According to Natasha's account, the students who belong to this informal group drop in on each other's dormitory rooms often, and sit for long hours of chatting into the night. "We rarely go out of the dorms for fun, though. We are simply lazy. Even when they have Russian-speaking movies in the theater we don't go. It's not that we're afraid or something,[12] we just prefer to talk."

The impression I received from that and similar sections of the interview was of a group of marginal individuals hanging out together, because this is the safest place for their somewhat fragile identities. Such a holding environment may have an extremely important role in supporting the necessary transition.[13] Natasha has reservations about the quality of these relationships, however, especially when comparing them to her lost friends. This is perhaps due to their marginality, a matter she gropes to explain.

"They are nice boys and girls, but I cannot reveal what is in my heart to them," she said at the beginning of the year. Related to that was the following observation, expressed with a lot of sadness: "I feel as if I am waiting for something, waiting for someone all the time. Waiting . . . as if these conversations we're having are not the real thing that I crave for."

In our second series of the interviews, she was able to clarify, using as a reference her different feelings among Israelis and in her own Russian group in Jerusalem:

> Among my Russian friends I feel more at ease. We all
> have our problems. [We are uprooted?] If one of us has
> a birthday, we celebrate it by going out together. But I
> feel this closeness is false, and I think I understand why.
> Because actually we are very different people thrown
> by sheer circumstances into this closeness of living
> together in the dorms; we were given no choice. I don't
> think we have much in common beside a language.[14]

As I listen to Natasha, I wonder about this longing for a more "true" relationship that I have sensed in Natasha all along. Is this longing a characteristic of Slavic people? An individual romantic trend in Natasha's personality? Probably both. The 10-or-so Russian students who define themselves as a group are but a tiny subgroup of all the young Russian new immigrants presently living in the dorms, so a selection process has been taking place. Moreover, I ask myself, how do people make friends other than through "circumstances"? How did Natasha make friends at the university in Kishinov? This expression of longing becomes even more intriguing for me after I discover she has a "boyfriend." The way I reason these contradictory messages, following some of the literature on immigration, is that Natasha's emigration created a deep loss that needs to be expressed, as in a mourning process, and as long as the process is not completed, no new relationship can be good enough to take the place of the missing ones.

False closeness is the term Natasha also uses for the description of her relationship with her Israeli roommate after 8 months together—one she had been reluctant to give up when I proposed to her that she transfer to the campus where her courses were given, rather than commute. About their kind of contact, Natasha relates:

> In Russia I saw some films about strangers who meet on a train and share their entire life story or their intimate problems, knowing that they will never meet again. Well, in our case too, sometimes we suddenly speak about deep things which bother us, and then we go back to our normal distance. But you can count the number of occasions this had happened on the fingers of one hand.

At the end of the year, Natasha still says she "misses terribly" her friends back in Kishinov, and finds some quality lacking in all her present relationships. Attributing this to the language barrier is not adequate, because she is speaking Russian to all her friends except for her roommate and David, her boyfriend.

A Boyfriend

Within 4 months of her arrival, Natasha had already formed a couple relationship. This, too, is fraught with ambivalence and uncertainty. David is the son of friends of Natasha's parents, who had emigrated from their town to Israel 17 years ago. He is wise and nice-looking, Natasha says, and is interesting to talk to. He understands Russian, but they speak to each other in Hebrew only (which is a remarkable feat in my eyes!). Through David, Natasha got to know several other young Israeli men and women, but she tells me that when she visits him at his university she does not feel at ease among them. An interesting comment she makes in this context is that David, who has grown up in Israel, also socializes mainly with Russian-born individuals. "This is so strange," she said, "perhaps it's due to his parents' influence. Every time I meet somebody new, whom I take for an Israeli, it later turns out that he or she originates from Russia (laughing)." This, of course, indicates that in Natasha's perception, even in an immigration country like Israel, lines of ethnic origin still underlie social interaction years after the actual transition. Or, another possible interpretation is that Natasha, who wants to change, feels trapped in her former national identity wherever she goes.

The fact that David is 1½ years younger than she bothers Natasha a great deal. Furthermore, she is not sure whether she really loves him. "Love is a word one tends to use too much," she said. (I remember how definite she sounded about her adolescent love in Moldavia!) "I've known him for 2 months, and I think that the word 'love' should be used only once in a lifetime. He is interesting to be with, and that's the most important thing."

Two months later, Natasha came to me asking for advice: she was afraid that her relationship with David was going to break up over the issue of phone conversations, and now that the relationship was threatened she realized that she really loved him. Yet she is still deeply bothered by the age difference, because "a guy should always be older than the girl." Toward the end of the year Natasha is still David's girlfriend, and still unsure of this relationship.

As I am writing this summary I find myself asking whether the fact that Natasha got attached to a younger and not-really-Israeli (in her eyes) man is another manifestation of her state of liminality between the two cultures. Perhaps this is the only couple-relationship she is capable of during her transition, a "transitional love," one might say. Once she has strengthened her self-esteem and status, will she be able to fall in love with someone she finds more adequate? Psychoanalytic literature about immigration seems to support my reasoning. Grinberg and Grinberg (1989) indeed borrow Winnicot's famous concept of "transitional object" to describe the immigrant's mental state of creating a transitional period (somewhat like Erikson's *moratorium*), in which the new culture is experienced as if in a game. From the point of view of the individual, it may seem like a regression; this is, however, a healthy strategy for adjustment.

New Career Plans

An area in which Natasha has gone through much changing during her first year in Israel concerns her career path. From the beginning, Natasha expressed reservations concerning her study program in Linguistics. Toward the end of the year she had worked out a new plan that she proudly outlined for me, although it was clearly going to take longer to complete. She will drop her major in Linguistics and adopt "General Humanities" instead. "I need to take this," she explains, her eyes shining, "because I lack so much background in Bible, Jewish History, Middle East Geography and History, etc. Once I become more informed in these subjects, I will apply to a program for the training of tourist guides, to become a tourist guide here in Israel." In answer to my question, Natasha told me that she did not disclose this plan to her parents yet, because she didn't want to "concern them."

Obviously, this is a dramatic change for Natasha: From the scholastic, introverted direction of her first choice—to an applied, people-oriented one. Further, it manifests Natasha's attachment to her new country, and her acquired confidence that, after adequate preparation, she, the newcomer, will be able to lead others in their tours. In this matter, more than in any other of the themes explored in our conversations, I was impressed with the blooming of Natasha's personality, her making use of the freedom that she gained in the new country, freedom of double significance: both from a generally restricting political system and from the overprotection of her parents.

New Gender Expectations

True, at the end of the year, Natasha is still conflicted about wearing a long skirt, a miniskirt or blue jeans, and she still finds it lovely to go out with an attentive gallant male. At the same time, some important transformation has occurred in a much more central area, namely Natasha's views about marriage and family life.

"Recently I realized that I am lucky to be in Israel," she said in one of our last meetings,

> because being 21 in Russia, I would already be expected to marry, and I really think this is too soon. In Russia, I would be by now done with my studies, and looking for a job. My [female] friends write to me that they are all in a rush to find a man and marry, because as single women they would be able to get teaching positions only in remote villages. This would have been my fate, too. I might have been married by now,

she said and shuddered dramatically. "Here I am free. My parents still hope that I'd marry soon, but they realize it is different here. I am so lucky. I have time. I do want to have kids, have a family—but not now. First I have to feel really well about myself."

It is hard to evaluate whether Natasha might have felt forced to marry had she stayed in the USSR, or done so willingly like most other young women of her age.[15] In Israel, Natasha perceives the woman's legitimacy for staying single and pursuing her own interests for another 5 years or so. Whether the change involves an entirely new option or the legitimization of a prior existing one, the change in Natasha's gender expectations for herself is apparent. Natasha made a long-term study plan that might last for another 4-5 years, and did not by any means consider her relationship with David as leading toward marriage. Both in terms of her career plans and her gender expectations, Natasha stresses her need for a time of "freedom" to prepare herself for assuming adult roles—what psychologists termed "moratorium" (Erikson, 1968; Josselson, 1988). Clearly, her transition to adulthood, which is superimposed on her transition to the new culture, might take longer for Natasha in her new society than what it might have taken her in the USSR.

Can We Speak About a Newly Acquired Identity?

By opening our second series of interviews at the end of the academic year, Natasha disclosed how she felt as follows:

> The other day I took a taxi, and the driver started a conversation with me. When we arrived he asked me where did I come from, offering a guess that I was from Argentina. When I told him I had come from Russia almost a year ago, he said: "No, this can't be true. You must have been at least 4 years here to speak Hebrew like that!" And indeed that is how I feel. I stopped counting the weeks or months since I moved here. I'm just here, it's my place. I feel much better, I'm entirely at home, I'm not a stranger anymore.

It was easy for Natasha to admit openly that she has changed in her sense of belonging to the Israeli society, because from her point of view this is an external change. From my point of view, however, following Erikson's (1968) concept of identity, the change in belonging naturally leads to a change in values, norms, behaviors, and choices, and is, therefore, of utmost importance for making a deeper transition. Or, put differently, one cannot shift one's sense of belonging without a parallel internal development.

Although numerous changes took place in Natasha during the first year of her life in Israel, it remained important for Natasha to claim repeatedly that she actually did not change, or changed very little. Clearly, loss of continuity or of the stability of one's self may be experienced as most frightening, because it gives rise to very early fears of internal and external discontinuities (see, e.g., Klein, 1987). Unconsciously, Natasha may have been feeling as if the new culture was about to swallow her up entirely. To remain the same in the midst of all these tremendous upheavals may be taken as an indication of one's established identity, or even one's sanity (Grinberg & Grinberg, 1989).

In some of our conversations, being somehow off guard, Natasha does admit some changes. One such highly significant instance occurred toward the end of our first series of interviews when Natasha reported that the only area in which she had changed was in her relationship with her parents. (This she compared to not having changed—in her perception—in her manner of behavior or dress.) Let us look more closely into Natasha's relationship with her parents toward the end of the year. "Regarding my parents," she said, "everything is simpler presently. They don't tell me what to do. They give me more freedom." The reason for that, in her view, is that they, too, have the "Russian chameleon syndrome," so they model their behavior after the predominant cultural pattern. I suggest that perhaps she has higher status in her family because she has made more progress into Israeli society than any of them, but she rejects my explanation. "I don't think so," she says, "they still don't see me as an independent adult, but they simply don't supervise my behavior. They don't talk so much about how I should behave as they used to."

Psychologically we know, of course, that this growing independence from one's parents is the essence of the transition to adulthood. In the process, we "lose" our parents as omnipotent figures who guide us, and "find" our autonomous selves. In Natasha's case, however, due to the additional losses associated with immigration, her new sense of autonomy is experienced both as a relief from former pressure and a privation of her firm hold on reality.

The process of growing up and apart from her parents is complicated further by the fact that Natasha is still partly depending on their financial support. Although all new immigrant students receive scholarships covering full tuition and rent expenses, they need to find their own sources for the cost of such things as food, transportation, clothing, and books. Most of the

Russian students in Jerusalem find jobs, and many of them even help in supporting their parents and siblings. Natasha, however, is not working, and takes a very modest weekly allowance from her mother.[16] In response to my question, Natasha tells me that she does not work because being a regular full-time student she has many courses and homework, and besides, she is "too clumsy to become a waitress, and tutoring jobs are too hard to come by." As in many places in the West, economic dependence on parents lasts much longer than psychological dependence, but in Natasha's case this is particularly significant because of her parents' poverty in Israel, and therefore the immense sense of guilt that Natasha describes as resulting from her need to be financially supported by them.

We returned, finally, to the discussion of change as our major topic at the end of our second series of interviews. At this time, Natasha is still often sad and self-doubting. She does not seem to be able to find "simple happiness in her life." At the same time, she looks so different—healthier, more tanned, less awkward in movement, more fluent in Hebrew, dressed like an Israeli. She seems more alive, or is not "a person in hiding," as I experienced her in our very first meeting. Yet she still claims that she did not change much. After this declaration, she goes into a monologue describing several areas of change, embedded in her sense of continuity:

> I have become a poor person. And I am still a member of a minority group. This is funny: In Russia we were told: you're different, you're Jews; Here we are told: you're different, you're Russian. I do feel I belong here by now, though I have much to learn about this society still. For example, had I had to vote for a party today, I don't know what I would do. On a personal level—I have fewer friends and I go out less frequently. I still worry too much about what would others think about me, a Soviet personality trait that I hate in myself. I envy the Israelis, even young children, who are unafraid to do and be as they like. I respect people who know what they are, and act in accordance with their true selves, regardless of the opinions of others. I am

> still my old self. In Russian they call me a "digger"—I
> think and reflect too much about myself and about all
> that is happening around me. That's why I want, in the
> future, to have such a job that would draw me out of
> myself. These self-ruminations do no good, they just
> lead me to nonsense.

To rescue her sense of continuity, Natasha is speaking here about traits she has long recognized in herself, such as her depressive moods and need to be accepted, that have probably been accentuated, but not produced, by the immigration process. "Feeling good about herself" is an aim she mentioned several times, which from the way it was brought up I understood as referring to a balance of feeling good as an individual, and making an adequate place for herself in her new society. "With luck," she says, "I will get to this point in my life."

This combination of subtle change in the midst of stability, together with changes that have occurred without acknowledgment, or without awareness, is very interesting to compare to more drastic types of changes that I was able to observe in some of my other interviewees. Several of the young students put "assimilation" as their major goal at present. They went after this goal with intense will to acquire the "Israeli identity" as soon as possible—what Natasha calls "the chameleon-type change." The external results of this process were often striking, even dramatic.[17] In comparison to these cases, however, Natasha is—to my mind—changing more moderately and profoundly at the same time.

Psychological theory about adolescence and the transition to adulthood on the one hand, and about the effects of immigration on the other, provide the framework for the story of Natasha. The attainment of ego identity in the transition to adulthood, according to Erikson (1968), implies a sense of meaning in relation to the social world. Other theories stress the process of separation from one's family of origin and the establishment of autonomy and individuality as a major feature of adolescence (Blos, 1967; Mahler, Pine, & Bergman, 1975). These two processes reflect the underlying themes of Natasha's narrative about her double transition—of growing up and of immigration.[18] At the same time, Natasha did retain her basic personality characteristics, as did the other young new immigrants in the midst of transition, thus providing additional support to the argument for "unity or consistency of personality" (Block, 1971, p. 268; see also Block, 1991).

Natasha experienced great losses due to emigration, yet a process of growth has promptly started the reconstruction of her personality. The mechanism of idealization of first impressions protected Natasha from reaching the breaking point under the experience of loss. Immediate acquisition of new skills and habits indicated the great plasticity of Natasha's character—probably resulting from three interdependent sources: The Soviet "chameleon personality," the documented plasticity of the age of early adulthood (Honzik, 1984), and Natasha's personal trait of malleability or courage, her awareness that "in comparison with my parents, I am not afraid to change." In a single year she became a member of a stable social network, including a number of people of similar background, and formed deep attachment to a young Israeli man. Although all these new relationships are highly ambivalent from her point of view, indicating an ongoing process of mourning for the loss of closeness of her former friendships, they support Natasha's well-being and self-esteem during the period of transition. Furthermore, as a result of exposure to norms and values of the new society, Natasha defined new goals for her professional life and a different concept of her gender identity. Celebrating her 21st birthday in Jerusalem, as mourning for her losses goes on, we see Natasha both more adult and more Israeli than a year ago.

The concept of transition implies both sameness and change in varying proportions. Balancing the two when developmental and cultural pressures interact is a complex and hazardous task that each young immigrant solves in her or his unique fashion.

Notes

1. It is beyond the scope of this chapter to review the extensive literature on the psychological aspects of emigration and immigration. Some of the classical

works on the subject are Handlin (1956), Fried (1977), and Grinberg and Grinberg (1989). The last book provides a psychoanalytic perspective of the topic, as do the articles of Garza-Guerrero (1974), Paris, (1978), and Stein (1985). In Israel, the classical sociological-psychological work on immigrants was done by Shuval (1963). It was based on survey research of the massive immigration of the 1950s. More recent sociological work includes Shuval (1982) and Horowitz (1989). On the subject of youth immigration to Israel one may consult a collection of papers edited by Gottesman (1988), particularly Klein (1988), whose approach is somewhat more psychological than the rest of the papers in Gottesman's volume. The great majority of previous immigration research in Israel is sociological. It is due to the initiative of Julia Mirsky (who emigrated from the USSR about a decade ago) of the Students' Counseling Service of the Hebrew University, that more attention has been paid to the psychological aspects of absorption, and specifically to adjustment problems of immigrant students from the USSR (Mirsky, 1990; Mirsky & Kaushinsky, 1989).

2. The acquisition of a new language is conceived as a central and a deeply meaningful aspect of the process of immigration. In addition to the more obvious functions of orientation and communication, Grinberg and Grinberg (1989) present language as the major instrument for the construction of inner and outer reality. Because all early memories and experiences are stored in the original language, learning a new one is not just a cognitive but a deeply emotional task for the immigrant. Thus difficulties in the process of language acquisition have cognitive and emotional factors in varying proportions in each individual case.

3. Both the crowded family housing and the important role of grandmothers in raising children are frequently noted in descriptions of Soviet families. See, for example, the excellent book by Du Plessix Gray (1990), *Soviet Women: Walking the Tightrope*.

4. This pattern of parental disregard of their children's wishes (even adult children!) in making the decision to emigrate is noted also by Mirsky, 1991.

5. Although no systematic data is available, clinicians working closely with the new immigrants in Israel formed the same impressions. Quoting from Mirsky (1991), in translation to English: "The relationship between parents and their children is authoritative to a very late age. Parents make decisions for their children, and children do not participate in making plans for the family. Most of the children and youth in the present immigration were not partners to the decision to emigrate" (p. 8).

6. On the changes in relationships within the immigrant's family, and their relevance to the process of successful adjustment, see Grinberg and Grinberg (1989). Mirsky and Kaushinsky (1989) analyze the same topic with particular attention to the dynamics of the Russian family in its move to Israel.

7. Grinberg and Grinberg (1989) present the multifaceted nature of learning a new language in the process of immigration, including the aspect of shame, which is central in the experience of Natasha's parents. See also Note 3, above.

8. At this point I would like to refer to personal communication with counselors working with the new immigrant students in the dormitories, in which they indicated the prevalence of promiscuity among female students from the USSR, probably a reaction to the breaking of former conservative standards and parental authority. This worried the staff, especially because Russian young

women did not use contraceptives and had frequent abortions (see also Du Plessix Gray, 1990, concerning Soviet women in general). The issue was denied by my interviewees, however, and no empirical "hard" data is yet available regarding this point.

9. A similar interpretation of the above can be derived from Grinberg and Grinberg (1989). In their view, immigrants have to give up part of their individuality in order to adjust to their new world, and this is an essential part of the adjustment process. The amount of "lost individuality" is proportional to the difference between the old and new societies.

10. The close linkage of loss and renewal has been pointed out by many theoreticians and researchers in the area of mourning. Moreover, these theoreticians described a series of steps ("the work of mourning") that enable the individual to emerge from the grief toward a gradual reconstruction of his wounded self. For one such example I refer the reader to Parks (1979), who counts "uprooting" among the common types of losses in human life.

11. Grinberg and Grinberg (1989) describe one type of immigrant reaction as "manic overadjustment." This involves fast adoption of the local habits and admitted forgetting of the "old ways." They observe that this type of immigrant tends to suffer from a postponed depression syndrome.

12. Notice that due to the war situation, foreigners often consider Jerusalem unsafe.

13. Similar observations were made by Mirsky and Kaushinsky (1989).

14. Because I interviewed several other members of the "group," and became friendly with some, I can offer some additional information on this point. As confirmed by others, Natasha is liked, even admired by her friends, yet she has a marginal position among them. For one thing, she does not study in the preparatory program, as do all others who "belong" to the "group." She is the only one who was admitted to the regular school program and commutes to another campus every day. In addition (partly because of her heavier course load), Natasha is the only one of the group who does not have a job and lives entirely out of her scholarship grant with some parental assistance. Others found part-time jobs as waiters, house cleaners, and so forth, and therefore have more money to spend. It is embarrassing for them to invite Natasha to go out with the group for the evening or for a longer trip out of town, they say, because often she cannot afford it.

15. For an up-to-date review of the situation of women in the USSR, see Du Plessix Gray, 1990.

16. It is interesting that only in this financial matter does Natasha's mother play an independent role toward her daughter, and not as part of the parental couple. I was unable to explore this point further, but it may be because in Natasha's nuclear family Father is considered as an "unpractical man," so that Mother, the former economist, became the cashier of the family.

17. Again, my impressions are confirmed by Grinberg and Grinberg's (1989) observations about types of immigrants' reactions in entirely different cultures. See Note 12, above.

18. This "intersection" of the transition of immigration and separation-individuation concerns in adolescence was labeled "third individuation process" (to paraphrase Blos's [1967] "second individuation process") by Mirsky (1990) and Mirsky and Kaushinsky (1989).

References

Block, J. (1971). *Lives through time.* Berkeley, CA: Bancroft Books.

Block, J. (1991, August). *Studying personality the long way.* Stanley Hall Award presentation, annual meeting of the American Psychological Association, San Francisco.

Blos, P. (1962). *On adolescence—A psychoanalytic interpretation.* New York: Free Press.

Blos, P. (1967). The second individuation process of adolescence. *Psychoanalytic Study of the Child, 22,* 162-186.

Du Plessix Gray, F. (1990). *Soviet women: Walking the tightrope.* Garden City NY: Anchor Books-Doubleday.

Erikson, E. H. (1968). *Identity: Youth and crisis.* New York: Norton.

Fried, M. (1977). Grieving for a lost home. In R. Lazarus (Ed.), *Stress and coping: An anthology.* New York: Columbia University Press.

Garza-Guerrero, A. C. (1974). Culture shock: Its mourning and the vicissitudes of identity. *Journal of American Psychoanalytic Association, 22,* 408-429.

Gottesman, M. (Ed.). (1988). *Cultural transition—The case of immigrant youth.* Jerusalem: Magnes Press.

Grinberg, L., & Grinberg, R. (1989). *Psychoanalytic perspective of migration and exile.* New Haven, CT: Yale University Press.

Horowitz, T. R. (Ed.). (1989). *The Soviet man in an open society.* New York: University Press of America.

Handlin, O. (1956). *The uprooting.* Boston: Little, Brown.

Honzik, M. P. (1984). Life span development. *Annual Review of Psychology, 35,* 309-331.

Josselson, R. (1988). *Finding herself: Pathways to identity development in women.* San Francisco: Jossey-Bass.

Klein, J. (1987). *Our need for others and its root in infancy.* London: Tavistock.

Klein, Z. (1988). Students and Aliyah: Changing patterns. In M. Gottesman (Ed.), *Cultural transition—The case of immigrant youth* (pp. 162-169). Jerusalem: Magnes Press.

Lieblich, A. (1978). *Tin soldiers on Jerusalem beach.* New York: Pantheon.

Lieblich, A. (1981). *Kibbutz Makom.* New York: Pantheon.

Lieblich, A. (1986). Successful career women at mid-life: Crises and transitions. *International Journal of Aging and Human Development, 23,* 301-312.

Lieblich, A. (1989). *Transition to adulthood during military service: The Israeli case.* New York: SUNY Press.

Mahler, M. S., Pine, F., & Bergman, A. (1975). *The psychological birth of the human infant: Symbiosis and individuation.* New York: Basic Books.

Mirsky, J. (1990). Individuation through immigration to Israel: Psychotherapy with immigrant adolescents. *Journal of Contemporary Psychotherapy, 20,* 47-61.

Mirsky, J. (1991, October). *Independence—A difficult language: Family and adolescence in the USSR [in Hebrew].* A lecture presented in Summit School Conference on Adolescence, Jerusalem.

Mirsky, J., & Kaushinsky, F. (1989). Migration and growth: Separation-individuation processes in immigrant students in Israel. *Adolescence, 24,* 725-740.

Paris, J. (1978). The symbolic return: Psychodynamic aspects of immigration and exile. *Journal of American Academy of Psychoanalysis, 66,* 51-57.

Parks, C. M. (1979). *Bereavement—Studies of grief in adult life.* New York: International Universities Press.

Shuval, J. T. (1963). *Immigrants on the threshold.* New York: Atherton Press.

Shuval, J. T. (1982). Migration and stress, In L. Goldberg & S. Breznitz (Eds.), *Handbook of stress, theoretical and clinical aspects.* New York: Free Press.

Stein, H. F. (1985). Culture change, symbolic object loss and restitutional processes. *Psychoanalysis and Contemporary Thought, 8,* 301-332.

Wiseman, H., & Lieblich, A. (1992). Individuation in a collective community. *Adolescent Psychiatry, 18,* 156-179.

❦ 6 ❦

Identity and Context

How the Identity Statuses Choose Their Match

Jane Kroger

Identity and Context

$\mathcal{F}$rank spent his late adolescence in the turbulent times of the late 1960s. As a young *pakeha* (European) New Zealander grow-ing up in his country's capital city, the media would have presented Frank with constant images of dissent and protest in the streets outside Parliament. American folksingers would have been heard sending their chorus of anti-Vietnam War lyrics over the radio waves that touched even the remotest of rural New Zealand ears; many views would have been heard, many opin-ions made known as students from the university on the hill met a more conservative wall of government officialdom in town. Speaking out, as such, was in vogue. Jobs were plentiful in those days and the welfare state prospered, so one's attentions could turn elsewhere.

Frank would likely have made his way past the protesters in the street, intent on getting to the seminary. In his last year of studies in a church-run high school, it seemed "just natural" to go on to the seminary. He did not mix widely with peers at school, many of whom ventured into more diverse fields upon graduation. Frank's parents were very religious as were their parents before them. Now, at age 40, Frank teaches in a religious school of the same denomination, satisfied with his life. Socially, he likes to "keep in touch with other things that are happening" and so visits his sister just down the road as well as one or two of his fellow teachers, who also board at the school where Frank lives and works. Sometimes Frank feels a little "flat," so varies his life by trying out different ways of teaching. Sometimes, too, he wishes he could be more assertive and tell others what he thinks, even though it might cause disagreement. But instead, Frank "just lets things slide." Generally, however, Frank finds his life at age 40 to be "comfortable and secure."

Elizabeth and her siblings were named after members of the British Royal Family, as were many of her classmates at school. Elizabeth began school at age 5 in the Depression and was 13 years old when World War II began. A strong sense of "King and country and all that" pervaded her adolescent years and she assumed that devout sense of duty that was instilled in her whole generation of contemporaries. Spending her late adolescent years in that same New Zealand capital city some two decades before Frank, Elizabeth's socio-historical context posed enormous restrictions on how she could be and who she could become in the world. Any political dissent was not expressed publicly and "there was a very strong traditional line" that one was expected to follow.

As a young woman, that traditional line was drawn even more sharply for Elizabeth when she considered her vocational future. In fact, little decision making was possible, as marriage was expected and employment was strictly controlled by the state. Yet at school Elizabeth had loved learning and immersed herself in as many subjects as possible. There was little money in the family and always present was the danger that her parents could afford to let only their sons finish secondary education. When money existed for only one more year of schooling for the girls, Elizabeth decided to leave high school and enroll at university (which was state funded, nearby, and open to her through her high marks at school). When unusual vocational opportunities later "came her way," Elizabeth explored them; when restrictions arose, Elizabeth worked within and around them to be able at age 60 to look back on her life with enormous satisfaction at the variety of contributions she had made to her various communities of residence. Although much of Elizabeth's enormous energy went into unpaid voluntary social work both before and after her husband's death, this work became a very meaningful commitment in Elizabeth's life. At the time of interview, Elizabeth had helped to establish several local and national organizations to deal with problems of child abuse, care for the physically disabled, and programs for the intellectually handicapped. Those pursuits, her children, and her network of friends made Elizabeth's life at age 60 feel very "fulfilled."

Frank and Elizabeth spent their late adolescent years in sociohistorical contexts that represented, perhaps, polar extremes in the messages they sent to young people on how to assume adult roles within the larger social milieu. For Frank and his generation of youthful New Zealanders, the 1960s was an era that promoted questioning and self-expression—a questioning of traditional values, a questioning of government leadership, a questioning of one's place in the world with its many options. Yet despite this general social climate, Frank pursued a narrow path toward vocational and ideological goals, without pause to look sideways. When opportunity knocked, Frank did not answer the door, preferring instead the familiar corridors of his internalized familial home values. By contrast, Elizabeth spent her late adolescent years in a social climate that imposed enormous limits on the young adult roles she would be permitted to assume. Despite such vast contextual constraints, however, Elizabeth found ever-changing ways to take calculated risks in developing new skills and talents that were personally challenging and expressive of her own considerable interests. When opportunity knocked, Elizabeth not only answered the door but went right on through—again and again and again. Although the socio-historical climate provided the general contexts within which these two individuals assumed identity-defining roles and values, the mechanisms that Frank and Elizabeth used to create their own personal niches within their broader milieus differed dramatically.

Frank and Elizabeth had both participated in a large retrospective study of identity formation by mid-life adults (Kroger & Haslett, 1987, 1991). My colleague, Stephen Haslett, and I had undertaken this work to learn more about how issues addressed in the identity formation process of adolescence described by Erikson (1968) might continue to evolve in the years beyond life's second decade. As the interviewer for the project, I brought with me a fascination for the life histories of interviewees, who were raised in a country in which I had not been born but had resided for the second half of my life; my experience of being among but not of New Zealand "stock" may have elicited additional reflections and clarifications from participants on their own socialization experiences as well as providing me with alternative frameworks in attempting to understand the interplay between identity and context. From statistical analyses of the retrospective data, Stephen Haslett and I found a very strong relationship between choice of life-style and the development of ego identity during adolescence and adulthood; when all major demographic variables in the study were held constant so that individuals in specific subgroups under study had similar opportunity structures, very different patterns of identity development still emerged across the various life-style options (balance of vocational/family interests) that people had chosen. What our statistical tests could not reveal, however, was whether choice of life-style determined the course of identity development from late adolescence through the middle adult years, or whether one's mode of approach to identity-defining issues determined choice of life-style pattern.

The Problem

Swann (1985, p. 100), has written that the "self [is the] architect of [its own] social reality." Frank and Elizabeth portray patterns of identity resolutions that suggest styles of approach to identity-defining issues may ultimately determine one's specific life context despite the constraints or opportunities accorded by the larger socio-historical milieu. Although it is likely that there is considerable interaction between identity and context, this investigation examines the means by which individuals may broaden or narrow future identity possibilities via the identity structure present in late adolescence.

Recently reengaging in several hundred hours of interview transcripts from this retrospective study, I have become intrigued by the relationship between identity and context, by the oftentimes obvious and sometimes very subtle ways in which individuals have created their own personal contexts of development within their broader cultural and historical settings. The purpose of this chapter will be to explore means by which three different modes of approach to identity-defining questions adopted during late adolescence have determined the characteristics of future life contexts. I return now to the narratives of Frank and Elizabeth and 98 other mid-life women and men to explore further the relationship between identity and context.

A Framework for Study

In so doing, I have made use of Marcia's (1966) ego identity status model. Marcia has expanded Erikson's (1963) formulation that the task of identity formation during late adolescence is a matter of finding some optimal balance between the bipolar extremes of role confusion and identity achievement, or achieving a sense of continuity, direction, and purpose in one's life. Marcia has proposed that there are several ways in which one can resolve the issue of life direction as well as several ways in which one can be role confused. In Marcia's terminology, identity achievement and foreclosure individuals both convey a sense of commitment to various identity-defining roles and values; identity achieved individuals, however, have arrived at such commitments on their own terms, following a period of active search and genuine exploration of a variety of possibilities. Foreclosed individuals, on the other hand, have assumed their identity-defining commitments without question or any real consideration of alternative possibilities. Many have merely assumed parental roles and values as their own to resolve the identity question. Moratorium and diffusion individuals both are uncommitted; however, moratoriums are in the process of actively searching for roles that fit, whereas diffusions are not.

Extensive research has been conducted on the identity formation process using Marcia's framework, and the four identity statuses have been examined in relation to styles of family interaction, developmental patterns of movement over time, and personality variables associated with each identity mode (see Marcia [1980], Marcia, Waterman, Matteson, Archer, & Orlofsky [in press], and Waterman [1982] for more extensive reviews of the identity status literature). Identity achieved adolescents have been characterized as coming from families that emphasize both individuality and connectedness in parent-child relationships (Grotevant & Cooper, 1985). Achievements are intimate in their interpersonal relationships and androgenous in sex role attitudes (Fitch & Adams, 1983; Kacerguis & Adams, 1980; Slugoski, Marcia, & Koopman, 1984). Once an identity achieved position has been attained, development through adulthood is likely to consist of repeated moratorium-achievement-moratorium-achievement (MAMA) cycles (Francis, Fraser, & Marcia, in press). Late adolescent moratoriums also have parents who emphasize individuality and connectedness in their child-rearing practices (Grotevant & Cooper, 1985). Moratoriums are likely to be more anxious than achievement or foreclosure adolescents (Marcia, 1967; Podd, Marcia, & Rubin, 1970). Intrapsychically, moratoriums are in the process of disengaging from parental introjects (Josselson, 1982; Kroger, 1990). Foreclosed adolescents come from families that are more authoritarian in their child-rearing practices; parents of foreclosures show little encouragement of individuality but high degrees of connectedness (Grotevant & Cooper, 1985). Foreclosures, themselves, are very authoritarian and conformist in their attitudes, stereotypic in their relationships, and use conventional moral reasoning (Cote & Levine, 1983; Marcia, 1966, 1967, 1980; Slugoski et al., 1984). Diffusion adolescents have often reported parental attitudes of rejection or disinterest toward them. Diffusions tend to be distant and withdrawn in their own interpersonal relationships (Marcia, 1980). Furthermore, they have low self-esteem, use less complex cognitive styles, and are conventional or preconventional in their moral reasoning (Hult, 1979; Marcia, 1966, 1967; Slugoski et al., 1984). These characteristics of the identity statuses have been replicated in geographically diverse samples within North America; cross-cultural evidence is mounting to support these findings from samples in Europe, Asia, and the Pacific (Marcia et al., in press).

One hundred participants (60 women and 40 men) took part in the Kroger and Haslett (1987, 1991) studies. Each individual was interviewed in some depth over the course of several hours regarding the development of present commitments or values within the domains of vocational choice, religious and political values, sex role beliefs, and values in intimate relationships. All participants were aged 40-65 years at the time of the interview and came from upper middle and upper income households; because socioeconomic status has been associated with differences in developmental change (Neugarten, 1968), the investigation was limited to those groups who were less likely to be constrained in their identity development by financial circumstance. Those taking part were selected through a network sampling technique, in which efforts were made to engage people representing a variety of life-style options. For each chronological year of age from 15 years to the present, an identity status rating was later assigned from the taped interviews. These ratings were made in order to examine patterns of identity status movement and change rate for the domains under study. Interviews with these individuals provide the data through which the nature of the relationship between identity and context will now be explored. The rating of "identity diffusion" was assigned too infrequently to these participants across most domains to permit generalizations regarding mechanisms for creating life contexts; however, strategies used by foreclosure, moratorium, and identity achieved individuals for such purposes will be examined in some detail below. Although names and identifying features of individuals have been omitted or changed to protect privacy, general features of the identity formation process have been preserved.

Case Studies in How Foreclosures Limit Their Life Contexts

Frank's approach to identity-defining issues reflects a prototypic foreclosure pattern in Marcia's identity status typology. Identifying strongly with parental or parental surrogate figures and never questioning potential alternatives, Frank has not only assumed a pastoral and teaching role within his father's Catholic church (which he decided to do in childhood), but has maintained political ties to the party of his father, grandfather, and many seminary counterparts. Frank's seven siblings also hold comparable religious and political views. In terms of sex role values, Frank has "changed with the times" to espouse a view of equal opportunity and responsibility, though this view has not been put to the test in his own life, which has remained celibate. A sister's enrollment in a women's studies course at university has helped him "broaden" his views on sex roles. In terms of values in a close friendship, Frank likes relationships that are "not too intrusive but compatible." He has always valued these qualities from the time of adolescence. Now, what he values in his most meaningful relationship (a friend he met at the seminary) is the way the friend can "reflect my moods and buck me up." Frank was rated foreclosed in all identity domains under study from age 15 years to the time of interview at age 40.

Frank's life history presents a clear example of how an individual has engineered vocational, ideological, and social contexts to allow few disruptions to an intrapsychic structure based on identifications with important childhood figures. Despite the climate of questioning in his wider cultural milieu, Frank managed to remain impervious to potential identity challenges. Through a closer examination of Frank's strategies, it may be possible to learn more of the mechanisms by which such engineering has been achieved.

Although any life is subject to vicissitudes, to uncontrollable fortunes and perils, Frank has carefully chosen his personal life contexts to minimize such possibilities as far as he can. As I have reflected on this interview, it became difficult for me to imagine ways in which Frank might further have restricted potential challenges to his values and internal identity structure, apart from total community isolation. His entire formal education has taken place within the confines of a single religious institution. Frank socializes only with his parents, siblings, and a few other teachers in his religious community where he lives. He has committed himself to a vocational role that prohibits his marriage. Frank did enroll in a course offered by a state-run educational institution, but he enrolled only upon the recommendation of a sister, who had taken the course herself in the preceding term. Although Frank presented himself in a confident manner at the time of the interview, it was difficult to imagine how Frank would cope if removed from the sanctuary of his present vocational and ideological havens. That Frank had agreed to be interviewed at all was intriguing, and his reasons for participation remain unclear to me now; could it be the dimmest glimpse of wider horizons that had brought this man to an opportunity for self-reflection? Frank was, however, the only participant who did not wish to receive follow-up information from the project. An initial mechanism for avoiding challenge to the foreclosure identity structure, then, may be to choose milieus that are highly structured and restrictive in their tolerance for diversity of opinion—milieus that are mirrors of childhood values, from which friends can be chosen to "reflect one's moods" and not be "too intrusive." Intrusion, after all, might make life uncomfortable and insecure.

The dearth of existing research that focuses on identity and context supports the notion that individuals adopt contexts or life-styles that are compatible with their degree of openness to experience. Research by Costa and Campos (1989) and Adams and Fitch (1983) has found that foreclosure university students appear to choose more restrictive college environments than moratorium or achievement individuals. From the Costa and Campos investigation, courses of study that were highly structured and discouraging of individual reflection in favor of rote learning had a predominance of foreclosure subjects. In examining different university departments and identity development among their majors, Adams and Fitch also found that certain departmental environments appeared to attract certain types of students; once in departments, however, different factors emerged to encourage the identity formation process. (For example, societal awareness, encouraged by peers or faculty, created one condition that facilitated a broadening of student perspectives.) Kroger and Haslett (1987) found that among women who had identical educational qualifications and family life structures, those who had opted for a full-time homemaker role throughout their adult lives had a high probability of being rated foreclosed at mid-life across all identity domains under study; women who had maintained full-time employment throughout their adult years or who had returned to full-time work after child-rearing had a high probability of being rated identity achieved across all domains at mid-life. It would seem that certain environments or life-style options that provide a broad range of experiences and encourage a reconsideration of one's views are unattractive to many firmly foreclosed individuals.

Frank reports only one occasion in the course of his life when he felt "really rocked." This event occurred for Frank at age 25, when a good friend decided to leave the seminary of his own volition. Frank reported having a few "wild" dreams but then just "got on with things again" after a few days. He did not try to learn of the reasons behind the friend's departure, nor was he interested in maintaining contact; Frank had decided that this person was not really that close a friend after all. It is likely that too close a scrutiny of the friend's decision would bring Frank up against the power of his own internalized parents and present too great a challenge to his own identity structure. Although the potential chaos of life without a structure derived from the internalized parents may have emerged unconsciously in the form of "wild" dreams, this prospect was quickly brought under control; Frank merely "shut out" the event by discrediting the closeness of the relationship and carried on with his life. A second strategy used by foreclosures to limit individual life contexts may be the ability merely to discredit or in other ways distance from information that might destabilize the existing identity structure.

Slugoski et al. (1984) provide some evidence from an interactional study that expands upon this observation. When seven groups of male university students—each comprised of one achievement, one moratorium, one foreclosure, and one diffusion subject—were observed attempting to reach consensus on several moral dilemmas, two foreclosure strategies were used to discount discrepant information: acquiescence and antagonism. Some foreclosure subjects avoided personal involvement by blanket concurrence with prevailing opinions, whereas others were antagonistic, attempting to discredit the source of the dissonant information or alternatively to set personal opinions beyond the reach of the group. Frank alters his views and devalues the closeness of a former friendship that has produced some discrepancy with his own life values by distancing himself from the relationship itself.

What happens, however, when discrepant life circumstances cannot be disregarded or otherwise altered for the mid-life adult foreclosure, whose intrapsychic structure is firmly derived from the values of the internalized parents? Such was the situation for Leo, as he struggled to maintain his internal equilibrium upon early retirement from the military.

Leo had been a career military officer since leaving high school some 28 years earlier. Now at age 47, he had decided to retire after some intensive deliberations. He recognized that opportunities for future advancement in the military would be limited and had decided to retire while he was young enough to begin another career. Leo describes the life he has known to this point: As a late adolescent, he had entered military college;

virtually all the male members of his extended family had served during World Wars I and II, and he had been an avid reader of war books as a child. When he joined the military, he understood that he was joining "for life." He had not seriously considered alternative pursuits. He comments at age 47, "In a few months, my first insurance matures that I took out when I was 19—because 47 was the youngest you could get out of the [military] at the time I enlisted." So at age 19 Leo had set himself up career-wise "for life."

The structure of the military appealed to Leo, as well as the security and regimentation. As he progressed through the ranks, he enjoyed the responsibility of being in command. "You own your people 24 hours a day, 7 days a week; if a guy has marital problems, they become your problems. He looks to you to help sort things out and you do it because ultimately it affects how he works as part of your unit." Leo and his wife had known numerous postings, enjoying the structure that his role provided in meeting these new situations. But now, at age 47, Leo and a military friend in similar circumstances had both decided to retire and go into partnership, setting up a small manufacturing business together. Between relying on a military management style and undertaking an operation for which they were undercapitalized, Leo was both personally and financially out of his depth. The military concept of being responsible for your men just was not working.

> When we took over this business, we found that the outside man doesn't think this way; that when we tried to display an interest in our staff's outside lives, it was resented. They didn't want us to be interested in what they did on the weekends or after work or whether we could do anything to help them with any problems. We were looked at with suspicion, which was a great disappointment. When we tried to carry the family concept over to the business, it just didn't work.

Financial concerns were also becoming all-embracing. "All the best theories in the world go out the window, really, and an iron lung becomes vital. It's frustrating because you know that if you just had the capacity to do this, you could do it. . . . We were biting off too much." Leo's identity predicament seems captured in the above lines as well.

I do not know the next chapter of Leo's life story. Certainly his plight would seem to require either a very fundamental and painful restructuring of ties with his internalized parents or a return to a structured, secure, extended family context for resolution—as well as a means of resolving financial difficulties.

Many other individuals in the study, like Frank and Leo, had remained firmly foreclosed across the course of their late adolescent and adult lives. In all such cases, personal life contexts or life-style patterns had been chosen or created with certain features in common. Vocational contexts were often highly structured and regimented, limiting reflective thought or exposure to alternative views. Among long-term foreclosed full-time homemakers, many women had created their own quite rigid time parameters to structure their days. Jean described the "breakfast, lunch, and dinner grids" of her life, during which time an invariant sequence of events had to occur. Unanticipated happenings could make havoc of the next time grid for Jean. Other vocations chosen were often those that emphasized the application of rote-learned material, with little scope for diversity in the solution of problems. As Leo said, "in the [military], you don't have to think." Additionally, the firmly foreclosed tended to socialize with a narrow range of others, often only family members and a few work colleagues or other homemakers holding similar views. Frank's social life revolved around his parents, siblings, and a few teaching colleagues who boarded in his religious community; Leo's socializing was solely with family and other (similarly ranked) military personnel; Jean's social life centered around her family, husband's business acquaintances, and one neighbor in circumstances similar to her own. In terms of qualities valued in intimate relationships, many interviewees of both sexes stressed harmony—no sharp differences between partners to potentially "rock the boat." In Dan's words regarding his marriage, "I'm not going for any fireworks there." Other, more superficial qualities were often mentioned as important in relationships, such as friendliness, "getting on" together, helping in the home; in no case was a partner valued for having her or his own center. Among those who had remained foreclosed across their late adolescent and adult years, most had chosen or created very insulated vocational, ideological, and social contexts for themselves within whatever broader climate of social attitudes existed at the time.

Case Studies in How Moratoriums Expand Their Life Contexts

Moira paused at some length when asked at the conclusion of her interview to describe herself to herself now at the age of 42. Although not a typical moratorium interviewee because of the length of her unresolved search for meaningful life directions, Moira's life story is presented here to allow a closer scrutiny of the means by which moratoriums may create personal contexts that allow suspension in identity commitments. As her nest empties and she realizes her part-time vocational employment in an early childhood day-care center is just not satisfying, life feels rather empty:

> I don't know where to start . . . perhaps that's my
> problem. I haven't gotten around to thinking of myself as
> any particular identity. It's more just a reaction to
> different things that crop up. I really don't know; I see
> myself as someone who's just starting—because my
> children, or some of them, are grown up, because I
> haven't had any clearly defined role that I've identified
> with or that's suited me, even in career terms—although
> the early childhood teaching I'm doing is fine, it satisfies
> me—but I still don't feel I'm really into that. I see myself as
> still trying to start to find my real direction in life.

> I'm somewhat freed from constraints of family, of
> children and marriage as it was—we're at a point where

I've got to, where we and therefore I have to find out what I'm doing, where I'm going, and why. My children's interpretation of me—much of what I've been saying this morning is not how they see me; they tend to see me as being all those things that I felt that I wasn't and disbelieved in. And so somehow or other, I've got to sort out what I really am in terms of my attitudes and values and what I'm concerned about and involved in or want to be involved in, and things that are just reflective of my age and stage—or are they really me? I almost feel as I did when I sort of embarked on my adulthood except that I'm running out of time now and I have to take more responsibility for making choices. I don't know, I suppose I just see myself as a middle-aged woman with that impetus to get on with the job of living and find the right direction, as time's running out.

But Moira's adult life has been characterized by such uncertainties. Some 8 years ago, she gave up part-time work as a nurse's aid; she knew she could do the job but felt she was not good enough. Four children and four vocational redecisions later, Moira is about to undertake retraining in social work. Moira married husband Thomas some 20 years earlier, but only on the basis that if she wanted a divorce, he would grant it straight away. Now, Thomas is frequently away on business, or otherwise unavailable to her. Moira loves her children, yet at the same time often feels estranged from them. Wholehearted commitment to a role or undertaking has rarely been a part of Moira's approach to identity-defining issues to date; only by setting up real or potential escape routes have new ventures been undertaken. Now, reflecting upon what she would value most in life at the present time, Moira responds:

I suppose the ability and strength to remain committed to and to work on the decisions I make this year and next. I have to make decisions I don't have control over totally; I can't control how my family will react or feel.

> When I make decisions about who I am and what I want
> to be and how I can best do it, I want to follow through
> instead of being overwhelmed by a sense of guilt or
> inadequacy or failure or those things that creep up on
> people as they do the things they think are right and
> then take the consequences. So it's some sort of
> internal strength that I would value most, I
> think. . . . That I won't succumb to other pressures that
> might impinge on what I want or what I am.

Moira describes feeling "quite lost now" with regard to sex role values; brought up to believe in sexual equality, Moira realizes that she and her husband at present have very clearly differentiated sex roles along traditional lines; she is both drawn toward and frightened by the Women's Movement. On religious issues, she finds things no longer "so black and white," and with regard to political opinions, she has become more firmly socialistic but at the same time more despairing than ever. However, religious and political values have never been crucial issues of concern for Moira.

Moira was rated in a prolonged moratorium state across four of the five identity domains under study. Only in the area of intimate relationship values did she evidence commitment to certain ideals following some exploration in late adolescence; however, her actual relationship commitment is to an often unavailable partner and the commitment was made at the outset only if divorce could be assured.

Moira's vocational, ideological, and relationship contexts within her larger cultural and historical milieus have all been created, in a sense, to provide a "passing" identity (Erikson, 1970). Moira obtained a B.A. degree, then chose part-time employment in four different fields that had high staff turnovers and could be entered and left easily at a time when positions were plentiful. The on-the-job training involved for her particular responsibilities within the vocations was not arduous and did not require extra time commitments on her part. Leaving each of the vocational settings after a few years of part-time work with the feeling of never being quite "good enough" or fully satisfied, Moira finds contexts that resonate with her reluctance to make long-term, wholehearted investments. By contrast, several other women of the same age range with children and engaged in part-time employment with the same educational qualification that Moira held had chosen work in such fields as microbiology, radiography, and special education teaching—all fields that required major commitments of time and energy on the part of the trainee. Likewise, in her relationships, Moira selected a partner while at the same time setting up a contingency plan for escape as well as choosing an individual who was likely to be unavailable much of the time. Moira realized that she "could not be happy being a full-time homemaker," but during the times in which she does assume that role, she does not appear deeply satisfied. She finds continuous problems in communication, with both her husband and her children. Moira's means of expanding her life contexts appears to be stuck in a cyclical pattern. Engaged in ongoing "approach-avoidance" conflicts within relationship and vocational domains, Moira uses mechanisms to distance herself from potential commitment. Only recently has Moira begun to hope that she can find "the strength and ability to remain committed to and to work on the decisions I make this year," despite the guilt this may bring.

Moira was the only participant in the study who remained in a prolonged moratorium process over her adult life, at least until the time of interview. However, her "approach-avoidance" style of engaging in commitments and finding or creating contexts where such behavior is tolerated or even encouraged has been a pattern noted in Hart's (1989) study comparing life contexts for subjects in the various identity statuses. For the one woman who remained a moratorium from late adolescence through mid-life in Hart's investigation, there was a similar pattern of feeling "unsuited" ultimately to all vocational endeavors undertaken. Also characteristic of the individual was ambivalence about intimacy and a rather fragile sense of self-esteem. Far more common among those undergoing a moratorium period of uncertainty and exploration in the present retrospective study, however, was ultimately finding some satisfying resolution at the end of the search—a resolution that remained in place commonly for a period of years until new life issues precipitated a further decision-making cycle.

"Sometimes you just have to feel ready to have your life shaken up," explained Mark, "so I went overseas." "Everything in my life had been so laid out for me, but there were stirrings there," reflected Emma. "It wasn't long, then, until I went overseas." Frequent among younger interviewees who had undergone a moratorium phase was the "overseas pilgrimage" (commonly taken in late adolescence but sometimes occurring at later ages as well); it was actually rather unusual to encounter a younger interviewee who had undergone a significant moratorium period within New Zealand itself. In fact, the term *O.E.* in New Zealand slang refers to "overseas experience," with the associated meaning of a "time out" before engaging in new life directions and commitments. For those interviewees who had experienced their late adolescence after the end of World War II, much cultural support existed for the O.E. Although war conditions made this experience impossible for older interviewees, many still engaged in overseas moratoriums during later periods of their lives. Where family circumstances or other responsibilities prohibited such geographical removal during a moratorium process, other means of distancing were employed to underscore a state of removal from the old life context. Ochberg (1986) reports the features of various contexts that moratorium students, who temporarily dropped out of college, found to gain a new sense of direction. The act of physical distancing from the old context was crucial to their moratorium processes as well. From present narratives, undergoing any moratorium process requires a level of readiness, openness to experience, and ego strength on the part of the participant, it seems. Such characteristics have frequently been found among moratorium subjects of both sexes in recent identity status research (e.g., Berzonsky & Sullivan, 1992; Ginsberg & Orlofsky, 1981).

For late adolescent Mark, it was his feeling of wanting to "break loose" from the institution for the disabled in which he had been raised that propelled him overseas. Mark was ready: "I found I was still too much into the custodial care, people fitted into slots routine . . . I was beginning to realize that I had control over my life, not them—it was an awareness sort of thing . . . I had to test it out." For Emma, it was marriage and moving to Australia that "somehow got me out of my mother's clutches," helping the young woman to feel more in charge of her life. Time and again, stories of seeking new physical contexts for the purpose of no longer being dependent was the hallmark of a beginning moratorium process (see Kroger, 1992, for a more extensive discussion of this issue).

From those few empirical studies exploring the relationship between identity and context, settings that are likely to provide a more diverse range of opportunities and experiences are often sought by moratorium subjects (Adams & Fitch, 1983; Kroger, 1983; Munro & Adams, 1977). Munro and Adams (1977) found that late adolescent moratorium and diffusion subjects were more frequently found in college environments (which were presumed to encourage exploration) than in work settings. Kroger (1983) found the moratorium identity status predominant among women enrolled in introductory university liberal arts courses for all three age ranges under study. Adams and Fitch (1983) noted that university departments that were less practical or community oriented and more academic and scholastic in their emphases were less likely to attract uncommitted (moratorium and diffusion) students than those committed to a life-direction (achieved and foreclosed). In addition, contexts that provide a "good fit" with existing expectations may not be the most optimal settings for identity development (Busch-Rossnagel, 1991).

Once the moratorium's struggle to disengage from the internalized parents began to subside, attention can be turned more fully to potentially satisfying life directions. Thus Mark returned to New Zealand to set up a small manufacturing business, commenting "it did feel right to come back," and bringing with him some of the skills he had begun to develop while in Europe. And Emma and her husband returned to their homeland, eager to start up a small sheep station where they could enjoy the beauty of the Southern Alps and the outdoor life they had so missed while in Australia. Josselson (1987), in her qualitative accounts of the movement from the moratorium to achievement status among young adult women, notes a similar sequence of issues. Moratorium women interviewed during their last year of college were absorbed in untangling family ties; for those who became identity achieved by their early thirties, the process of realizing and consolidating personally expressive life directions could occur only after differentiation struggles had subsided.

For those moratoriums who eventually found satisfying life directions expressive of their own talents and interests in the present sample, there appeared, once again, certain commonalities among the contexts that were created or chosen for a furthering of development during the process. Frequently important was the initial creation of physical distance between the "old" and "new" environments, particularly when the moratorium period occurred during late adolescence before family responsibilities had been assumed. Furthermore, the new context was often a foreign land or at least unfamiliar territory—a place where one was not known, a place where the old rules no longer applied, where one's ability to survive was put to the test. It is noteworthy that for those few moratoriums who did not satisfactorily resolve their search for satisfying life directions and either returned home (in the intrapsychic sense) or, infrequently, gave up to drift or become hospitalized, contexts seemed to be sought more for purposes of testing independence from the internalized parents and/or caregivers of reality rather than for finding expression of personal interests and abilities. Again, within pre- or postwar socio-historical climates that discouraged or supported self-realization, respectively, those who entered a moratorium phase created or found the conditions for expansion suited to their own developmental needs at the time.

Case Studies in How Achievements Stabilize Their Life Contexts Following Exploration

Elizabeth's narrative, begun earlier, presents a very clear example of a prototypic identity achievement pattern in Marcia's identity status typology. Here, contexts were sought which ultimately allowed an integration of societal expectations and opportunities with personal talents and interests to provide for Elizabeth a personal sense of deep fulfillment and satisfaction—at least until the next developmental passage. Elizabeth has tried through her life to emphasize and validate a role that women have had in New Zealand, "largely undervalued and yet tremendously important to the community." She notes with some sadness during her interview that the present generation of young women seem to devalue the largely voluntary endeavors in which many women of her generation engaged:

> Now, if you're not paid, you're not worth anything. And yet for many women who haven't had the opportunity to do anything else, it was a perfectly valid expression of their own talents, running these organizations—you know, actually raising sufficient money to build a hostel or day-care center. Now it might sound old hat, but at the time they were doing it they were sort of acting on a hunch that they were doing something really important.

Looking back at the social climate that existed during her teens, Elizabeth comments:

> I went to a girls' school that imbued in us a very strong sense of duty. . . . We were a guilt-laden generation, because very often in our school [during the war] we were told things like sailors were dying so that our school textbooks could come out by ship from England, and we were imbued with the fact that we must do our part to rebuild the world. You know, we were a generation that was spared, and the obligation was on us to rebuild things and be useful.

Thus, in her identity formation process, Elizabeth was faced with the job of sifting through such demanding social messages and integrating her own talents and interests with the vocational, ideological, and relational opportunities that existed within her cultural milieu at the time. Elizabeth's contexts seemed to have had a way of presenting a number of interesting and unique opportunities for her consideration. No doubt, the young woman's eagerness for new experiences and challenges to exercise her talents did much to attract such "opportunities," which were considered at some length until just the right outlet for her combination of interests was found. Elizabeth's own words best describe the process:

A teacher told me about a job that came up at school. They [the government] wanted some women to go and train as metallurgists in [a government laboratory]. Women had finer fingers and essentially what they wanted us to do was make sort of gauges and various measuring instruments that I think were used in munitions making. You would get certain hours off school to go to university and study for a science degree, too. And I had a terrible job trying to make up my mind. I loved working with my hands and I loved science. Should I go in this science direction? But what about my languages? I loved languages. And I can remember weeping and wailing trying to make up my mind.

And then the vocational teacher at school turned up with a chance to become a librarian [at a major national library]. Now these jobs were VERY, VERY rare, they were. This was a job opening up with all these wonderful books and languages—and I said, "Oh, yes, please!" But even though I was offered the job, I decided in the end to go on to university, for there was money for one more year of schooling. Then the vocational counselor at school came back to me after that year, with a chance to be an education officer at the museum—that had been all shut up because the Air Force had taken over the building during the war. All the exhibits and everything had been all lumped together, all the young men working there had gone off to war. And now they wanted to reopen it to the

public. . . . So at long last, here was my love of science
and languages all put together!!

So I got that job and loved preparing exhibits and
taking them around to schools. I just loved my work at
the museum. I was the only person who could read the
Greek dictionary, and every time someone discovered a
strange animal or plant, I, you know, had to look up the
Greek root so they could name these plants and things.
And I would translate the odd bits of Spanish and Italian
out of the journals for them.

I could get 5 hours off a week, so I went back to the
university after work. . . . I never ever wanted to give
away my study. At the end of that year, though, I knew
what I wanted to do. I wanted to do social work. What
had happened was during the war, everybody was
involved with the servicemen, but there was a whole
generation of adolescents growing up whom nobody was
interested in and this is where I wanted to put my time.

From this point, Elizabeth continued her interests in social
work on a voluntary basis, in tandem with her marriage (at age
21) and her husband's rural veterinary practice. Even when
having to move to a very remote country area, Elizabeth notes,
"I still regarded myself as a social worker. . . . And I said to
myself, oh well, I'll go and do some social work in the wop-wops
now." And that she did, working with individuals and groups,
so that eventually her interests drew much recognition both
locally and further afield. The birth of a child with special needs
saw Elizabeth building a national support network for other
parents having children with such difficulties. Marriage was very
much a partnership for Elizabeth, as she and her husband often
worked side by side, undertaking different tasks associated with
his veterinary practice as well as some domestic chores. As
necessary, the young woman would involve herself in counseling work with animal owners, as well as assisting her husband
with some of the more scientific tasks. Although maintaining
fairly traditional sex roles within the marriage, Elizabeth and her

husband considered these roles merely as convenient divisions of labor rather than as [an unequal] power balance for decision-makin' purposes. Elizabeth's religious and political interests were ultimately woven into the fabric of her middle adult years. Her life at age 60 has evolved from a pattern of ongoing reflection followed by an adaptive response to continually changing situations and circumstances. Following her husband's death, Elizabeth has maintained active involvement in her life's interests and important relationships. What she values most in her life now is, "Integrity, I think. To thine own self be true—that's what I mean by integrity."

What mechanisms does Elizabeth use to stabilize new identity-defining commitments following periods of reconsideration, which have reoccurred throughout her adult life? It is interesting to note through Elizabeth's narrative that her identity formation process entails an ever-expanding integration of issues or interests that were not dealt with in previous decision-making periods. Initially, Elizabeth struggles with the task of finding a means to integrate her science and language interests in a vocational direction, setting aside interests in political and religious domains. She then marries, creating a context that enables her to pursue her scientific interests via involvement in her husband's work, while building upon newfound interests in social work that grew from war and postwar experiences—work that eventually carried her abroad, enabling expression of her linguistic talents. At the same time, she carries with her messages from internalized others of "being useful" and contributing service. Such cultural messages appear, however, to have coincided with Elizabeth's own genuine interests in offering service and assisting others within her community. Later in Elizabeth's life, religious and political interests are reintegrated as she finds political contexts in which to lobby support for her projects and renews commitment to a religious faith that provided much comfort through the death of her husband and a child.

Contexts that Elizabeth has created following decision-making periods have many elements in common with those of other participants who ultimately found psychosocial niches "that fit"—at least until the next decision-making phase. New contexts were often sought in response to the need for reintegrating personal interests or talents that had been left behind in the staking of earlier contextual claims. Such contexts often had to enable the expression or realization of quite disparate identity elements. Late adolescent Elizabeth is not able to commit herself fully to a vocational setting until she finds one that will allow the realization of both her scientific and linguistic interests.

Similar to Elizabeth's, Al's narrative gives evidence of an identity formation and reformation process spanning several decades; the creative capacity for reintegrating lost identity elements ultimately brings him much peace and pleasure by mid-life, though the cost of the quest has been great. In his midteens Al felt depressed. He was considering work in journalism, but in a small rural farming community there was little scope for such work. Al's father had always stressed the importance of financial security, so Al finished high school to begin work as a clerk in a bank, a job that his father had arranged. After 2½ years, however, Al's urge to write could no longer be suppressed; he sought employment as a reporter for the local paper, though he was offered and took a position doing only clerical work for that news agency. About this time, Al underwent the experience of a religious conversion that began to make his 19-year-old-life feel more secure. By age 20, however, he felt frustrated by the lack of small-town opportunities and, on his own, shifted to a large city some distance away. Al had never lived away from home before, and it was not long until he formed a strong identificatory relationship with a minister in his new locale. His social life soon revolved around the church as he engaged in many of its causes. He had taken a job in clerical work, which provided little satisfaction, so it was not difficult for Al to develop a strong feeling of attachment to the ministry. Through time, this attachment developed into a feeling of being "called" into a career in the ministry. Al adopted a "crusader line" in his approach to life's activities, which ultimately brought him into contact with his wife-to-be. However, upon marriage Al soon "lost the call," moved to a new community and settled down to work toward a position as bank manager and to begin a family. But "the call" did remain as a whisper in the very quietest of times. By his late twenties, Al could no longer ignore the call that had become by now a relentless roar, even at the busiest of times at the bank. After enormous difficulties, he was accepted into theological school, where he moved with his family to study for the next 6 years and ultimately begin work in a small church parish. Al undertook his new responsibilities at breakneck speed, crusading all the while for worthwhile causes. Exhaustion eventually took over, and he was forced into several months of rest. During this time, writing interests began to surface once again, as he dabbled with the parish newsletter.

In his late thirties, Al became plagued with many theological doubts, and sought answers in the human potential movement. He could by now no longer abide by the teachings of his church (and probably internalized parent) and turned against "the whole religious establishment." High and low points came over the next 5 years as Al and his wife experienced relationship difficulties and began experimenting with open marriage. Journalism interests were also pressing more strongly for a hearing, slowly becoming realized in various vocational contexts. Al met his second wife-to-be at an encounter group one weekend, but it was not until age 45 and time in the hospital that Al "began to find [himself] again." Over the next 10 years, Al was at last able to "put the crusader to rest." He sought to bring religion back into his life by adopting what he now calls a "humanistic Christianity." Vocationally, he is self-employed as a free-lance journalist, which allows him the realization of his writing talents.

Asked to describe himself to himself now, at age 55, Al replies:

> The first word that comes to mind is OK. I feel more at peace with myself, more self-aware than I've ever been in my life before. I've got these themes, these major elements in my personality, and now they are all able to play a part in who and what I am today. So I'm a pretty happy man, really.

[What do you value most in your life right now?]

Peace of mind, really. Acceptance of myself as a person, acceptance of the people around me, particularly my wife. And her acceptance of me, warts and all.

Achieving a sense of identity on one's own terms seems to involve the ability to integrate and reintegrate often quite disparate elements into a "new unique Gestalt, which is more than the sum of its parts" (Erikson, 1968, p. 158).

New contexts were often sought or created by interviewees in response to external events that had destabilized the meaningfulness of existing life directions as well. Precipitating such a crisis for many women and some men was the breakdown of a marital or otherwise important relationship. Ultimately, this challenge often produced a more strongly defined sense of self—either in or out of subsequent relationships—a strong sense of identity achievement becoming the eventual reward. After her husband's affair, Ruth at age 45 was forced to examine her life and her expectations of marriage. "Every tub has to stand on its own bottom," is the conclusion she came to 2 years later. Before Ruth and her husband could recommit themselves to a relationship, now quite changed in form from earlier years, each had to find a personal center of gravity. Similarly, a marital crisis at age 46 eventually brought Joan to the realization that "even in the most comfortable of relationship situations, you're still on your own. You just can't sink too much into somebody else." At age 50, Joan reflects that she has "had to leave the thought of remarriage alone to build myself up in other ways." It was through professional counseling at age 44 that Sarah located one source of dissatisfaction with her marriage—her socialization for dependency and continually self-sacrificing activities for her partner and children. Now at age 62, Sarah is able to find pleasure in seeking gratification of her own needs without guilt and in bringing into balance both self- as well as others' interests. Growth to the awareness that "I am whole without a man" ultimately allowed Adele to engage in a satisfying relationship after a series of disappointing involvements in her thirties. John did not marry until his late thirties, for he had "wanted to find [his] own independence first." Development or growth as an individual were continuing themes among those who had undergone and successfully resolved a relationship crisis.

Ruth summarizes an important sex difference in relationship values, however, that often appeared across the themes from men and women:

> My sense of values is quite different to his. I think if we're together, the time together matters; he thinks to ACHIEVE something in that time is important. That if we're going somewhere we should get there. You know, start doing it, whatever IT is. And I think it wouldn't matter if we didn't go anywhere—we could just take a walk, or talk, and it wouldn't need to be planned, and you wouldn't need to achieve something at the end, but some understanding. I don't know whether that's my husband or a male approach to things. I mean just driving in a car, he wants to get there—he doesn't stop to look at things on the way, or say, "Hey, that's interesting; let's stop." You know, there's a path that's laid . . . take it. And that may be a male way of going for life. Men often achieve goals because they won't be interrupted, I think.

Such different values regarding expectations of intimacy has been a frequent source of conflict for couples rated identity-achieved in this study.

There has been minimal research on the relationship between context and identity achievement for the years of adulthood; results of studies cited earlier by Adams and Fitch (1983) and Costa and Campos (1989) for student populations, however, show some similarities to features of adult life contexts for the interviewees described in this section. Settings that allow for reflection and/or exposure to a range of viewpoints characterize the environments of identity achieved individuals from the present investigation. From qualitative descriptions in Hart's (1989) and Josselson's (1987) longitudinal work, identity achievement women at mid-life had adopted contexts that helped them grow in "breadth and depth." By contrast to the insulated worlds of the adult foreclosures, identity achievements in the present study had created or chosen vocational, ideological, and relationship niches that are likely to produce ongoing opportunities for reflection and development. Studies of relationship style for the various identity statuses have consistently found more differentiated and intimate forms of relatedness among the identity achieved than other identity statuses (Kacerguis & Adams, 1980; Orlofsky, Marcia, & Orlofsky, 1973). Descriptions of values held in an intimate relationship from this study's identity achieved persons stress themes of individuality and partnership, of support and recognition for personal effort. More superficial qualities, which predominate in foreclosure descriptions, are rarely mentioned by the identity achieved here.

Thus the contexts in which the identity achieved stabilize their newly emerged senses of self have the common features of enabling the actualization of often quite disparate identity elements as well as being supportive of a greater need for personal autonomy and deeper form of intimacy. Additionally, they provide ongoing opportunities for exposure to new people, situations, and ideas. Contexts are often experienced as restful or peaceful havens, allowing for diversity while at the same time producing a feeling of stability and satisfaction in the creator.

Conclusions: Identity and Context

Stewart (1980) has noted that personality variables, considered either alone or in combination with situational factors, have been largely unexamined in predicting women's life-style patterns. Her work has shown that although family situation variables, such as being married and having children, may set broad limits on probable behaviors, personality variables predict the choice of particular behavior patterns within those broad limits. Results from Kroger and Haslett (1987, 1991) have further refined the concept of "family situation" to show that choice of life-style (in terms of balance between full- or part-time paid employment and marriage/child-rearing responsibilities over the course of adulthood) is strongly linked to the development of ego identity; what has remained unclear from these results, however, is whether the choice of life-style determines the course of further identity development or whether one's mode of resolving identity issues determines the life-style choice itself.

The present qualitative examination of narratives from participants in the Kroger and Haslett studies suggests that even though there is considerable interaction between identity and context, individuals using different modes to address identity-defining questions have created personal contexts within their larger socio-historical milieu that differ quite markedly. For those individuals who remained firmly foreclosed across the course of their adult lives, personal niches had certain features in common. Vocational contexts were often highly structured and regimented, allowing little opportunity for reflective thought or input of alternative views. For some full-time homemakers, where such a structure did not exist externally, many created quite rigid time parameters to their days. Relationships were valued for more superficial qualities, often for meeting nurturance needs alone; little recognition of individuality appeared in these relationships themes. For those entering a moratorium process, undertaking an O.E. (overseas experience) was common, as was entering a new and unfamiliar physical environment where one was not known. This exercise was frequently undertaken by both men and women as a personal test of their ability to disengage from the power of internalized parents. Upon feeling some success or satisfaction with this task, energy could then turn to issues of finding satisfying life directions that allowed the realization of personal interests and talents. When periods of re-decision-making were precipitated by external life events, it was often the ending of a relationship that propelled individuals into more differentiated senses of self. Among contextual features of the identity achieved were settings that would allow the expression and integration of often quite disparate identity elements. Often, entire domains of life values, long left behind, were reintegrated into adult contexts at mid-life. The contexts created also were ones in which ongoing exposure to new ideas and situations were probable. Relationships were valued according to the support for individual autonomy they provided as well as for the sharing of deeper experiences that they allowed. The mechanisms by which individuals in different identity statuses create their own life contexts within the broader socio-historical milieu await further description.

References

Adams, G. R., & Fitch, S. A. (1983). Psychological environments of university departments: Effects on college students' identity status and ego stage development. *Journal of Personality and Social Psychology, 44,* 1266-1275.

Berzonsky, M. D., & Sullivan, C. (1992). Social-cognitive aspects of identity style, need for cognition, experiential openness, and introspection. *Journal of Adolescent Research, 7,* 140-155.

Busch-Rossnagel, N. (1991, April). *The goodness-of-fit of identity processes and the contextual demands of late adolescence.* Paper presented at the Biennial Meeting of the Society for Research in Child Development, Seattle.

Costa, M. E., & Campos, B. P. (1989, July). *University area of study and identity development: A longitudinal study.* Paper presented at the 10th Biennial Meetings of the International Society for the Study of Behavioural Development, Jyvaskyla, Finland.

Cote, J. E., & Levine, C. (1983). Marcia and Erikson: The relationships among ego identity status, neuroticism, dogmatism, and purpose in life. *Journal of Youth and Adolescence, 12,* 43-53.

Erikson, E. H. (1963). *Childhood and society.* New York: Norton.

Erikson, E. H. (1968). *Identity: Youth and crisis.* New York: Norton.

Erikson, E. H. (1970). Autobiographic notes on the identity crisis. *Daedalus, 99,* 730-759.

Fitch, S. A., & Adams, G. R. (1983). Ego identity and intimacy status: Replication and extension. *Developmental Psychology, 19,* 839-845.

Francis, J. E., Fraser, E., & Marcia, J. E. (in press). Lifespan identity development: Variables related to moratorium-achievement-moratorium-achievement (MAMA) cycles. *Journal of Adolescence.*

Ginsberg, S. D., & Orlofsky, J. L. (1981). Ego identity status, ego development, and locus in control in college women. *Journal of Youth and Adolescence, 10,* 297-307.

Grotevant, H. D., & Cooper, C. R. (1985). Patterns of interaction in family relationships and the development of identity exploration in adolescence. *Child Development, 56,* 415-428.

Hart, B. (1989). *Longitudinal study of women's identity status.* Unpublished doctoral dissertation, University of California at Berkeley.

Hult, R. E. (1979). The relationship between ego identity status and moral reasoning in university women. *Journal of Psychology, 103,* 203-207.

Josselson, R. L. (1982). Personality structure and identity status in women as viewed through early memories. *Journal of Youth and Adolescence, 11,* 293-299.

Josselson, R. (1987). *Finding herself: Pathways to identity development in women.* San Francisco: Jossey-Bass.

Kacerguis, M. A., & Adams, G. R. (1980). Erikson stage resolution: The relationship between identity and intimacy. *Journal of Youth and Adolescence, 9,* 117-126.

Kroger, J. (1983) A developmental study of identity formation among late adolescent and adult women. *JSAS Catalogue of Selected Documents in Psychology, 13,* Ms. No. 2537.

Kroger, J. (1990). Ego structuralization in late adolescence as seen through early memories and ego identity status. *Journal of Adolescence, 13,* 65-77.

Kroger, J. (1992, February). *On the nature of structural transition in the identity formation process.* Paper presented at the Wellington Identity Conference, Wellington, New Zealand.

Kroger, J., & Haslett, S. J. (1987). A retrospective study of ego identity status change by mid-life adults. *Social and Behavioral Sciences Documents, 17,* Ms. No. 2797.

Kroger, J., & Haslett, S. J. (1991). A comparison of ego identity status transition pathways and change rates across five identity domains. *International Journal of Aging and Human Development, 32,* 303-330.

Marcia, J. E. (1966). Development and validation of ego identity status. *Journal of Personality and Social Psychology, 3,* 551-558.

Marcia, J. E. (1967). Ego identity status: Relationship to self-esteem, "general maladjustment," and authoritarianism. *Journal of Personality, 35,* 118-133.

Marcia, J. E. (1980). Identity in adolescence. In J. Adelson (Ed), *Handbook of adolescent psychology.* New York: John Wiley.

Marcia, J. E., Waterman, A. S., Matteson, D. R., Archer, S. L., & Orlofsky, J. L. (in press). *Ego identity: A handbook for psychosocial research.* New York: Springer.

Munro, G., & Adams, G. R. (1977). Ego identity formation in college students and working youth. *Developmental Psychology, 13,* 523-524.

Neugarten, B. L. (1968). Adult personality: Toward a psychology of the life cycle. In B. L. Neugarten (Ed)., *Middle age and aging.* Chicago: University of Chicago Press.

Ochberg, R. L. (1986). College dropouts: The developmental logic of psychosocial moratoria. *Journal of Youth and Adolescence, 15,* 287-302.

Orlofsky, J. L., Marcia, J. E., & Lesser, I. M. (1973). Ego identity status and the intimacy versus isolation crisis of young adulthood. *Journal of Personality and Social Psychology, 27,* 211-219.

Podd, M. H., Marcia, J. E., & Rubin, B. M. (1970). The effects of ego identity and partner perception on a prisoner's dilemma game. *Journal of Personality and Social Psychology, 82,* 117-126.

Slugoski, D. R., Marcia, J. E., & Koopman, R. F. (1984). Cognitive and social interactional characteristics of ego identity statuses in college males. *Journal of Personality and Social Psychology, 47,* 646-661.

Stewart, A. J. (1980). Personality and situation in the prediction of women's life patterns. *Psychology of Women Quarterly, 5,* 195-206.

Swann, W. B. (1985). The self as architect of social reality. In B. R. Schlenker (Ed.), *The self and social life.* New York: McGraw-Hill.

Waterman, A. S. (1982). Identity development from adolescence to adulthood: An extension of theory and a review of research. *Developmental Psychology, 18,* 341-358.

❦ 7 ❦

Altered Views

Fathers' Closeness to Teenage Daughters

Terri Apter

*A*fter 2½ years' research and observation of adolescent daughters and mothers in a family setting, I concluded that girls seldom get from their fathers the kind of emotional support and intimacy they get from their mothers (Apter, 1990). Many girls said that their fathers tended to communicate with them by issuing orders, [1] and some girls said that the father was "the last person" they would go to with those adolescent problems or queries that make embarrassment bite hard and deep. The very idea of confiding in him could be outrageous and hilarious. "He'd be as uncomfortable as we would," 14-year-old Mary insisted. "Can you imagine having a heart-to-heart with Dad? About sex!" she squealed to her 16-year-old sister Louise, who concurred, "He'd say 'Yeah, yeah,' squirm in his seat, and change the subject."

Many fathers were shocked when they heard what their daughters had said. One father—whose daughters were not part of this study—wrote to *The New York Times Book Review* declaring that he had forbidden his daughters to read the book. [2] Less drastic paternal indictments described my findings "sad." [3]

A father whose daughter was part of my study challenged her when I returned for a follow-up interview. "But what about you?" he demanded of his daughter. "Didn't you say things were different with us?" As he put his arm around her shoulders he managed a simultaneous hug and push. "Close," he stood beside his daughter and stooped for a moment to touch his shoulder against hers. "How are we not close?" he repeated as he left the room, allowing us to talk in private.

Naomi, 15, admitted that when she saw how hurt he was she "felt kind of dizzy" and no longer knew if she had spoken the truth. "He's sulky, sort of surprised—I mean, when I explained what I'd said and why you were coming again. Well—I guess I wasn't really thinking about what I thought about him. Not so much about him." His dismay shocked her into a new perspective in which she could see what she had previously overlooked. But what had she overlooked, and why were adolescent girls prone to overlook it?

It was not a direct refutation of my conclusions that has stimulated me to reassess them, as much as the fact that many fathers have been hurt by them. This concern speaks more persuasively than any rebuttal. The discrepancy between the daughter's casual assurance that they were not "close" and the fathers' amazed, pained denials, needs to be addressed. Emotional closeness is not always reciprocal, but the fathers were protesting not simply that they felt close to their daughters, but that their daughters seemed to be close to them.

Fathers apparently believe they know more about older children, and feel more comfortable and competent with them, and are often more interested in them—though they do not spend more time with the older children (Lamb, 1986; Pleck, 1985). Yet research on adolescent girls has shown that the girls themselves feel less close to a father during adolescence than in childhood, that they view their fathers as issuing orders, that they do not feel open and comfortable with their fathers (Apter, 1990; Harris & Morgan, 1991; Youniss & Smollar, 1985). Did the fathers deceive themselves, or were their daughters obtuse?[4] If so, why did the daughters who spoke with such depth and clarity about their mothers, show such blindness about their fathers?

The puzzle deepened as I spoke to older women about their parents (see also Rossi & Rossi, 1991). It became clear that in retrospect woman saw their fathers as having played an important part in their adolescent development, and, as adults, felt love and gratitude for his role. Why did adolescent girls grudge their fathers a forthright acknowledgment?

This query pointed to a gap in the published research. Girls' own experience of their relationship with their fathers has barely featured in the stories told in the social sciences about this bond. Instead, the relationship is described as an unconscious grounding of heterosexual desire (Freud, 1976) or as a mechanism through which cultural notions of femininity and masculinity are transmitted to children (Parsons, 1955). Recently, as the family has been seen, or supposed, to undergo change, research has addressed questions about fathers' new involvement with child care (Cowan & Cowan, 1987; Hochschild, 1989; Pleck, 1985), and what effect this has on the mother (Hoffman, 1983; Hochschild, 1989; Grossman, Pollack, & Golding, 1988) and on the child's development (Bronstein et al., 1987; Radin, 1976, 1986, 1988). Questions have also been asked about what types of fathers, under what circumstances, show more involvement than do traditional fathers (Barnett & Baruch, 1988; Orthner & Lewis, 1979). And, as more children experience the divorce of their parents (the majority of whom live with their mothers) research has investigated the effects on girls of father absence (Hetherington, 1972; Laiken, 1981; Wallerstein & Kelly, 1980).

These studies investigate the effects of this relationship, but they leave the daughters' subjective stories untold. Though adolescent attitudes towards parents have been covered through detailed, well constructed questionnaires (Youniss & Smollar, 1985), the results of these leave out the microresponses that would allow further description and interpretations. They also leave untouched that sharp discrepancy between daughters' experience of the relationship with a father, and fathers' assessments of how close they are to their daughters.

The New Study

Fathers were part of my original study only as significant parts of the mother/daughter pair. I had of course asked these girls to describe what they felt toward their fathers. Most of them said they loved him, and many admired him "more than any other man." The few who disliked a father had good reason—her parents were divorced, she lived with her mother, and rarely saw her father who, she judged, contributed little or nothing to the family's well-being. Yet these father-loving girls measured closeness largely in terms of whom they could "talk to" or "tell things"—that is, to whom they could disclose their confusion, doubts, secrets, and hopes. This ability to explore ideas and feelings involved trust. This trust involved the expectation that she would "have a chance to explain," that what she said would "not be held against" her, that her words would not "be taken away and held in a bad light." When this trust was lacking, or unstable, a girl often decided she would suppress her impulse to talk. Her conviction that someone did not really know her could provide some protection from unfair interpretations of her speech and actions.

In reconsidering my views on fathers and daughters I returned to seven adolescent girls whom I had already interviewed as part of a mother/daughter pair, and I contacted seven other girls to speak about their fathers, of whom I chose four to interview extensively, and to observe with their fathers. The girls' ages ranged from 15 to 18. The socioeconomic status of my sample ranged from (blue-collar) working class to professional middle class. They were drawn from the East Anglia region in England, and the Chicago area of the United States. Among the new group were two sisters, aged 16 and 17, who had been living with their father since their parents divorced 2 years before. Since, in my original study, all the daughters of divorced or divorcing or separated parents lived with their mothers, I was happy to take a step toward filling in this gap. They remain unrepresentative in that most daughters of separated parents live with their mothers, but cases that are unrepresentative in one feature may share many things with more common cases. I wanted to discover how different this atypical case was. Single custodian fathers have been reported as feeling more emotionally involved with their young children than their own fathers had been with them. They believe they are making a conscientious effort to be more expressive and affectionate with their children (Hanson, 1985, 1988). But what, from the daughters' point of view, are the results of such conscientious effort?

I sought out new subjects for two reasons. First, I already knew a great deal about my original sample—though not enough, I decided, about the daughters' relationship to the father. Prior knowledge is on the whole an asset. New things can be understood in a wider context. But presumptions of knowledge may stall the spotting of different patterns, and this was precisely what I wanted to discover. Furthermore, I had to accept the unlikely possibility that my treatment of fathers and daughters had been minimal because the relationship, in my original sample of 67 mother/daughter pairs, was uncommonly sparse. After all, the mothers and the daughters had to consent to being interviewed and observed, and those who consented might have done so because this was the stronger relationship. In the end I did not conclude that this was the case, but I could not know that at the outset.

The standard procedure involved at least 3 hours of interviews with the adolescent girls, and at least an hour's interviewing time with the father. These were conducted on either two or three separate occasions, with intervals of between 2 and 5 weeks. I frequently spoke to sisters together about their father. The agreement between them was remarkable—and not, I believe, coincidental, because they built their image of their father together, suggesting interpretations of his behavior, and one reminding the other of something omitted by a specific narrative. I also sought time to observe the daughters with their fathers. Though this was agreed in every case I used, the definition of "time together" tended to be loose: often in the time they were allegedly spending together, they were not in immediate contact with one another, but simply in the home at the same

time. Hence I was often observing mothers and daughters inter-
acting with one another while the father was in the background.
In addition, when I spoke to daughters about their fathers, they
spoke about their fathers with reference to their mothers—what
they would tell a mother rather than a father, what was easier
with a mother than with a father, how they felt with a mother
in contrast to how they felt with a father. Conversations about
fathers involved mothers as reference points, so much of what
I say about daughters' relationships with fathers takes their cue:
I often contrast, as the girls themselves did, exchanges with
fathers and exchanges with mothers. The five girls—which included two pairs of sisters—and three fathers whose patterns of
interaction and problems in communication I describe here
were selected because the problematic mix of attachment and
irritable defensiveness highlights in different ways prominent
features of father/daughter relationships I found generally. In all
these pairs there were paths to connection and problems that
arose from them. In all these cases the adaptation to the difficulties came from the daughters, though the fathers made use of
the new opportunities to connection offered by the daughter's
maturity. The father's inflexibility, or insensitivity, or belief that
the daughter had no just grounds for complaint, itself became a
problem. To remain close to their fathers, these girls had to
adjust to his terms of connection. In so doing, they felt that their
bond had specific limits.

Projected Embarrassments

As Mary, who had been 14 when I first spoke to her, expressed embarrassment at the notion of "having a heart-to-heart
with Dad . . . about sex,"[5] she was registering both her feelings
and what she supposed her father's feelings would be. It would
be embarrassing to Mary and her sister Louise to speak about sex
to their father because he would be embarrassed. In anticipating
his embarrassment they explained that he would not know what
to say. He would be cast in a role he could not play. He would

not know how to respond to their confessions or their appeal for advice. He would be embarrassed because "a heart-to-heart . . . about sex" would reveal his ineptness. In supporting her claim against him, Mary creates a character out of past experience, though the character she creates is undoubtedly exaggerated and simplified. "His eyes go all over the room when you start talking to him." She looked up at the ceiling and rolled her eyes in imitation of her father. "It's as though I'm not there, as though all this–," and she looked down at her well developed body, "hadn't happened." Mary looked for confirmation to her older sister, who was amused by these antics. Louise explained, "That's his way of being polite."

When I returned to Mary and Louise 2 years later, they both defended what they had said then, yet also modified it. "The thing is," Mary said, "he really thinks of himself as someone who wants to talk to you, and then when you do, he gets all antsy. There's no way he would've recognized himself by what I said about him. He thinks he's all there for us."

"He is for the important things," Louise, now 18, reminded her sister.

"For important things. Yeah. But that's part of it. Most of the time with someone you know well you can talk about lots of things."

"You can't really have a frivolous conversation with him," Louise said.

"I never show him clothes I buy," Mary continued, ". . . I can't ask him how he thinks I look, because that's not important, I guess. But it's worse than not important. It's like I'm not there, and I'm not there because something's wrong with the way I am there. Well that's how I feel!" she snapped at Louise who began to sigh with disagreement.

"No, I don't talk to her for hours on end like her mother does," the father admitted, "but most of what she talks about is drivel. You try to listen to it. You've listened to it! It's nothing. It goes on and on, and it's nothing. But that's such a small part of the whole thing."

The trouble is, to a teenage girl it is not "nothing" and it isn't small. Her special closeness to her mother is built on small things that, on some scales, weigh nothing at all, and amount to "nothing." Small, apparently inconsequential or "frivolous" conversations can lead to more important matters. Casual discussion allowed girls to send out "feelers" to test whether the time was right to make a request, to explore a problem, or to make a confession. At this phase of development, when the girl matures through responses of people close to her, it is the mother who does most of the exhausting and exacting work—listening to her "drivel," or reacting to her varied (sometimes clumsy, sometimes shocking, sometimes aggressive) self-presentations. The mother may say, "I'm not going to put up with this," but when she does, she does not mean it the way a father does. The father will say those words and walk away. The mother may be warning the daughter she has gone far enough. She is not concluding, but merely seeking a breather from the ongoing conversation that is so important to her daughter's development.[6]

> My Dad says he wants to talk. He's into talking and
> being open and that sort of thing. But I never know
> where a conversation's going with him. Things sort of
> get broken—I don't know—I'm exaggerating—I guess
> that's what Louise would say, because it does get to me,
> the way he thinks he's such a good father, but
> something closes up. It's not just sex and boyfriends
> and other stuff—like I told you before. It's feeling him
> suddenly go cold, and you don't know why. I mean—is
> he disapproving, or bored or what? I end up feeling so
> silly, and then I guess I start to act silly. He has an awful
> laugh. It's not even like he can't help it. It's not the kind
> of thing that you just can't help, but like he means it,
> like he's telling us something with it. Once Mom was
> away and I had to ask him whether I could go on this
> boating party. He asked a few questions about it and
> then just laughed—I guess that meant "no," like it was
> all too ridiculous. I just told my friends I couldn't go. I
> didn't want to bring it up with him again.

Mary was confronting a question about her father's feelings toward her. Was "he disapproving, or bored or what?" She feels a tension, which irritates her, between his idea of himself as someone who is open to talk, and her experience of his edginess when she tries to talk. His perception of himself as someone who is available for communication poses further questions about herself: If he is available for communication and goes cold when she starts speaking on her own terms, then is the problem to be located within her? Is there something wrong with what she says ("like it was all too ridiculous") or is she failing to communicate anything ("I seem to disappear")? She half believes what he says about being willing to talk, but as it clashes with her own experience of talking to him she either has to correct and criticize his self-image, or she has to conclude that she is not communicating in appropriate or real terms. This uncertainty between sympathy with her father's self-presentation and her own experience leads to uncertainty about "where the conversation is going." His edginess and lapse of interest are felt as criticism.

On the "important" issues, which Louise said their father did have time for, Mary judged him as

> not much better. He sits down with me, and listens—but it's like he only listens, and you realize you're having half a conversation. I know he has opinions—about what electives I should take, or whether I should join a sorority, or what colleges to apply to. So he sort of leads me on, but only so far. He just leaves me. "It's your decision," he says, and I guess I should be flattered, but what I feel is that he's not really tuned in. You start to explain something to him, and he tells you he's sure you can figure it out yourself. Then when you make a decision which he likes he sort of takes the credit: "I knew you would come to that conclusion." But if he doesn't like what you're doing he says, "Well, it's up to you," and that means it isn't right. I just wish I knew where he stood. I feel—yech! horrible, squelchy—when he doesn't let on how he feels.

For adolescent girls, conversation—talking—is an important measure of intimacy. Friendships among girls are graded according to what can be told to a friend, whether a friend understands, and whether a friend can be trusted with the communication—that is, whether she can "keep a secret." They also value the practice sessions with friends as they make themselves known to others, but to be sure that their self-presentation has succeeded, they need a responsive audience. Hence Mary feels she is left with "half a conversation" because her father does not make his own view known. She feels anxious because she may be making the "wrong" decision—in that what she decides may not turn out right, or, in a more simple way, it may be wrong because her father "really disapproves." A mother's company is valued through what she says: Daughters usually feel they can talk to her, that she is reassuring and supportive, and older teenage girls, contrary to the adolescent stereotype, often praise her as advisor.

Mary's father did recognize the value of this "drivel," although his recognition did not make him a willing participant. My final interview with Mary and Louise took place on the day that Louise had returned from summer camp. For me this was propitious. I knew that reunions were wonderfully illuminating. Even commonplace reunions—the mother returning home from work, the daughter returning from school or from a date—sparked a fascinating range of expectations and disappointments. Though I had explained that I now wanted to observe father/daughter pairs, I found myself in the living room while the mother and Louise talked nonstop, and the younger sister Mary sat on the floor, making sporadic claims for attention like a cautious but hungry cat. The older girl spoke about her outings, activities, and adventures, though sometimes her revelations got her into trouble, and the mother declared that she was "crazy" or "irresponsible" and "would not be allowed to go there next year." However, these little bids for control and correction were submerged in the general euphoria of the daughter's return.

The family had kept its word—the father was home, but he remained based in the upstairs den. He seemed to crave a series of snacks, however, and to get to the kitchen he had to pass the living room, which was visible from the stairwell. The sound of his footsteps was a signal for conversation to stop, and there was a lull until he retrieved whatever it was he wanted from the kitchen and returned upstairs. But each time he passed the living room he would bestow a smile on Louise. She responded with a grimace—clearly he was interrupting their good time. He cast the grimace back to her, but added affection and humor, so that it was more like the exaggerated mouthing offered to a baby than a hostile exchange. This eased her irritation, but her laugh was somewhat uncomfortable, for she did not know where the joke lay. On his third passage through the room he paused and said, "I just want you to know I sure am enjoying this conversation." The mother's faced reddened with laughter, and Mary lowered her forehead into her hand, indicating she thought him a "lost cause."

Yet the father was expressing his genuine sense of belonging while displaying diffidence about his participation. He felt the warmth and intensity of the mother/daughter conversation, which may to him seem so perfectly formed that he does not want to disturb it. Hence he expressed closeness, and kept his distance. To the women so adept at conversing with one another his criss-crossed stance is a hoot. Girls often keyed in to the father's diffidence in approaching them or joining them on their terms. "I have to try to get my homework out of the way by Saturday," Naomi explained, "because if my Dad's free on Sunday, he sort of hops about, wanting to join in anything I'm doing." It may be that even much younger children, who call their father "funny" or "silly," may be laughing less at the jokes he tells than at his attempts to "join in." The amusement is stimulated by inept efforts rather than by an adept comic.

Sex and Rejection

The terror that Mary expected to strike her father were she to discuss sex with him touches one common assumption about father/daughter relationships. The distance between fathers and daughters is thought to increase at a girl's puberty because the father actually responds in kind to the daughters' own reactivated oedipal desire. These incestuous feelings in parents are seen as normal, but the father himself may be disturbed by them, and distance himself from the daughter in order to protect the entire family from them (Ferenczi, 1949; Johnson, 1969; Pincus & Dare, 1978). Growth and maturity, which she expects her parents to delight in, push her father away. Sexual maturity, too, can strike fear in a parent, making him more aware of his daughter's vulnerability; hence he may increase restrictions and supervision rather than grant her the greater freedom she expects as she matures. Her own ambivalence about her sexual maturity is increased by her confusion at other's responses to her (Brooks-Gunn & Petersen, 1983).

The fathers' own accounts of their behavior, however, have a readily accessible logic. The consensus among fathers was that they understood a daughter's increased need for privacy. "I don't want to intrude." "I have no business prying into that sort of thing." "It hasn't changed our relationship, I don't want her to think it has. But I can't barge in her bedroom like I used to." Fathers felt powerless to help their daughters with problems that did arise. Her maturity increased parents' fear on her behalf. The fathers believed that daughters needed a woman's advice. "It's hard—thinking back on how I thought about girls when I was a teenager. I wasn't a bastard, but let's just say that their well-being wasn't my first priority. She needs a mother to explain what's going on." The two fathers in my study who did not think the daughters' mothers were equipped to give them good advice, did not bank on their own advice, but relied on their daughter's "independence" and ability to "know her own mind" or "look after herself." Partly through feeling inadequately equipped to give a daughter advice, and partly through sensitivity to her changing needs, he sees new points of distance, yet believes that these do not affect his closeness.

The daughter's own ambivalence about her physical maturity may lead her to exaggerate a father's response. Other girls described, as did Mary, a father as "not knowing where to look" when she wore a new swimsuit or appeared in the first light T-shirt of the summer. But perhaps the father learns not to look at the daughter. After all, girls of 14 and 15 described their pain at being observed. "When I walk into a room other people's eyes feel like sandpaper." Others' glances are like "barbed wire pressing into me" or "sort of scrape my nipples and making me want to scream." Because girls often punished their mothers for looking at them too intently—by glaring back at them or grimacing—the father may well have been responding to the girl's own rejection of his glance.

Different Measures of Closeness

Though conversation and communication are important measures of intimacy, teenage girls who decide not to talk to fathers because the results are so unsatisfactory ("It's like feeling him go cold, and you don't know why.") seek other scales of measuring intimacy, in order to remain close to a father. The new maturity of adolescence allows fathers to communicate with daughters in a wide range of ways. The fathers in this study saw a daughter's adolescence as offering opportunities to extend their relationship with her. One father was pleased by his daughter's increased stamina that allowed him to take her on rigorous hikes. Another said that when she was little he could not ski throughout the day "without her throwing a tantrum every time she fell. I'm enormously impressed by her determination—and all this is new. As a young kid she would give up something after one try. Now she's game for anything. It's a treat to be with her." Another father welcomed his daughter's intellectual maturity that allowed them to discuss general ideas. Still another father welcomed the opportunity to teach her things: Her science projects were now "more interesting," and she was "good with her hands" in carpentry.

Daughters appear to be highly responsive to this new interest fathers show in them. In view of the daughter's responsiveness, it is not surprising that fathers are often cited as having played an important role in their daughters' intellectual development (Landy, Rosenberg, & Sutton-Smith, 1969; Radin, 1986; Radin & Sagi, 1982).

New Closeness and Old Problems

The new opportunities for companionship that are opened to fathers and adolescent daughters still come up against the problems daughters feel in conversation. "I really do love my Dad," said 15-year-old Naomi,

> and I like doing lots of things with him. There's something about the way he gets so involved. It's so serious. That's what makes it fun! And then sometimes, all of a sudden, he can hurt me so bad. . . . We were putting up the tent last night, and I'm suddenly a "pain in the neck" because I wasn't getting the spikes in fast enough, and he sent me off to do something else, because I'm a real failure. . . . He's not mad the way Mom would be. She can get nasty, but then she knows she's hurting me. To him, my feelings don't count—not while he's setting up that tent. Most of the time this doesn't matter, but when it comes, it's "wham"—just like a slap. And there's this lump of angry me he won't even see, no matter what I say or do.

The teenage girl, who concentrates on what a parent manages or fails to "see," appreciate, hear, or understand (Apter, 1990), is as offended by the father's decision that she is "a real failure" as she is by his ignorance of how this decision has hurt her. She makes good use of his preference for "doing things with her" or "going places with her" over "just talking"; but here too Naomi comes up against the need to defend herself against him.

> I used to just cry when that sort of thing happened, and not really understand, I guess, why I felt so sad. Now it's still a shock, because so much of the time—more now, really than ever—he's so much fun. But I clam up for a long time when that hits me. I'm not as forgiving as I used to be. I don't just forget.

Though she described herself as guarded and careful and closed with him—especially after he had hurt her in some way—

Naomi did not give up on him. In spite of the pain of having her anger ignored, and her frustration at being unable to express it ("Because he only gets mad when he sees I'm mad. He'll shout, or tell me to buzz off") she is willing to come back to try again. His anger passes and the "fun" returns. The evening after the weekend camping trip, not half an hour after she had described how he hurt her and how she, in response, would "clam up for a long time," Naomi was getting help from her father with a school project that involved some carpentry. It was Sunday night, the project was due the next day, and in preparation for the new school week, Naomi was musing on other social problems. She began to complain that a girlfriend had been making snide remarks. She spoke to her father for some time, watching him while he worked. Eventually he glanced up and said, "Well, you'd better stay away from her then!"

"Stop ordering me around!" she snapped. Her father looked up at her, seemed to wonder whether this was worth a reprimand, decided it wasn't, and continued to sand the wood. From the father's point of view, he was protecting her, suggesting a way of solving her problem. The daughter, however, wanted a chance to talk, to explore her feelings.

None of the fathers in this sample was able to find a balance between ordering and neglecting: though Mary felt unsupported ("horrible, squelchy") when her father refused to express his own views, Naomi felt her father was taking her problem up and solving it for her, making it more simple than she felt it to be.

Discussion about the problem she was having with her friend would allow her to weigh things up: Was the friend more trouble than she was worth, or might she be able to preserve the friendship without suffering further humiliation? The father's peremptory remark was perceived as an order, directing not only her actions but also putting a stop to her implicit request for discussion. She responds more to the authoritative than to the supportive aspect of his advice because the advice is inappropriate to her feelings. Her clear invitation to "talk it over," or explore through discussion, is ignored—or, perhaps in her eyes, "rejected." Her father's solution was too simple. Complaints about friends indicate a puzzle—a sense that something isn't in the right place. Giving up on the friend is rarely the answer. "This can't go on" is a decision based not on unkindness but breach of trust. Secrets told, trust betrayed, these are unforgivable in the girl's code of friendship. Other complaints are problems to be overcome. Sometimes they are "worked out" in gossip sessions. The problem is reconstructed. "Her trouble is, she just wants to show off," or, in a more sophisticated vein, "Criticizing people makes her feel good. It sweeps the field free of competition." Complaints about a friend have several facets: the need to whine, to share the discomfort; and the need to confirm that the friend's hurtful behavior is unjust. There is often another element—the need to smooth the wrinkle in the relationship.

Her father took the pencil box base from the vice and told her to fit the top to it and see if it was a smooth and level fit. Together they made marks on where the screws would go into the base, and he made holes with a hand drill. Naomi was silent while they adjusted the screws—not too tight—to allow the top to swivel from the base. As soon as it was finished, she took it to her mother. She handed it to her, then drew it back. "Don't mark it—it hasn't been varnished yet. I have to take it apart to do that." The mother and daughter exchanged vaguely irritable glances. "Dad told me not to mark the wood," Naomi explained. Her mother wiped her hands, but did not reach for it again, and admired it. As Naomi searched through a drawer to find something to wrap the box in, I recorded the following exchange:

> Naomi: Meg's being really mean to me now. She's always going on about how Debbie teases everyone, and thinks teasing is real smart. Well, she was with Debbie when I came out of Chemistry—I was late because I had to clean up—and when I passed her she starting talking in this loud voice about how some people hang around to brown nose the teacher.
>
> Mother: Well, was she really talking about you?
>
> Daughter: Yes! I was passing her and she was looking at Debbie but that voice was "notice me" loud.

Mother: So what did you have to clean up?

Daughter: Jo and I spilled some ammonium chloride.

Mother: You spilled it?

Daughter: Yes, Mom, I spilled it. (Her voice exaggerates regret.) We had to wipe it up. No big deal.

Mother: So you weren't in trouble with your teacher?

Daughter: No! I wasn't in trouble with my teacher (mimicking a goody-goody).

Mother: Well—so Meg said that. . . . So what do you care?

Daughter: I don't! Except sometimes she seems to want to be my friend, but then she pals up with someone else and sets herself against me.

Mother: Mmmm.

Daughter: Don't say "Mmmm"! I hate it when you say "Mmmm."

Mother: Oh, Naomi!

Daughter: Like she's always messing with me.

Mother: Okay—not "Mmmm" but "Okay"—Okay? So some people are like that. You have to take care. You live and learn. Right?

Daughter: (Walks up close to mother and measures their respective heights.) Shrimp.

In this conversation the mother sees the complaint as a window onto her daughter's school life, and checks potential problems ("You're not in trouble with the teacher?"). This tactic is potentially irritating. It veers away from the daughter's intended direction, and implies criticism and control rather than the empathy she is seeking. Her strong "No!" not only silences her mother's worry, but also redirects her to the daughter's purpose. (The mother winces at this abrupt denial. In fact, mothers tended to be highly sensitive to a daughter's shouting.

It clearly inflicted pain. They would respond either by getting angry themselves, and shouting more loudly than the daughter, or, after a moment's pause, would take a placatory position.) The mother then offers support by giving her avoidance advice ("What do you care?"), but it is less peremptory than the father's and the daughter responds to the more open-ended advice. "I don't [care]!" is a kind of decision not to be bothered by it, as well as a defensive move against the mother's implicit challenge (Do you care what other people think when you know they are wrong?). Then she goes on to explain why she does care: Meg's messages are confusing, and she does not know how to weigh friendship against this insult. Her complaint against her friend and her growing awareness that she is not presenting her case in a way that gets her the response she thinks she deserves makes her angry with her mother. The dialogue becomes an altercation, whereby she attacks her mother ("Don't say 'Mmmm'!"), but she backs down a tiny bit after the mother's counter move ("Oh, Naomi!") and returns to the initial topic. The mother accepts this move away from a quarrel, placating her daughter but holding her ground ("Not 'Mmmm' but 'Okay'—Okay?"). Even the final piece of platitudinous advice ("You live and learn") is offered as a suggestion, linking in to the daughter's own experience. Naomi does not admit that she thinks the mother is right, but she does not counter her advice. Instead, she seems to accept it by changing the subject: she reminds her mother that she is now the taller of the two ("Shrimp.")—though to do so she stands close to her mother, thus affirming their attachment as she underlines her "superior" height. The daughter has a great deal of control over this conversation, which permits indecision about her future behavior, even while the mother takes the role of advisor.

Not only confidences and complaints but other exchanges, too, seem—for the daughter—easier between her and her mother than between her and her father. Mary said that when she apologized to her mother, she knew her mother understood that she was apologizing for the pain or worry she had caused her. She was saying she was sorry that they had quarreled. When she apologized to her father, he "went all smug" because he thought she was admitting she was wrong. Naomi too felt that her mother was less likely to pull rank with her than her father was:

> She shouts a lot, especially when she's flustered, like when she's lost her way in the car, or is in a hurry. It gets harder to take as you get older. They shouldn't—you know they shouldn't shout at you like a naughty little kid. My Dad still does it. "HEY YOU GIRL!" Do they know how much that hurts? I think my Mom does—there's a broader picture, and she's sorry after. She knows what his shouting feels like too, and tells me he doesn't mean anything by it, that I shouldn't take it personally. But he lays it on—then when it's over for him he thinks that's the end of it. There's no point in trying to tell him what it's like. He just wouldn't see.

The Limits of Love

The problems that Mary felt in getting close to her father and the problems Naomi expressed ("There's this whole lump of angry me he won't even see") stem from the father not knowing the daughter well enough, not seeing what she is feeling. When the father becomes the primary parent, would this change?

I found that Emma and Elizabeth, aged 17 and 18, who lived with their father after their parents' divorce, faced problems with their father similar to those felt by Mary and Naomi, and the problems were intensified rather than mitigated by the father's special position.

Even with the father as primary parent, it was the mother who acted as mediator to the daughters on behalf of their father's love. Just as Naomi's mother tried to soften the blow of her father's impatience by reminding her not to "take it personally," Emma's mother "was the one who told me that he really loved me even though he doesn't show it." Just as Mary and Louise went to their mother—and definitely not their father—to discuss a boyfriend or any query relating to their bodies, Emma and Elizabeth "saved things like that for Mum" and "talked to her a lot," either during their weekly visits or during telephone calls.[7]

The sisters were 14 and 15 when their parents separated. Their maturity and independence, they said, made the decision to stay with the father possible:[8] they were "beyond the tucking-in stage." But they appreciated care-taking gestures—like keeping their dinner warm in the oven if they were out late, coming home to have lunch with them if they were ill, and showing them how to mend and maintain their bicycles.

As Emma and Elizabeth spoke about their relationship with their father they had to sift out time spans—what they felt when their father and mother first separated, how things were for a while after that, and how things had changed when their father remarried. At 16 and 17 years old, they could look back on what they had felt, and why, and whom they had hurt, and who had hurt them. Their decision to live with their father was—he said—a result of the mother "being unable to cope." This English idiom does not imply instability, but can describe the more moderate condition of simply having enough on one's plate already. The daughters, however, described their decision as "practical" because their mother was already working in the North of England when the couple separated, and they were in school in the South of England, where their friends were, in a town they already knew their way around, and very different from the large city of Manchester where their mother now worked and lived. But because their father was at home while the separation took place, "and he was here like he was supposed to, cooking the meals and being home for us," they initially blamed the mother for going off. Now they realize that they hurt her by blaming her. The desire to repair the harm done, and their sense of understanding things more deeply (of which they were proud, for it was a measure of their maturity), increased their appreciation and their closeness to the mother. The sisters believed that the problems they had with their father—and that had intensified after his recent remarriage—were also problems in the first marriage. They believed that the father's reserve played a part in the breakup of the marriage, and as they too experienced it, they felt closer to their mother.

Their assessment of the role the father's emotional reserve played in the separation of their parents may have been worthless as a marital analysis, but it expressed their feelings. "I came home from orchestra practice one night at about 9:30," Emma said.

> My sister was still out, and as I got to the door I could see someone moving inside. I knew it wasn't my sister. I could see that, and I thought maybe my Dad had come back from the conference early. But I knew he hadn't. I knew he was still in Birmingham. And then I could see whoever it was hear me and run out the back. I ran inside, up and down the stairs—everything seemed so spooky. . . . I phoned my Dad straightaway. He was so cool. He told me what to do, call the police, get a glazier to mend the window. Was anything taken he wanted to know. Was the house vandalized? "So everything's all right," he said. He didn't think about how I felt. He didn't seem to care. I rang Mum, and she had a fit. "Oh, my baby darling!"—that sort of thing.

"She uses a kind of baby talk when she's worried about us," Elizabeth explained.

> She was really good, really involved. She told me to stay by the phone, and assured me he won't come back, that I'd frightened him off. Five minutes later she got back to me. She'd already arrange for me to spend the night with a friend of hers, and she came down the next day. It was like she knew how I must feel—not measuring everything from the outside, the way my father does.

The arguments she and her sister continued to have with their father often revolved on this issue: his not knowing how she felt, and in the steps he took not to hear her feelings out. Their quarrels (or "rows") were sparked off, Emma thought, by her trying to tell him what she felt. One hot topic was the father's plan to sell the house.

> We moved here only two years ago, after we sold the house that was our home as a family. Now my Dad wants to sell this one. When I start to tell him how sad that makes me feel, he slams the table and says, "We've been through all this before!" Like it's been decided and that's that and there is no point in discussing it. Then he flew out at me because I hadn't tidied my room. I really meant to—I did! But that's the kind of thing that's easy to forget. Someone came to see the house and he showed them round and opened the door onto my messy room. He told me I'd done it on purpose because I didn't want to move. I felt that something awful had happened, because he didn't trust me, that he really thought I'd done that on purpose.

Emma may not have understood her father's accusation. Perhaps she imagined that he was accusing her of some plot, but he may have been complaining of a half conscious wish getting the upper hand. The row was sparked by her neglect to do as he had requested—or ordered—a common enough adolescent/parent tension. From her point of view, the accusations he had made pointed not simply to her failure to do as she was told, or even as she should have done—which she acknowledged, but also to a subversive motive. At the same time she resented him imputing this motive to her, she felt that she had every right not to want to move, and that it was inappropriate for him to get angry with her because of what she wanted or did not want. The complex focus of his anger made her feel cast in a role that was far worse than she deserved, and also addressed issues that he had no right to control:

> He can shout at me for not tidying my room. I understand that. But the idea that I did something sneaky to prevent them selling the house—that he thinks I would do that . . . and he's always doing that now, thinking I'm doing something to get at him or [his wife].

At the same time that he guessed she was being underhanded in expressing her reluctance to move, he was refusing to discuss her feelings. "He looks at it from the outside. The decision's been made, that sort of thing." She felt then that he was both giving her feelings a wicked force they did not have, and denying them a legitimacy that they did.

For Emma, growing up and dealing with her father involved learning the limit of his love. Life, for this academic scientist, was rational and you proceeded through it in an orderly and rational fashion. These are not simply different communicative styles, but different expectations about what is involved in love.

> I know I'm the most important thing in my mother's life now. I know I'll always have a home with her. My father loves me even less than I thought he did. That new home with his wife won't be my home. "You can always come to stay," he says [about the new home], and doesn't understand why I feel so low about it. He talks about having done his duty, and we're old enough to be independent, and our mother can take her turn now.

The reference to "duty" separated his care, which she had once appreciated, from love. It again showed how her father was looking at the relationship "from the outside," which to him gave it structure, and which to her took away the foundations.

Her growing sense of his coolness and his mistrust of her motives forced upon her a series of decisions. "I could move in with Mum and never speak to him again," she said lightly. "We sometimes feel like that," Elizabeth laughed. "But that's like punishing him by giving him what he wants." Then the sisters modified their assessment of what he wanted: "He does want us around—but sometimes . . ." Emma said. "On his terms," Elizabeth added. Then, rather than plotting revenge, they continued to speak regretfully about how things had changed. "The dinner table used to be quite an institution in our house," Elizabeth explained,

but now we keep a low profile. So does he. I don't
know what he thinks about like I used to. He used to
tell us what he was doing, how his experiments were
going—that sort of thing. Maybe his job takes up more
time now. It seemed that he used to have more time. It
gets harder and harder to tell him anything about
myself. At first I thought he'd notice I was keeping
something back, and try to find out what was up with
me. But he doesn't even notice. I could disappear inside
and he wouldn't notice.

Whereas mothers do tend to notice when a girl is reserved,
and see it as a danger signal, fathers normally take a silent girl at
face value. Mothers pry and nag and cajole a sulky daughter into
speech, however negative; fathers are likely to let a girl remain
silent if she wants to. They see that as "her choice." The sisters'
father at first said he had not noticed they spoke less at dinner.
Then he added, "when they do talk, they just make waves."
Hence keeping silent was a way of keeping the peace. From
Emma's point of view this acceptance of her silence was another
rejection. He was allowing her to grow more distant.

The loss that Emma described was certainly real for her, yet
watching her and her sister and her father and her father's new
wife together, it seemed to me that the sisters and the father shared
a powerful bond that had been left out of the girls' story—and that
was humor. The father's jokes were not especially funny to an
onlooker. He concocted doggerel rhymes, or coded remarks like
initials used in place of words, and they instigated guessing games
about what the initials signified. The father would signal that such
a game was about to begin with a tone of voice or a look. Both girls
would have his full attention, and he enjoyed their quickness; even
wrong guesses delighted him. Later I asked whether the mother
had ever joined them in this shared humor (as the new wife
certainly had not). "Oh, no," Emma laughed, "that's always been
just me, my sister and my Dad."

Emma may have been discovering the limits of her father's
love, but she was finding her way round a fairly substantial

object. The daughters in this study understood the value of connection with the father. While the father worked to extend the relationship as the daughter matured and took advantage of new opportunities for connecting to her in new ways, the daughters eagerly accepted these "extension offers," but also had to develop defenses against their limits. The burden of the adaptive work seems, in this preliminary study, to be placed on the daughters. They can withdraw and isolate themselves from the father in defence against or "punishment" of the father, without giving up connection on the father's terms. Mothers often reassure daughters of love that the father does not express, and this may protect both the father and the daughter from disappointment or frustration in the relationship. Adolescent girls' tendency to describe themselves as "not close" to their fathers may be strictly inaccurate. Fathers are dismayed by these descriptions because they do not see their points of accuracy.

The study of fathers' changing roles and influence is multi-faceted: It can be measured through the fathers' descriptions of his activities, through observation of his behavior, through measured differences in the development of children from different types of fathers. What has been relatively neglected is the child's assessment of and responses to the fathers' behavior. Even the observation that fathers do give more directives and imperatives (i.e., "orders") to children than do mothers (Bellinger, 1982; Bright & Stockdale, 1984) does not expose the important point that daughters construct "orders" from their fathers' expectations, conversational manners, and expression of interest (or lack of interest); and that a fathers' ignorance of the fact that—from the daughter's point of view—he is insensitively authoritarian, increases her sense of distance from him.

Interpersonal relations consist, to a high degree, of "interactions that are conceptually organized by the participants into structures" (Youniss & Smollar, 1985, p. 2). These structures are observable, and become more profound and complex the further we look into them. Research on fathers should not neglect the relationship as experienced by their daughters.

Notes

1. Also reported by Youniss and Smollar, 1985.
2. Robert McEliece, August 12, 1990, "What fathers do." Letters, *New York Times Book Review.*
3. "A Good Read," BBC, Radio 4, July 19, 1990.
4. Recently Ruthellen Josselson (1992) reported the "men experience themselves as tending and nurturing . . . but others do not experience men as nurturing" (pp. 236-237).
5. This case is discussed in Apter, 1990, p. 67.
6. Sharon Rich (1990, p. 267) found that "mothers who are perceived as being unresponsive to what daughters say harm the relationship."
7. Single custodian fathers who generally feel competent parenting their daughters nonetheless seek outside advise on issues such as sex education and clothing (Lynn, 1979).
8. When fathers do have full custody of their children upon divorce their children are more likely to be adolescent (Hanson, 1988).

References

Apter, T. (1990). *Altered loves: Mothers and daughters during adolescence.* New York: St. Martin's.

Barnett, R. C., & Baruch, G. K. (1987). Determinants of fathers' participation in family work. *Journal of Marriage and the Family, 49,* 29-40.

Barnett, R. C., & Baruch, G. K. (1988). Correlates of fathers' participation in family work. In P. Bronstein & C. P. Cowan (Eds.), *Fatherhood today: Men's changing role in the family.* New York: John Wiley.

Bellinger, D. (1982). Sex differences in parental directives to young children. *Sex Roles, 8,* 1123-1139.

Bright, M. C., & Stockdale, D. F. (1984). Mothers', fathers', and preschool children's interactive behaviors in a play setting. *Journal of Genetic Psychology, 144,* 219-232.

Brooks-Gunn, J., & Petersen, A. (Eds.). (1983). *Girls at puberty: Biological and psychosocial perspectives.* New York: Plenum.

Bronstein P., D'Ari, A., Peiniadz, J., Franco, O., Duncan, P., & Frankowski, B. (1987, April). *Parenting behavior as a predictor of early adolescent school functioning.* Paper presented at the Society for Research in Child Development, Baltimore, MD.

Cowan, C. P., & Cowan, P. A. (1987). Men's involvement in parenthood: Identifying the antecedents and understanding the barriers. In P. Berman & F. A. Pedersen (Eds.), *Men's transition to parenthood.* Hillsdale, NJ: Lawrence Erlbaum.

Ferenczi, S. (1949). Confusion of tongues between the adult and the child. *International Journal of Psychoanalysis, 30,* 225-230.

Freud, S. (1976). New introductory lectures on psychoanalysis. In J. Strachey (Ed. and Trans.), *The complete psychological works: Standard edition* (Vol. 22). London: Hogarth Press.

Grossman,, F. K., Pollack, W. S., & Golding, E. (1988). Fathers and children: Predicting the quality and quantity of fathering. *Developmental Psychology, 24,* 82-91.

Hanson, S.M.H. (1985). Single custodial fathers. In S.M.H. Hanson & F. W. Bozett (Eds.), *Dimensions of fatherhood.* Beverly Hills, CA: Sage.

Hanson. S.M.H. (1988). Divorced fathers with custody. In P. Bronstein & C. P. Cowan, *Fatherhood today: Men's changing role in the family.* New York: John Wiley.

Harris, K. M., & Morgan, S. P. (1991, August). Fathers, sons, and daughters: Differential paternal involvement in parenting. *Journal of Marriage and the Family, 53,* 531-544.

Hetherington, E. M. (1972). Effects of father-absence on personality development in adolescent daughters. *Developmental Psychology, 7,* 313-326.

Hetherington, E. M., Cox, M., & Cox, R. (1976). Divorced fathers. *Family Coordinator, 25,* 417-428.

Hoffman, L. W. (1983). Increased fathering: Effects on the mother. In M. Lamb & A. Sagi (Eds.), *Fatherhood and social policy.* Hillsdale, NJ: Lawrence Erlbaum.

Hochschild, A. R. (1989). *The second shift.* New York: Viking.

Johnson, A. M. (1969). Parental influence in unusual sexual behavior in children. In D. S. Robinson (Ed.), *Experience, affect and behavior: Psychoanalytic explorations of Dr. Adelaide McFayden Johnson.* Chicago: University of Chicago Press.

Josselson, R. (1992). *The space between us: Exploring the dimensions of human relationships.* San Francisco: Jossey-Bass.

Laiken, D. (1981). *Daughters of divorce.* New York: Morrow.

Lamb, M. E. (Ed.). (1986). *The father's role: Applied perspectives.* New York: John Wiley.

Landy, F., Rosenberg, B. G., & Sutton-Smith, B. (1969). The effect of limited father absence on cognitive development. *Child Development, 40,* 941-944.

Lynn, D. B. (1979). *Daughters and parents: Past, present and future.* Monterey, CA: Brooks/Cole.

Orthner, D., & Lewis, K. (1979). Evidence of single father competence in child rearing. *Family Law Quarterly, 8,* 2704-2708.

Parsons, T. (1955). Family structure and socialization of the child. In T. Parsons & R. F. Balkes (Eds.), *Family, socialization and the interactive processes.* Glencoe, IL: Free Press.

Pincus, L., & Dare, C. (1978). *Secrets in the family.* London: Faber & Faber.

Pleck, J. H. (1985). *Working wives, working husbands.* Beverly Hills, CA: Sage.

Radin, N. (1976). The role of the father in cognitive/academic and intellectual development. In M. E. Lamb (Ed.), *The role of the father in child development* (2nd ed.). New York: John Wiley.

Radin, N. (1986). The influence of fathers upon sons and daughters and implications for school social work. *Social Work in Education, 8,* 77-91.

Radin, N. (1988). Primary caregiving fathers of long duration. In P. Bronstein & C. P. Cowan (Eds.), *Fatherhood today: Men's changing role in the family.* New York: John Wiley.

Radin, N., & Sagi, A. (1982). Childrearing fathers in intact families in Israel and the USA. *Merrill Palmer Quarterly, 28,* 111-136.

Rich, S. (1990). Daughters' views of their relationship with their mothers. In C. Gilligan, N. Lyons, & T. Hammer (Eds.), *Making connections: The relational worlds of adolescents girls at Emma Willard School.* Cambridge, MA: Harvard University Press.

Rossi, A., & Rossi, P. (1991). *Of human bonding: Parent-child relations across the life course.* Hawthorne, NY: Aldine de Gruyter.

Wallerstein, J., & Kelly, J. (1980). *Surviving the breakup: How parents and children cope with divorce.* New York: Basic Books.

Youniss, J., & Smollar, J. (1985). *Adolescent relations with mothers, fathers and friends.* Chicago: University of Chicago Press.

❦ 8 ❦

Narratives of
the Gendered Body
in Popular Autobiography

Mary M. Gergen
Kenneth J. Gergen

One of the commonplace truths of contemporary culture is that people are born either male or female, and that these two groups of people exhibit differing characteristics related to their sexes across the life span. Except for rare instances, people identify themselves in the most profound ways as either male or female, and become acutely aware of qualitative changes in what it is to be a man or a woman as they age. Yet, how we understand these matters is subject to broad debate. Let us contrast two positions, the one stressing *essence* and the other *meaning*. It is frequently presumed that facts about gender differences, along with views about human development more generally, are (or should be) derived from systematic observation of behavior. What we believe about gender development is, ideally, a reflection of the actual essence of gender differences across the life span (cf. reviews of sex difference research in Maccoby & Jacklin, 1974; Money & Ehrhardt, 1972). Scientific knowledge on this account represents a distinct advancement over folk psychology because scientific observation of essential differences is more systematic and rigorous.

Yet, though the essentialist view is commonplace, it is also delimited. A growing body of scholarship now places central emphasis on the formative effects of understanding itself. That is, what we take to be knowledge of gender and development over the life span are not reflections of the essences; rather, our presumptions of knowledge enter, reflexively, into daily affairs to shape the contours of human activity (cf. Steier, 1991). On this latter account, the possession of full breasts or a bald head is of no necessary consequence in itself—no more, let's say than other observable facts, such as having brown eyes or large toes. However, if full breasts and a bald head come to demark discrete stages of development, and the members of such classes are thereby defined as more or less emotional, rational, passive, sexy, or moral, then having full breasts or a bald head may importantly shape one's life chances, activities, and satisfactions.

Further, as people live out their lives, engaging in various courses of action, they often support the matrix of preexisting meanings attached to various physical characteristics. In this way the current cultural meanings, whatever they are, exert their effects on others, even into future generations. In a broad sense, one is thus born into a culture composed of interlocking patterns of meaning and action (Bruner, 1986). These meanings give specific significance to various biological characteristics, rendering them socially visible or insignificant, deeming them valuable or debilitating, using them to designate differences or similarities. The result of this process of cultural construction is a deep sense of the *natural* differences between men and women as they develop and age over the life span.

From the social constructionist perspective, meanings are not private and subjective events, but public and shared.[1] Meanings are generated through the discursive practices of the culture, transmitted from adults to children within various cultural contexts. Because such practices are inherently fragile and subject to continuous alteration, various significations can be foregrounded in one cultural enclave but overlooked in another. Cultural patterns of speaking and acting at any time may be viewed as a patchwork of discourses, each with its different history and context of usage.[2] In order to carry out relationships, it is thus necessary to borrow from various repositories of discourse to achieve mutual coordination of action.[3] At the same time, most recognizable cultures also contain a body of more or less interdependent, enduring, and broadly sustaining discourses. Thus, for example, in the United States a common discourse on justice may enter into relationships in the courtroom, the classroom, or the living room. In this case, each localized usage may support a more or less pervasive array of cultural meanings.

In the present offering we explore a small repository of discourse within the culture; although relatively insignificant in the literary landscape, this body of writing provides significant bearings for negotiating the life course. Our particular interest is in narrative construction, and most focally, the stories people tell about their lives. In our view, the narrative is the central means by which people endow their lives with meaning across time.[4] Thus, as people are exposed to the popular narratives within the culture, they learn how to regard themselves, how to make themselves intelligible to each other, and how to fashion their conduct. In Paul de Man's (1979) words, "We assume that life produces the autobiography . . . , but can we not suggest, with equal justice, that the autobiographical project itself may produce and determine life?" (p. 920).

To the extent that narratives are gendered, furnishing different structures of meaning for men as opposed to women, so do they contribute to cultural patterns that differentiate between the genders and prescribe both what is likely and unlikely during a lifetime. Thus, as men and women tell the stories of their bodies—what they mean and how they should be considered—so do these stories affect the course of their relationships with others, their career potentials, and their life satisfactions. If the stories of embodiment differ importantly between men and women they may also generate estrangements. To live in a different story of the body from another can render an impasse of understanding. Male and female actions toward each other may be misunderstood, and relationships dwindle into lonely alienation.

Autobiography and
the Fashioning of the Life Course

One of the most accessible forms of narrative available to contemporary North American readers is the autobiography. Highly marketable in the United States, the best-seller list each week usually includes at least two autobiographies in the top 10 nonfiction books (cf. *New York Times,* 1990-1992 booklists). These autobiographies vary in their instantiations, but best-sellers are frequently based on formula formats prescribed by publishing houses. These forms allow celebrities, often abetted by professional writers who specialize in this form, to tell their life stories in a revealing and engrossing way. Despite their mass appeal, we believe the popular autobiography is far more than a mode of public entertainment. Rather, such works operate much like secularized primers for the "good life" (Stone, 1982). They provide an idealized model of the life course—furnishing direction, sanctioning deviation, and providing benchmarks against which the common person can measure and judge their development. Autobiographies such as these are not, of course, the only such sources for rendering the life course meaningful. However, because they bear an intertextual relationship with other popular sources of narrative—television documentaries, Hollywood films, and magazine stories, as well as other fictional fare—their significance is noteworthy.

The function of the autobiography as a life course model is revealed in the narrators positioning of self vis-à-vis the reader. As Eakin (1985) points out, the autobiographer typically takes "the stance of the wise and fatherly elder addressing the reader as son or niece" (p. 29). The principal form of the autobiographical relationship is expert to novice, elder to younger, master to apprentice, or powerful to powerless. The edifying principle behind autobiographies is also revealed in their central themes and the personages selected to write about themselves. The central emphasis of the autobiography is on success and failure, and particularly how to achieve the former and avoid the latter. The authors are typically figures widely recognized for their cultural achievements (Olney, 1980). Classical autobiographies almost exclusively delineate the life of cultural heroes—those who have achieved greatness through their accomplishments (Jelinek, 1980). Readers benefit by being able to fantasize about the pleasures of escaping their humdrum circumstances and learning the ways and means to a notable life.

The Emergence of the Female Voice

What kind of image of the life span does the popular autobiography present? There has been no systematic study of this question, but the answers can be ascertained, in part, by reference to the historical development of the autobiographical form itself. Although the history of autobiography is in its infancy, scholars suggest that its particular form took shape with the rise of the bourgeoisie, and the accompanying concept of the self-made man (Lejeune, 1971; Pascal, 1960). Similarly, Weintraub (1978) argues that the development of autobiography is closely linked in Western culture with the emerging value of the unique and independent individual. "The fascination with individual specificity leads to deep intrigue with life stories" (Eakin, 1985, p. 204). In this view, autobiographical figures represent a culturally and historically situate model of an ideal self.

With the emphasis on individual achievement, autobiographies tend to follow the classical lines of the "monomyth," a form that Joseph Campbell (1949/1956) has designated as the most fundamental in Western civilization. In its clearest form, the monomyth is the saga of a hero who triumphs over myriad impediments. When applied to the life span, the monomyth is a heroic trajectory. It thus tends to recognize youth as a preparatory period, early and middle adulthood as induction and struggle to attain one's goals, and mature adulthood and old age as full achievement and later consolidation and appreciation of one's successes. The form of the heroic life span is indeed like a skewed arc, with the apex at the climactic moment of highest attainment. The particular time in the life span is dependent upon the goals, but in the popular autobiography it is usually formed so that this point is approximately three quarters of the way through the text. In the autobiography, the form of the story is singular, linear, and progressive to the climax, and usually stable thereafter.

Yet, it is also clear that this account of the autobiography is most relevant to—if not the unique provenance of—prominent public figures; in almost all cases, the high status man. The chief features of the monomythic tale speak most directly to the life span of a man, not a woman (Gergen, 1992). As Mary Mason (1980) has described, "the self presented as the stage for a battle of opposing forces and where a climactic victory for one force—spirit defeating flesh—. . . simply does not accord with the deepest realities of women's experience and so is inappropriate as a model for women's life-writing" (p. 210). Included in the monomythic story are several women's roles, none of which is considered heroic. Women are cast in roles that are defined as stable, passive, or service oriented. Women are thematized as fair maidens to be wooed and won, mothers and wives, witches and sorcerers.[5] Women tend to be objects of quest, or forces that impede the hero in pursuit of his quest.

Earlier work on gendered forms of autobiography (M. Gergen, 1992; in press) indicates that in contrast to men's accounts, women's story lines are multiple, intermingled, ambivalent as to valence, and recursive. Whereas men's stories concentrate on the pursuit of single goals, most often career oriented, women's are more complex. Women's stories usually weave together themes of achievement, along with themes of family obligations, personal development, love lives, children's welfare, and friendship. Whereas men's stories are rarely revealing about emotional experiences, traumas, self-deprecation, self-doubt, and self-destructiveness, women's stories often express these aspects. Because of these multiple themes and self-expressions, the tone or movement of women's stories are never unidirectional, focused, or contained. Thus the content and the form of men's and women's autobiographies are distinct. The men's stories, however, exhibit the cardinal characteristics of the idealized form of autobiography. Women's forms are deviant.

Gendered Narratives of the Embodied Self

Although there are substantial differences in the narrative forms located in male as opposed to female autobiographies, our special interest is in a specific form of content, namely embodiment. As reasoned above, the body doesn't "speak for itself." Rather, as a culture, we invest it with meaning—giving it importance (or not), treating its changes as significant (or not), and elaborating these meanings in such a way that life satisfactions blossom or are obliterated. The question, then, is how these culturally acclaimed authors embody themselves over the life span. How do they define, elaborate, and give significance to their physical being? How do males and females differ in the model they provide for the experience and treatment of one's body through the life course?

To explore these issues we shall consider how famous men and women account for their bodies from their youth, through adulthood and old age. A sample of autobiographies of 16 men and women published in the United States in the past 7 years will serve as the basis for this discussion. These books were chosen to reflect the range of autobiographies available in the popular market. This selection includes people who have accomplished noteworthy activities, and are not merely associated with or related to famous people. The authors of this sample do vary in age, primarily because many of them—in particular the athletes and performers—became famous in their youth. The male autobiographies include those of: Ansel Adams, John Paul Getty, Lee Iacocca, T. Boone Pickens, Ahmad Rashad, Donald Trump, Jr., Thomas Watson, Jr., and Chuck Yeager. The female autobiographers are Joan Baez, Sidney Biddle Barrows, Nien Cheng,[6] Linda Ellerbee, Gelsey Kirkland, Martina Navratilova, Joan Rivers, and Beverly Sills. Although the full complexity of these accounts cannot be conveyed in this chapter, illustrative quotations will allow dominant themes to become apparent.

Bodily Inscription From Childhood to Puberty

Remarkable differences between men's and women's accounts of their bodies begin to emerge from their earliest reminiscences of childhood. Two facets of this difference deserve notice. First, men have very little to say about their physical beings, except to note how effective their bodies were in attaining their goals. Second, men display little affect when making these descriptions. Perhaps the time lag between event and reportage has stifled any sense of connectedness that once may have existed for the author, and/or the inclusion of any emotional reactions might seem inappropriate. In any case, the body is virtually an absent figure in their reminiscences. Women's stories tend to be far more embodied. Beginning with the early years, women include greater detail in the descriptions of the body, and they are often emotional in describing their embodied lives.

A typical example of the "indifferent" male author is Thomas J. Watson, Jr. (1990), powerful long-term boss of IBM. After looking at a homemade film of his first grade class in 1921, Watson (1990) reports only, "I'm the tallest, long boned and ungainly" (p. 4). More poignant to the reader, but apparently not to the owner, is photographer Ansel Adams's (1985) account of how he acquired his misshapen nose:

> On the day of the San Francisco earthquake [April 17, 1906] . . . I was exploring in the garden when my mother called me to breakfast and I came trotting. At that moment a severe aftershock hit and threw me off balance. I tumbled against a low brick garden wall, my nose making violent contact with quite a bloody effect. The nosebleed stopped after an hour, but my beauty was marred forever—the septum was thoroughly broken. When the family doctor could be reached, he advised that my nose be left alone until I matured; it could then be repaired with greater aesthetic quality. Apparently I never matured, as I have yet to see a surgeon about it. (pp. 7-8)

For Adams, the contorted nose that punctuated his face simply became irrelevant to his life.

For women, the physical tribulations of childhood are often felt strongly and deeply, sometimes for many years. Feelings of present day self-worth seem strongly conditioned by the physical nature of the person they were. For example, comedienne Joan Rivers (1986), now a Barbie-doll look-alike, has made a career out of comic references to her misbegotten self. As she describes a family photograph,

> When I make jokes . . . about being fat, people often think it is just my neurotic imagination. Well, on the right, with her mother and sister during a vacation trip to Williamsburg, Virginia, is the thirteen year-old fat pig, wishing she could teach her arms and hips to inhale and hold their breath. (p. 183)

Fat also plagued the prima ballerina, Gelsey Kirkland (1986). She describes her dancing debut at camp as a form of self-defense for her misshapen body: "The other children taunted me about the disproportions of my body. I never let them know how much I was stung by their disparagements . . . I turned my abdominal bulge to advantage by performing a belly dance to amuse those in my cabin." (p. 10). Tennis star Martina Navratilova (1985) had the reverse problem: being too small. "I was tiny, not an ounce of fat on me—nothing but muscle and bone—just sheer energy. In school I was kind of embarrassed about being so small, but on the tennis court it didn't really matter that much" (p. 24).

In terms of development over the life span, the impact of physiognomy for both boys and girls often turns on the extent to which its effects are intensified or altered in puberty. For men in contemporary Western culture, the adolescent challenge largely takes place within the arena of athletics. The body's abilities to measure up to the competition is all-important in athletics particularly. For these males, it is in this period that body and identity are more closely linked than at any other time in the life span. Chuck Yeager (1985), the man with the "right stuff," looks back with pleasure: "By the time I reached high school, I excelled at anything that demanded dexterity. . . . In sports, I was terrific at pool and pingpong, good in basketball and football" (p. 11). Having an athletic body also helped ease a racially tense social scene for footballer Ahmad Rashad (1988), as well as contributing to his self-esteem. "If you lived in my neighborhood, . . . you tended not to go to Eastside—they would kick your ass over there. Because of my brother and my athletic ability, the law of the street didn't apply to me" (p. 47). T. Boone Pickens, Jr. (1987), the billionaire "take-over" tycoon describes himself: "Fortunately, I was well coordinated. . . . Only five feet nine inches tall, . . . but a basketball player" (p. 17). In effect, being short was a threat to adolescent identity; being coordinated was a fortunate compensation. Donald Trump (1987), New York's bad-boy builder, avoids any physical description of himself as a youth, except to relate that he was physically aggressive, to the point of giving a music teacher a black eye when he was in second grade "because he didn't know anything" (p. 71).

Lee Iacocca (1984) turned the story of his youthful illness into gains in the realms of gambling and sex. "I came down with rheumatic fever. The first time I had a palpitation of the heart, I almost passed out—from fear. I thought my heart was popping out of my chest. . . . But I was lucky. Although I lost about forty pounds and stayed in bed for six months, I eventually made a full recovery" (p. 16). While convalescing, he started playing poker and reading books. "All I could remember about the book [*Appointment in Samarra*] was that it got me interested in sex" (pp. 16-17).

An exception to the bravado and self-assuredness of the vast majority of autobiographers, Watson (1990) portrays himself as unathletic. "While I was skinny and taller than most other kids, I was no athlete. My eye-hand coordination was terrible, so I hated baseball." Late in his life he proves himself by going sailing in dangerous waters away from medical supports, in part to overcome his fears of dying following a heart attack. A theme of overcoming his bodily and psychological defects is a stronger undercurrent in his book than in others. His success in mastering himself is illustrated, however.

For the adolescent girl, character is not made so much on the playing fields as in private chambers. Because girls seem more fully identified with their bodies, bodily changes at puberty become an enormous issue for identity formation. It is as if the body, which seemed a reasonably stable and controllable aspect of the girlhood self, begins to undo one's identity in adolescence. Spontaneously, it can make one hideous or desirable, both of which are problematic shifts in identity. Unlike men, it is a rare woman whose personal narrative is not concentrated on the unsettlement of adolescent transformation. As Navratilova (1985) comments, "The girls started to fill out in the sixth or seventh grade, but I didn't wear a brassiere until I was fourteen— and God knows I didn't need one then. I was more than a little upset about developing so late" (p. 24). Later she gains in stature: "My new weight gave me some curves I never thought I'd have, and they gave me the idea that I was a full-grown woman at seventeen" (p. 122). Joan Baez (1987) described her entry into junior high school as marked by rejection, which stemmed from her physical appearance. Without much pathos she recounted her image: "Joanie Boney, an awkward stringbean, fifteen pounds underweight, my hair a bunch of black straw whacked off just below my ears, the hated cowlick on my hairline forcing a lock of bangs straight up over my right eye" (p. 30). In high school her self-evaluation echoed a degree of self-confidence, mixed with doubt: "On the one hand I thought I was pretty hot stuff, but on the other, I was still terribly self-conscious about my extremely flat chest and dark skin" (p. 43). Beverly Sills (1987), the great opera singer and director of the New York City Opera, describes her anguish:

> I developed breasts earlier than any of my classmates, and that was a great source of anguish for me. I was already feeling tall and gawky, and when it became obvious in gym class that I was the only girl who needed a bra, I didn't just become miserable, I became *hysterical.* I was so unhappy with the sheer size of me that my mother bought me a garter belt, which was about seven inches wide, and I wore it around my chest. (p. 17)

As a more general surmise, through the period of childhood and adolescence, boys and girls develop dramatically different interpretations of their body. Boys describe their bodies as separated from self, and as more or less useful instruments to attain their will. Whereas the male's identity is alienated from physical form, females tend to define themselves in terms of their body. This tendency is congenial to the views of many object relations theorists who hold that daughters are much more strongly linked to their mothers' identities through the similarities of their bodies, but sons are taught that they are distinct and separate from their mothers. Boys must suppress their identification with their mothers and cleave to the unknown world of men outside the home (cf. Chodorow, 1978; Dinnerstein, 1977). To elaborate in the context of autobiography, it is possible that the distinctiveness that men acquire of self from mother becomes fulfilled in their alienation from their own bodies. That is, they echo their mother's actions in regarding their bodies as "other." In support of this complex relationship, theorist Jane Flax (1990) speculates that men desire the unity with the mothering figure that characterizes girl-mother relationships, and their rejection of the "female" in themselves and others [including their embodied natures] is a constant discipline required "to avoid memories of, longing for, suppressed identification with, or terror of the powerful mother of infancy." She cites "a long line of philosophic strategies motivated by a need to evade, deny, or repress the importance of . . . mother-child relationships" (1990, p. 232).

The Adult Years: Living Within and Beyond the Body

The tendency in narrative for men to distance themselves from their bodies intensifies in adulthood. The major plot in adult male autobiographies is focused on career development; these careers are typically defined independently from the body. The discourse of career tends toward the transcendent—emphasizing ideals, goals, values, and aspirations as opposed to organicity. The body, if mentioned at all, tends to be characterized as servant to the master's plans and purposes, whether for career or pleasure. For most of one's activities the body is simply taken for granted; it seems not to be a matter of particular interest or concern. Metaphorically, the body is considered a machine possession, and like one's automobile, its normal operation should enable one to get on with the real business of life. Only on occasion does the body enter the register of meaning, and that is when it serves as an asset or a liability to ends that lie beyond. Thus, as Yeager (1985) describes, "Being in our early twenties, we were in good physical shape and at the height of our recuperative powers—which we had to be to survive those nights. That was our Golden Age of flying and fun. By the time we reached thirty, our bodies forced moderation on us" (p. 180). In effect, one simply goes on until the machine begins to break down. Watson (1990) describes an attempt to turn a disenabling threat into a career gain: "I developed a pain in my right side that turned out to be appendicitis. Getting operated on gave me an chance to postpone taking the exams by six weeks, so I was able to study and pass" (p. 47).

At times the male autobiographer is surprised to find the body makes a difference. Donald Trump (1987), commenting on his early efforts to join a prestigious Manhattan club (with a lack of modesty about his body that is not found in women's autobiographies), is shocked to find his body is a consideration: "Because I was young and good-looking, and because some of the older members of the club were married to beautiful young women, [the officer of the club] was worried that I might be tempted to try to steal their wives" (p. 96). Having a good body can thus be a career impediment. It can also cause other troubles, especially for the man who takes too much pride in his athletic abilities. Consider J. P. Getty's (1986) attempt to pass himself off as a boxer. Enticing his friend Jack Dempsey to spar with him, he finds himself in difficulty in order to impress some young ladies:

> A few moments after we began to spar, I realized that Jack was pulling his punches. My *macho* was taking all

the punishment, for there were two or three very attractive young women friends watching at ringside. I wanted not only to test my ability as a boxer but also to prove myself . . . "Damn it, Jack, treat me just as you would any professional sparring partner.". . . I swung my lefts and rights as hard as I could. Jack . . . moved back a pace or two.

"Okay, Paul," he said, "If you insist . . ."

The first punch was hard. Jack swung again—and connected. That was that. . . . I picked myself up off the canvas, fully and finally convinced that I would thenceforth stick to the oil business. (pp. 276-277)

One might also note from this little tale that Getty was willing to subject his body to abuse in order to satisfy his "macho" needs.

Because the body as an asset is taken for granted—much like the beating of a heart—it is only its potential for failure that must be confronted. The male reaction is expressed in two major ways: *anxiety* and *denial.* Among autobiographers, overtly expressed fear of dysfunction is largely reserved to men whose career success is closely linked to physical condition. Thus Rashad (1988) comments,

injuries are the ultimate reality for a pro athlete—they throw a shadow over your days. . . . Football is like the army in that you know that a third of your men will become casualties. You just hope it isn't you that gets hit. Football is not just a job, it's an adventure—until it comes time to get killed. (pp. 118-119)

However, by far the more common reaction to the threat of dysfunction is denial. Again consider Rashad:

"On a pass play early in the game, Ferguson threw to me. . . . As I caught the ball, cornerback Jimmy Marsalis undercut me, rolling with his full body weight on my left knee.

> The pain was excruciating, but the invulnerable Keed
> did the natural thing: I bounced up off the turf,
> pretending nothing was wrong. I didn't want to be
> hurt, and I insisted on walking it off. That provided the
> next real sign that something was wrong: I couldn't put
> my foot down. . . . As the trainers came out, I insisted
> to them, "Nah, it ain't too bad. It'll be all right. There's
> nothing wrong with this baby." (p. 179)

A more dramatic illustration of defensiveness at work comes
from Chuck Yeager's (1985) account of his emergency exit from
a crashing plane. Yeager's parachute caught on fire as he ejected
himself from the cockpit. Upon hitting the ground, he wanders
toward a passerby who has seen him land.

> My face was charred meat. I asked him if he had a
> knife. He took out a small penknife, . . . and handed it
> to me. I said to him, "I've gotta do something about my
> hand. I can't stand it anymore." I used his knife to cut
> the rubber lined glove, and part of two burned fingers
> came out with it. The guy got sick. (p. 360)

Yeager himself registers no reaction.
    Women's accounts of embodiment in the adult years stand in
marked contrast to men's. The woman's sense of identity remains closely tied to her physical condition. It is not so much
that the body is used instrumentally—as a means to some other
end outside the body. Rather, to be in a certain bodily condition
is to "be oneself." Consider the detail in which Joan Baez (1987)
describes her bodily being as she readies herself for a major
performance:

> I am in my room by two o'clock, tired, wired, and
> thinking about what to wear. I turn my suitcase upside
> down, littering the floor from wall to wall to get a good
> look at my entire out-of-date collection of rags and
> feathers. By three o'clock I have finally ironed a yellow
> parachute skirt and cobalt blue blouse, dug out the belt

with the big silver circles and the necklace made of
spoon ladles linked together, and the nineteen-dollar
black sandals bedecked with rhinestones. I spend an
extra twenty minutes hunting down my half
slip. . . . They escort me to the green room. All the
saliva in my mouth evaporates on the way. I have to go
to the bathroom desperately, but it's too far and won't
do any good anyway, so I sit tight, sip water, and ask
Mary not to let anyone talk to me. (pp. 355-357)

This is not to say that women do not speak of using their
bodies as instruments of achievement. For women, appearance
constitutes an integral part of every story they tell and they are
often keenly aware of shaping their bodies for ulterior ends. In
the dramatic tale of survival in a Chinese detention prison during
the era of the Cultural Revolution, Nien Cheng (1986) described
the day her long ordeal with the Red Guard began. Two men
from her company arrive unannounced at her home to take her
to her "trial." She delayed going downstairs to have more time
to think what she should do to preserve herself in this tense
situation. She strives to create an impression of herself through
her appearance. "I put on a white cotton shirt, a pair of gray
slacks, and black sandals, the clothes Chinese women wore in
public places to avoid being conspicuous. . . . I walked slowly,
deliberately creating the impression of composure" (p. 8). Effects of appearance on career goals continues to be especially
relevant to women in the public eye. Comments by Linda Ellerbee
(1986), a television journalist, are telling:

I was told to lose weight if I wished ever to anchor again at
NBC News. I wonder if anyone's ever said that to Charles
Kuralt. . . . Regarding my hair—I have lots of hair—I've paid
attention to commands to tie it back, bring it forward, put
it up, take it down, cut it, let it grow, curl it, straighten it,
tame it—and I stopped doing so before someone asked me
to shave it off. . . . Maybe I'd just gotten older, not
mellower, or maybe I'd had it up to here with men telling
me to do something about my hair. (p. 119)

Because women describe themselves as deeply embodied, they are more often candid than men about the discomforts and threats to their bodies. A typical example is furnished by Beverly Sills (1987), as she describes her bout with ovarian cancer at the age of 45: "I was lucky. I had a tumor the size of a grapefruit, but the doctor removed it entirely." Then she adds a gratuitous aside from a medical standpoint: "After my operation, I probably weighed about 125 pounds. I don't think I'd weighed 125 pounds since I was four years old" (p. 264). Returning to the stage very quickly, she mentions the pain she suffered. "To be blunt about it, I was in agony . . . the pain was almost unbelievable," but she did it anyway. "The plain truth is that if I had canceled, I would have worried that I was dying" (p. 267).

After her arrest and imprisonment, Nien Cheng (1986) minutely describes her experiences in prison as embodied ones of privation. Her description is rich with details of her bodily states, her illnesses, and her deteriorating condition: "After some time, hunger became a permanent state, no longer a sensation but an ever present hollowness. The flesh on my body slowly melted away, my eyesight deteriorated, and simple activities such as washing clothes exhausted my strength" (p. 185).

Given women's close identification with their bodies, it is also possible to appreciate why violations of the body are so unsettling for the woman: They represent invasive negations of one's identity. Consider Sidney Biddle Barrows's (1986) account of how nude photos were taken of her and published in national newspapers. With a boyfriend in Amsterdam:

> We went to the houseboat and sampled our new friend's excellent hashish. After a while, [the friend] tactfully disappeared, leaving us together in the shimmering afternoon sun. . . . I was delighted to have him snap some shots of me in my skimpy summer clothes. Pretty soon, he started flattering me: I looked so terrific, the light was just right, so why didn't I take off my clothes and let him shoot some nude photographs? (p. 22)

Later when Barrows was arrested for running a high-class escort service, her former boyfriend sold the photos to the *New York Post:*

> I was devastated. I could live with being called the Mayflower Madam, and I could even tolerate having my real name known. But now nude photographs of me were being splashed across two of the largest newspapers in the country! I couldn't believe that Rozansky had so shamelessly betrayed me, and I was disgusted that I had ever given him the time of day. (p. 290)

Other intimacies of the body were shared by Ellerbee (1986), who describes her illegal abortion.

> I'd been one of those women . . . who'd gotten pregnant, then gotten the name of someone through a friend of a friend, paid six hundred dollars cash, and waited, terrified, at my apartment until midnight when a pimply-faced man showed up, exchanged code words with me, and came in, bringing cutting tools, bandages and Sodium Pentothol—but no medical license I could see. I was lucky. I did not bleed uncontrollably. I did not die. I recovered. I was no longer pregnant. But I wasn't the same, either. No woman is. (p. 96)

From the standpoint of the unity of mind and body, it is also possible to understand why women's stories—and seldom men's—often contain instances of bodily alteration, mutilation, or destruction. When a woman is unhappy with her identity—feeling like a failure, wishing for a change in identity—the frequent result is some form of bodily obliteration. Ballerina Gelsey Kirkland (1986) described a period of despair: "I wanted to lose my identity. . . . [at night, sleeping] I was able to dream my way into somebody else's body. I was no longer Gelsey" (p. 205). At another point, when she has lost her boyfriend, "I went through another round of cosmetic surgery. I had my earlobes snipped off. I had silicone injected into my ankles and lips" (p. 126). Joan Rivers (1986) turned such events into comedy:

> That winter, in fact, suicide become one of my options; a way to strike back at all the people who did not appreciate me, a way to make them pay attention and be sorry. . . . I wanted to do something terrible to myself, expend my powerless rage on my body, so I went into the bathroom and with a pair of scissors crudely chopped off my hair. (p. 249)

Summing up the narratives of embodiment for the adult years, we find that the man's bodily self fades even more into the background as career interests expand. The career is typically tied to ideas and ideals, power and prestige, and not to corporality. In contrast, women typically remain wedded to their bodies regardless of their career interests and abilities. In their identification with their bodies, self and bodily activities are one.

Embodiment in the Latter Years

Because popular autobiographies tend to embrace the traditional criteria of the well-formed narrative,[7] their endings are extensions of that which proceeds. Especially for the male, the story line is a coherent one, with the writer describing early events in such a way that later outcomes are almost necessitated. Thus, in accounting for the body in the later years, much of the groundwork has already been laid. For the younger male autobiographer, the life account will be notable for its absence of body talk. Discursively, career success serves almost as an epiphany, enabling the male to achieve a state of the pure ideal. For males who do write from a more elderly position, however, matters are more complex. For here there are pervasive signs of what the culture defines as bodily deterioration. Issues of embodiment, then, begin to break through the seamless narrative of career advancement.

Three primary reactions tend to dominate the male autobiography. First, there is a *self-congratulatory* theme. If one's body has remained in reasonably good health, one may offer it (as separated from "I, myself") some form of adulation. Like a motorcar that has outlasted those of one's friends, one may feel proud to be the owner of the machine. This orientation flavors Getty's (1986) commentary on aging: "I am eighty-three. Cold, damp winters do bring on attacks of bronchitis . . . I can't lift weights or swim for hours or walk five miles at the brisk pace I did ten years ago. . . . Luckily, I can afford the best medical care available" (p. 275). With a "touch" of the "chronic," Getty appears to revert to the earlier defensive posture.

Among those writers who are not so fortunate as Getty, two other orientations are taken toward the body. One is *begrudging admission* that one has a body, and that it must be given its due. This approach is taken by Chuck Yeager (1985):

> My concession to aging is to take better care of myself than I did when I was younger. . . . Nowadays, I hunt as much for the exercise . . . as for the sport. . . . I'm definitely not a rocking-chair type. I can't just sit around, watch television, drink beer, get fat, and fade out. (pp. 422-423)

This begrudging interruption of the heroic narrative is more dramatically illustrated in Ansel Adams's (1985) revelations of his chronic and increasingly disabling problems: "As I cleared the decks for future projects, I found an ever-present complicating factor: Health. My mind is as active as ever, but my body was falling farther and farther behind" (p. 365). (The reader may note that the "real" Adams is the mental form, and the body is a recalcitrant fellow-traveller who is lagging behind.) Adams (1985) describes his heart surgery (a triple bypass and valve replacement). "Without surgery I was fast reaching an embarrassing state of inactivity; I could not walk a hundred feet without the crippling symptoms of chest pains and shortness of breath" (p. 366). Yet, the sense of bodily infringement on the idealized masculine narrative is revealed in Adams's (1985) description of recovery: "My only complaint was a pestiferous vertigo. . . . . In two months the vertigo vanished and I was able to drive the late Congressman Philip Burton to Big Sur for his first view of that marvelous region; he soon became one of the leaders in the fight for its preservation" (p. 366). Back to business as usual.

A third orientation to the aging body is often encountered in the male autobiography, essentially a *trauma of broken defenses*. Because of the ravages to the body in the later years, the picture of the self during the middle years—detached from natural anchors—can no longer be maintained. With the disruptive sense of being the victim of "a dirty trick," the male at last confronts the possibility of finitude. Watson's (1990) description of his heart attack is illustrative:

> In mid-November, I was in my office and Jane Cahill, my executive assistant, started to come in the door. Then she stopped cold, because I had my head down on the desk, "Are you all right?" she asked.
>
> I'm fine. I'm tired.
>
> That night I woke up with a pain in my chest. It wasn't very intense but it wouldn't go away. Olive was in the Caribbean with friends, so I drove myself to the emergency room at Greenwich Hospital . . . having a heart attack. (p. 392)

Employing the metaphor of the body as the serviceable machine, Watson also reveals his sense of vulnerability; "When you have a heart attack, you realize how fragile your body is. I felt that mine had let me down, damn near entirely, and for several months I had very volatile reactions to insignificant things" (p. 394).

It would be useful to make broad comparisons between older male autobiographies and those written by older women. Unfortunately, however, few women write popular autobiographies when they are past 60. For this genre of literature, women's reputations tend to result from achievements of the early years.

Lifetimes that culminate in professional heroics are rarer for women than for men. For those older women who do contribute to the genre, the body continues to figure importantly in two ways. First, although one might anticipate a drawing away from bodily identification as it become more problematic, this does not seem to be the case with women. Instead, the writers continue to "live their bodies," in spite of the body's transformation. Beverly Sills's (1987) account of her body's reaction to her chores in the management of the opera company after her retirement as a diva is illustrative: "I was working like a horse, my blood pressure was way up, and I was eating six meals a day. . . . I came into my job as general director weighing 150 pounds; on June 16, 1984 when I visited the endocrinologist, I weighed 220 pounds" (p. 345).

There is a second theme located in the accounts of women, including those in later years, that is far more subtle in its manifestation, but pervasive and profound. Because the woman's body is so closely identified with the self, one's bodily relations with others essentially extend the self. In the same way that violations of the body are defacements of identity, so are investments of the body in others' modes of unifying self and other. Thus, in pondering the preceding years and the meaning of one's life, women are more given to thinking about their children, lovers, and parents—those with whom the body has been intimately shared—and others, such as friends, who are now part of oneself. Nien Cheng's (1986) autobiography is a continuous knitting of her life to her daughter's especially. After the memorial service for her daughter, killed by the Red Guard, she describes a night without sleep.

> Lying in the darkened room, I remembered the years
> that had gone by, and I saw my daughter in various
> stages of her growth from a chubby-cheeked baby . . . to
> a beautiful young woman in Shanghai. . . . I blamed
> myself for her death because I had brought her back to
> Shanghai in 1949. (p. 495)

This recounting of significant connection is not wholly reserved for the old age, however. Even when the younger women think back on their lives, their ruminations tend to center on those related through extensions of the body. When Navratilova (1985) won the Wimbledon Championship, she expressed her first thoughts on winning as: "For the first time I was a Wimbledon champion, fulfilling the dream of my father many years before. . . . I felt I was on top of the world" (p. 190). Joan Baez (1987) writes an epilogue in which she describes her family and friends, those who have been important in her life. In the final pages she talks of going to a party in Paris with her son. When she returns home,

> Mom will have a fire going in the kitchen and perhaps a Brahms trio on the stereo. Gabe will fall into bed, and I will sit in front of the fire, dressed like a Spanish princess, telling Mom how the sun rose, piercing through the mist over the lake . . . and how there was peace all around as the castle finally slept. (pp. 377-378)

For men, rumination about the significance of intimates plays but a minor role in their stories. When one is on the grand highway of monomyth, it is important to travel light. Thus Yeager and Getty, for example, speak only in passing of deaths and illnesses within the family; Trump describes himself, his family members, and his then wife, Ivana, as "rocks." The major exception to this general disregard is the father's death, which often receives considerable attention. The importance of the father's death can be traced to the threat it symbolizes to the male portrayal of invulnerability. Because one can see within the father's death the possibility of one's own finitude, added attention is needed to keeping the defenses strong. There is no male autobiographer who could write as Nien Cheng (1986), who is an old woman when she is finally allowed to leave China. Leaving Shanghai harbor she continues to speak of bodily sensations, the feeling of the heavy rain, her lack of umbrella or raincoat, her "staggering up the slippery gangway," the "wind whipping my hair while I watched the coastline of China receding." She ponders her daughter's fate. "I felt guilty for being the one who was alive. I wished it were Meiping standing on the deck of this ship, going away to make a new life for herself" (pp. 534-535).

Embodied Selves Over the Life Span

The popular autobiography is both a repository of cultural meanings and a model for future lives. As the present analysis indicates, autobiographical stories differ dramatically in the meanings they impart to the male as opposed to the female body over the life span. The male autobiographer suggests that the man should be "above bodily concerns," more invested in culture than nature, in rationalities and values as opposed to the corporal.[8] To be fixed on one's body would be unmanly, narcissistic, and perhaps effeminate. To put matters of corporality aside is also highly functional for the male in terms of career. More hours can be devoted to achievement, and with fewer complaints. It is only in the later years that the male autobiographer admits an important relationship between self and body, and it is often an admission of shock, fear, and sorrow. The grand story is being brought to a close by a secret villain, and that villain dwells within.

Female autobiographers present a life story in which body and self are more unified. To be a woman is to be embodied; to fail in attending to one's corporality would be to ignore the cultural codes of being. Bodies serve a more central role in women's lives and consciousness than they seem to in men's. As Adrienne Rich (1977) has put it: "I know no woman—virgin, mother, lesbian, married, celibate—whether she earns her keep as a housewife, a cocktail waitress, or a scanner of brain waves— for whom her body is not a fundamental problem" (p. 14). This embodiment lends itself to a far greater sense of unity with others—particularly with those who have shared the flesh. To be embodied in this way is thus to be in significant relationship with others. At the same time, the discourse of embodiment sets the stage for deep unsettlement during puberty, for self-mutilation during periods of disappointment, and for a more profound sense of aging in the later years.

Inevitably an analysis such as this raises questions of the cultural good. For if one lives the life course within frameworks of meaning, and these meanings invite and constrain, celebrate and suppress, then one may ask whether it might be otherwise. If we could alter the forms of meaning—whether in autobiography or elsewhere—should we do so? From the female standpoint, there is much to reject in the male version of life and the practices that they favor. The male life course seems a strange "out of body" experience, one that devalues potentially significant aspects of human life. For the male, the female's mode of indexing life seems often irrelevant to the tasks at hand, and lends itself to emotional instability. However, rather than conceptualizing themselves as participants in "the longest war," perhaps both genders might benefit from new syntheses that would expand life story options for all. At the same time, however, further attention is needed to the cultural patterns in which these discourses are embedded. So long as the power relationships between men and women appear to favor the male version of reality and value, so long as the workplace makes little allowance for embodied selves, and so long as relationships are treated in a utilitarian manner, new stories might not be able to survive. Yet, one might hope that within dialogues, through reciprocal and reflexive endeavors, and via political and social changes, new stories might encourage new practices and prospects—and we might hope that embodied stories would be available to all (see K. Gergen, in press).

Notes

1. For further discussion of meaning as discursive rather than psychological, see Gergen (1991).
2. See Bakhtin's (1981) concept of *heteroglossia*.
3. For more extended accounts of the mutual management of meaning, see Pearce and Cronen, 1980.
4. See also Bruss (1980), Rabuzzi (1988), Russ (1972), Sprinker (1980), and White (1978).
5. See Frye (1957) and Rich (1977).

6. Nien Cheng's (1986) autobiography, *Life and Death in Shanghai*, is exceptional within this group because she was not well known before her book was published, and she did not write with the help of a professional writer. Her volume was selected for inclusion in this sample because it was a best-seller and, in addition, she was a businesswoman and an older woman author. These characteristics are difficult to find in best-selling autobiographies by women.

7. See Gergen and Gergen (1983, 1988) for further discussion of these criteria.

8. It should be emphasized that the subject of concern here is how embodiment is described in autobiographies. It is possible that in private spheres men express their embodiment much as women do in print. This possibility remains to be explored.

Autobiographical References

Adams, Ansel, with Mary Street Alinder. (1985). *Ansel Adams. An autobiography*. Boston: Little, Brown.

Baez, Joan. (1987). *And a voice to sing with: A memoir*. New York: New American Library.

Barrows, Sydney Biddle, with William Novak. (1986). *Mayflower madam*. New York: Arbor House; London: MacDonald.

Cheng, Nien. (1986). *Life and death in Shanghai*. New York: Penguin.

Ellerbee, Linda. (1986). *And so it goes: Adventures in television*. New York: Berkley Books.

Getty, J. Paul. (1986). *As I see it: An autobiography of J. Paul Getty*. New York: Berkley. (Original work published 1976)

Iacocca, Lee, with William Novak. (1984). *Iacocca. An autobiography*. New York: Bantam Books.

Kirkland, Gelsey, with Greg Lawrence. (1986). *Dancing on my grave*. Garden City, NY: Doubleday.

Navratilova, Martina, with George Vecsey. (1985). *Martina*. New York: Fawcett Crest.

Pickens, T. Boone, Jr. (1987). *Boone*. Boston: Houghton Mifflin.

Rashad, Ahmad, with Peter Bodo. (1988). *Rashad*. New York: Penguin.

Rivers, Joan, with Richard Meryman. (1986). *Enter talking*. New York: Delacorte.

Sills, Beverly, and Lawrence Linderman. (1987). *Beverly*. New York: Bantam Books.

Trump, Donald, with Tony Schwark. (1987). *Trump: The art of the deal*. New York: Warner Books.

Watson, Thomas J., Jr., & Petre, Peter. (1990). *Father son & co. My life at IBM and beyond*. New York: Bantam Books.

Yeager, Chuck, and Leo James. (1985). *Yeager, an autobiography*. New York: Bantam Books.

General References

Bakhtin, Mikhail. (1981). *The dialogical imagination: Four essays* (Michael Holquist, Ed.). Austin: University of Texas Press.

Bruner, Jerome. (1986). *Actual minds, possible worlds.* Cambridge: Harvard University Press.

Bruss, Elizabeth W. (1980). Eye for I: Making and unmaking autobiography in film. In J. Olney (Ed.), *Autobiography: Essays, theoretical and critical.* Princeton, NJ: Princeton University Press.

Campbell, Joseph. (1956). *Hero with a thousand faces.* New York: Bollingen. (original work published 1949)

Chodorow, Nancy. (1978). *The reproduction of mothering: Psychoanalysis and the sociology of gender.* Berkeley: University of California Press.

de Man, Paul. (1979). Autobiography as de-facement. *Modern Language Notes, 94,* 920.

Dinnerstein, Dorothy. (1977). *The mermaid and the minotaur: Sexual arrangements and the human malaise.* New York: Harper & Row.

Eakin, Paul John. (1985). *Fictions in autobiography: Studies in the art of self-invention.* Princeton, NJ: Princeton University Press.

Flax, Jane. (1990). *Thinking fragments.* Berkeley: University of California Press.

Frye, Northrup. (1957). *Anatomy of criticism: Four essays.* Princeton, NJ: Princeton University Press.

Gergen, Kenneth J. (1991). *The saturated self.* New York: Basic Books.

Gergen, Kenneth J. (in press). *Social construction: Critique and re-creation in the postmodern community.* Chicago: University of Chicago Press.

Gergen, Kenneth J., & Gergen, Mary M. (1983). Narrative of the self. In T. Sarbin & K. Schiebe (Eds.), *Studies in social identity.* New York: Praeger.

Gergen, Kenneth J., & Gergen, Mary M. (1988). Narrative and the self as relationship. In L. Berkowitz (Ed.), *Advances in experimental social psychology* (Vol. 21). San Diego, CA: Academic Press.

Gergen, Mary M. (1992). Life stories: Pieces of a dream. In G. Rosenwald & R. Ochberg (Eds.), *Telling lives.* New Haven, CT: Yale University Press.

Gergen, Mary M. (in press). The social construction of personal histories: Gendered lives in popular autobiographies. In T. Sarbin & J. Kitsuke (Eds.), *Constructing the social.* London: Sage.

Jelinek, Estelle C. (1980). *Women's autobiography. Essays in criticism.* Bloomington: Indiana University Press.

Lejeune, Philippe. (1975). *Le pacte autobiographique.* Paris: Seuil.

Maccoby, Eleanor, & Jacklin, Carol. (1974). *The psychology of sex differences.* Stanford, CA: Stanford University Press.

Mason, Mary G. (1980). Autobiographies of women writers. In J. Olney (Ed.), *Autobiography, essays, theoretical and critical.* Princeton, NJ: Princeton University Press.

Money, John, & Ehrhardt, A. A. (1972). *Man & woman. Boy & girl.* Baltimore, MD: Johns Hopkins University Press.

Olney, James. (1980). *Autobiography. Essays theoretical and critical.* Princeton, NJ: Princeton University Press.

Pascal, Roy. (1960). *Design and truth in autobiography.* Cambridge, MA: Harvard University Press.

Pearce, W. Barnett, & Cronen, Vern. (1980). *Communication, action, and meaning.* New York: Praeger.

Rabuzzi, Kathryn Allen. (1988). *Motherself. A mythic analysis of motherhood.* Bloomington: Indiana University Press.

Rich, Adrienne. (1977). *Of woman born: Motherhood as experience and institution.* New York: Norton.

Russ, Joanna. (1972). What can a heroine do? Or why women can't write. In S. Koppelman Cornillon (Ed.), *Images of women in fiction.* Bowling Green, OH: Bowling Green University Popular Press.

Sprinker, Michael. (1980). Fictions of the self: The end of autobiography. In J. Olney (Ed.), *Autobiography: Essays theoretical and critical.* Princeton, NJ: Princeton University Press.

Steier, Frederick. (Ed.). (1991). *Method and reflexivity: Knowing as systemic social construction.* London: Sage.

Stone, Albert E. (1982). *Autobiographical occasions and original acts. Versions of American identity from Henry Adams to Nate Shaw.* Philadelphia: University of Pennsylvania Press.

Weintraub, Karl J. (1978). *The value of the individual: Self and circumstance in autobiography.* New York: Random House.

White, Hayden. (1978). *The tropics of discourse.* Baltimore, MD: Johns Hopkins University Press.

Index

Acquiescence, as foreclosure strategy, 140
Adams, G. R., 135, 139, 148, 157, 158
Adolescence
  diary, function of for girls, 32, 39-40
  embodiment and narrative, 199-202
  father/daughter relationships, 163-187
  identity making, contexts of, 130-133, 147-148, 154
  identity-achieved individuals, 135-136
  separation-individuation in immigration, 99, 103-104, 122-123, 124-125
Aging, embodiment and narrative, 209-214
Allport, G., 31
Antagonism, as foreclosure strategy, 140
Anti-Semitism. *See* Holocaust
Approach-avoidance, in moratorium individuals, 146
Art
  interpretation of, 10-11, 12, 14
  memory, function as, 21-24
  narrative, function as, 22-24, 27-28.
  See also Literature
Astrophysics, use of narrative in, viii
Autobiography
  as life model, 194-195
  history of, 195

in women's psychology, 195-196. *See also* Biography; History; Narrative; Women's psychology

Bach, S., 44-45, 50
Baumeister, R. F., 38
Bellinger, D., 187
Berger, P., 25
Bergman, A., 124
Bertaux, D., 59
Berzonsky, M. D., 147
Biography
  analysis of, 61, 66-88
  embodiment, function in, 191-215
  identity, relationship to, 6-9
  interviewing. *See* Interview
  narrative, function of, xi, 1-19, 53, 59-90
  reconstruction of life history, 68-69
  research. *See* Interview
  social science research in, 59-88. *See also* Autobiography; Diary-keeping, the psychology of
Block J., 125
Blos, P., 99, 124
Boundaries
  use of diary in dissolving, 41-43
  use of diary in setting and maintaining, 35-38

About the Contributors

Terri Apter is the Betty Behrens Research Fellow at Clare Hall, University of Cambridge. She received her Ph.D. from the University of Cambridge. The author of *Altered Loves: Mothers and Daughters During Adolescence,* she is now working on a book about women in mid-life.

Amos Funkenstein was born in Israel in 1937. He studied at the Hebrew University and at the Free University of Berlin. He has been a professor of history at UCLA and at Stanford University. Since 1991, he has held the Koret Chair of History at the University of California, Berkeley. He is also a member of the faculty of the Tel Aviv University. Among his many publications is a book entitled *Theology and the Scientific Imagination From the Middle Ages to the 20th Century.*

Kenneth J. Gergen is Professor of Psychology at Swarthmore College. His work on social constructionism has been extended into a book series (Sage, London) that he edits with John Shotter. He has coauthored several articles and chapters on the narrative in psychology with Mary M. Gergen, and is the author of several books, most recently *The Saturated Self.*

Mary M. Gergen is Associate Professor of Psychology and affiliated with the Women's Studies Program at Pennsylvania State University, the Delaware County Campus in Media, PA. In 1988 she edited *Feminist Thought and the Structure of Knowledge.* She has written extensively on narrative form and popular autobiography. Currently she and her husband, Kenneth J. Gergen, are working on developing a duography, a narrative form for a relationship.

Ruthellen Josselson is currently Visiting Professor at the Harvard Graduate School of Education. She is also professor of psychology at Towson State University where she is director of the Clinical Concentration Program. She is author of *Finding Herself: Pathways to Identity Development in Women* and *The Space Between Us: Exploring the Dimensions of Human Relationships.*

Jane Kroger is currently Reader of Human Development in the Department of Education, Victoria University, Wellington, New Zealand. She received her Ph.D. in Child Development in 1977 from Florida State University. She is the author of *Identity in Adolescence: The Balance Between Self and Other* and editor of *Discussions on Ego Identity.* Her current interest is in identity development from a life span perspective.

Amia Lieblich is a member of the faculty of the Department of Psychology at The Hebrew University, where she served as the chairperson in 1982-1985. She is author of several psychology books that deal with the specific issues of the Israeli society, such as the war, military service, and the kibbutz. Her work uses mainly the narrative form.

Gabriele Rosenthal received her Dr. rer. soc. in Sociology from the University in Bielefeld, the Federal Republic of Germany, in 1986. She presently teaches at the University of Kassel, F.R.G. Teaching and research interests address interpretive sociology, methods, and biographical research. She is currently investigating life histories of Holocaust survivors and their families in Israel.

George C. Rosenwald received his doctorate from Yale University. He is a Professor of Personality and Clinical Psychology at the University of Michigan and a psychotherapist in private practice. He recently co-edited (with Richard Ochberg) *Storied Lives: The Cultural Politics of Self-Understanding* as part of a larger interest in the political conditions of individual and social development.

Guy A. M. Widdershoven is Associate Professor of Philosophy and Head of the Department of Health Ethics and Philosophy at the University of Limburg, Maastricht, The Netherlands. His research concerns the philosophy of health and the philosophy of the humanities. He wrote a dissertation on the relationship between action and rationality in phenomenology and hermeneutics and edited several books on philosophical hermeneutics and the foundations of the human sciences.

Wendy J. Wiener received her master's degree and is currently pursuing doctoral studies in the Clinical Psychology program at the University of Michigan. She is studying the role of culture in emotional experience. She has had a long-standing interest in diaries.